A TWO-PART MEMOIR

OUT OF WEDLOCK 1948

Nancy A. Fredrickson

BEAVER'S POND
PRESS

A TWO PART MEMOIR

OUT OF WEDLOCK 1948

Nancy A. Fredrickson

BEAVER'S POND

Is there a reality *not* made of memories?

This is a work of creative nonfiction. The events portrayed are to the best of Nancy Fredrickson's memory. While all the stories in this book are true, some names and identifying details have been changed to protect the privacy of the people involved.

Edited by Kris Kobe

ISBN 13: 978-1-64343-695-1
Library of Congress Catalog Number: 2022914037
Printed in the United States of America

First Printing: 2022
25   25   24   23   22   5   4   3   2   1

Book design and typesetting by Dan Pitts.
This book is typeset in Minion

BEAVER'S POND
PRESS

Pond Reads Press
939 Seventh Street West
Saint Paul, MN 55102
(952) 829-8818
www.BeaversPondPress.com

To Order, visit https://www.amazon.com
Or for an autographed copy, visit www.gordonfredrickson.com

CONTENTS

PREFACE

As my husband and I reminisced during road trip vacations or over a glass of wine at home in the evenings, I opened up to him about growing up as a bastard, and I admitted how intensely aware I had been of the stigma.

Of course, he knew some of the details already, but the more we talked, the more I remembered, and eventually he urged me to remember his mantra: "A story *not* told is lost forever."

He asked me a simple, thought-provoking question: "Nancy, do you want your bastard stories to be told or lost forever?"

I agreed that if I said nothing, the opportunity for my experiences to enlighten anyone would be lost, and the shaming of my mom and me by nuns and a few members of the church-led community would go unchallenged forever. I thought that maybe people needed to read about how malicious behavior toward innocent children affects them.

Reluctant to make my problems public, I agonized over the decision for months. Did I want to dig into those horrible memories and relive details that I had kept to myself all these years? Telling my stories to my husband was fairly easy and even therapeutic, but did I want to expose my bastard moments to strangers? Did I want to risk alienating friends and relatives? Eventually I reconciled my reluctance with what I understood to be the importance of telling a story that must be told. Gordy and I planned our process: I would write details of what I remembered and help Gordy create a true narrative that was more than just a chronology of events.

At this point, I need to unequivocally state that the vast majority of people in New Market, Minnesota, the town where I grew up, were kind to my mother and me. In fact, I think many were especially kind because of our circumstances. At the time, New Market had about two hundred people and a number of businesses that supported the area's farm economy. It was a great place to grow up. People in small towns tend to know a great deal about one another, but in the end, there is a bond between them that goes beyond whether or not they approve of their neighbor's past. But if church leaders assume the duty of scorning others, some of the "faithful" will enthusiastically pick up the torch and carry it various distances. Fortunately for Mom and me, only a few picked it up. Most did not.

Until now, I had kept these stories to myself because I did not want to whine or to appear weak. I did not want to complain to my mom, who had to bear scorn every day since she became pregnant with me, her bastard child. Silence became our cover and our survival. When I was a child, my questions about my father were met with evasive and often inconsistent answers, right before Mom abruptly changed the subject. I never doubted her love for me, but many times when I was alone, I cried because I knew my father didn't want me. There is no antidote for that poison.

I didn't write this memoir to evoke pity for my past. Pitying someone is the worst kind of scorn. And I didn't write this memoir to create a tool of belated revenge, which is why I use aliases for those who perpetrated my pain. Instead, I wrote this book because it's a story that must be told for all bastards, for all people scorned, for all children of single parents, and for all children and adults who are different in some way. And I write especially to enlighten the self-righteous, to illuminate the damage they do when they find a way or a reason to elevate themselves above others.

BASTARD MOMENTS: EARLY YEARS

Part 1

CHAPTER 1

LEARNING MY BASTARD IDENTITY

First Bastard Moment

Summertime was joyful for me. I played freely in our small backyard with little girls and boys my age and younger, each of us reveling in the fairy-tale life of innocent children. Busy making small mounds of dirt on which we could sit to have tea, we were too preoccupied to notice two tall boys entering our make-believe world.

"Who's your father?" the taller of the two boys demanded. "What's his name?"

He started to call me names. I did not know all the words he used, but I knew they were bad. They made me feel ashamed and afraid that the boys might hurt me.

The tall boys urged the other kids to repeat the names, and they soon joined in, all of them eventually chanting, "Who's your father? What's his name?" as if it were a new game.

Clasping my hands over my ears, I fled to the back of our ground-level apartment, opened the wooden screen door, and closed it quickly. A few steps behind me, the group stopped at the door and stood outside as they continued calling me names. Angry and frightened, I tried yelling at them to leave, but the two tall boys kept up the chant.

"Who's your father? What's his name? Who's your father? What's his name?"

Terrified, I raced to my bed, buried my head under a pillow, and cried.

After what seemed like an eternity, they gave up and left.

When Mom got home from work, I told her what had happened. She took me on her lap, comforted me, and told me to stay home and play inside the house the next day.

The following day, before leaving for work, she instructed, "Don't yell back at anyone, and stay in the house."

I did as Mom instructed. I stayed in the apartment, but it was hot. And because the windows on the three outside walls of the old building could not be opened, I had to leave the front and back doors open for ventilation. I closed only the screen doors, which still allowed a breeze to blow through. Stretching to reach as high as I could, I managed to fasten the hook latch on each screen door. With the doors securely locked, I played with my doll in the small front room.

Outside, the narrow sidewalk hugged our building, with no grassy strip separating the sidewalk from the street. Over the next few days, the two tall boys returned to call me names through the front screen door, never sticking around for too long. A few of the younger kids joined them briefly on the first day, but on subsequent visits, the two tall boys were alone. A few days later, only the taller boy came to yell at me. I stayed in the house a few more days before my young friends returned to play with me in the sand and grass behind our building. No one mentioned the incident, but it remained on my mind.

To this day, whenever that horrible memory surfaces, I can still hear the chanting clearly, as if the boys were outside my door: *Who's your father? What's his name? Who's your father? What's his name?*

This was my first bastard moment, a terrifying first of many moments where others shamed me because of the circumstances of my birth, making me feel unworthy, disgraced, and powerless to do anything about their cruelty.

The Environment

When that first bastard moment happened, I was seven years old and living with my mother in New Market, Minnesota, a bustling town with several grocery stores, full-service filling stations, feedstores, and taverns as well as a bank, a hardware store, a café, a Catholic church, a Catholic elementary school, and a population of about two hundred. We'd moved there when I was three, in 1951.

Curiosity is natural, especially when someone new moves in. But given New Market's Catholic leaning, especially during that era, it was inevitable that the locals would single out an eight-year divorcée with a three-year-old. Although the specific details of Mom's past and my birth were a mystery to most everyone—including me, even now—when it comes to a scandal, even the people who aren't good at math suddenly become good at math. No one needed a pencil and paper to compute that I was not old enough to be a child of Mom's first husband.

"The chanting boys," as I now refer to the incident, happened the summer before I began second grade. Although it is my first specific bastard memory, my experiences in the first grade gave me reason enough to believe I was an outsider, disapproved of by some and only tolerated by others. There was no kindergarten in those days, so at age six, I started first grade at St. Nicholas Catholic School in New Market, which was run by St. Nicholas Catholic Church. The three teachers were nuns of School Sisters of Notre Dame, an international women's congregation.

For grades one, two, and three, I was in Sister Mary Arthur's classroom. She was kind, caring, and energetic and treated every child with respect. However, everything we learned in school was geared toward children with both a mother and a father, which made me painfully aware I was different. I had no father nor any memories of having one, and it didn't help my situation when Mom lied, telling me my father had died in a car accident. She probably lied to keep the explanation simple, but she continued stifling further discussion of the topic for years. If she lied to anyone else in town about my father, I was not aware. It only became clear to me years later that people in town were unsure if my biological father was Mom's first husband or someone else. And I remained confused as to why she failed to unveil the mystery to them or to me.

The M&M's Episode

Although Sister Mary Arthur created an atmosphere that fostered learning at St. Nicholas Catholic School, the school's constant emphasis on a "complete" family seemed to give license to some of my classmates to treat me as inferior. I felt it daily in the classroom, at lunchtime, and at recess. Bastard moments seemed to pop up at strange times, even outside of school. When I was about seven or eight years old, New Market Bank was having some type of open house celebration where children who came in with an adult were given a free individual bag of M&M's. Maybe a bag of candy doesn't sound like much, but to us kids, an individual bag of M&M's was a big deal. Mom worked at her regular job during the bank's open house celebration, so I thought I would be unable to attend, but a neighbor lady kindly offered to take me along with her and her daughter. Her daughter was in my grade, so I knew her well. We were friends, although when we played together, she always made it clear that she was superior to me.

At the bank, we girls were both given a bag of M&M's. Following instructions from my mother, I was polite and did not open the bag of M&M's at the bank. The other girl followed my lead and did not open her bag either. After a short stay at the bank event, we all walked back to their house. Once her mother left the room, my friend insisted that we open our bags of M&M's and count the contents. That confused me. I'd never had anyone tell me to count the pieces of candy inside a bag before I could eat any. The girl insisted, explaining that we had to count them to ensure that we had the same number of candies. As it turned out, she had received two more M&M's than I did. She was happy with that result, but she didn't offer to share her extras with me. I'm not sure whether this was a bastard moment, but she clearly felt herself to be more deserving. In any case, I didn't expect her to share her windfall with me, but I always wondered what she would have ordered me to do had I received the two extra candies in my bag. I think I know the answer.

Learning Confession

Before we made our first communion in the second grade, we had to make our first confession. The nuns had us rehearse the ritual—what to say to the priest and when to answer him—before they marched the entire class over to the church to give our first real confession to the priest.

After I completed my confession, I watched my classmate (I'll call her "Pat") go into the confessional. Suddenly, the priest's door flew open as he rushed to open the side where Pat was kneeling. He grabbed her arm and pulled her out of the confessional. The nun came running over and dragged Pat to where the rest of us couldn't hear what was said, but the volume of their voices confirmed both the nun and the priest were viciously scolding Pat, who by this time was sobbing uncontrollably. Finally, she was allowed back into the confessional, and the priest went back inside his section. After a short time, Pat came out and knelt by me in the pew to say her prayers— her penance.

As we walked back to school, I asked Pat what had happened. She started to cry again as she explained. "I thought it was a practice session, so I made up a bunch of things." To this day, I do not understand why the nun and the priest made such a dramatic event out of a seven-year-old's mistake. Maybe she didn't explain her mistake very well, but I wonder how well they listened to her. Why did they feel it necessary to scold her so? If their goal was to frighten a little girl, they succeeded. I always wondered whether that experience traumatized Pat and how her memory of it differed from mine.

Protection from Bullies

Pat's older brother was a strong farm boy who was kind to her and protected her at school. He stood up for me as well. One day during recess in third grade, a couple of older boys decided to pick on me by calling me names on the playground. As they became more aggressive, I became frightened. When I ran, they followed me until Pat's brother intervened. I don't know what he said to the boys, but they left quickly.

No one ever picked on me again when Pat's brother was around. Pat and I stayed friends during elementary school and would see each other after church every Sunday. Her mother would always make a point of stopping by to say hello and chat with my mother at New Market Produce, or "the Produce," where she worked. Many years later, when Pat's mom and my mom were both widows, they lived in houses next door to each other in New Market.

Christian Mother Society

I was in the second or third grade when I became aware of an important upcoming event scheduled by the Christian Mother Society at the St. Nicholas Catholic Church in New Market. When I asked my mother whether she would participate, she told me she was not allowed to be a member. I asked why without any clue how much pain it may have caused her to answer. Mom said that because the Catholic Church did not allow divorce, she was not considered a fit mother and couldn't join the society. She never said anything negative about the other women in the society, nor did she disparage the church or its teachings.

I'm sure this episode hurt Mom, but she seemed to accept what she could not change. But at the young age of eight or nine, I lacked her tolerance. The news hurt me terribly, and I became angry as I struggled to think how anyone could see my mother as anything less than the most wonderful mother in the world. Mom wouldn't allow me to express any anger or talk to anyone about it. She said to just forget it because it really didn't matter. Her method of coping was to keep things to herself.

Well, it mattered to me that they rejected my mother. The event had a huge impact on my young mind, and when I look back at it now, I recognize it as a turning point in my life. I never again looked at the Catholic Church, or Christianity in general, with the same blindness. How could I? If I loved my mother but the church proclaimed her "unfit," how could I, her child, reconcile the authority of the church with what I knew to be true about my mother? Of course, I had no idea then, nor do I now, if her membership was blocked specifically by the priest, the nuns, the other members, or an organization charter stipulating divorced women were ineligible for membership—or some combination. As an adult, I now understand that denying a divorced woman membership in a Christian mothers' society is totally consistent with the Catholic belief that disallows divorce. As a child, though, I blamed the priest and nuns.

I began to question the legitimacy of the nuns judging my mother and me, and I began resenting their privileged life. I had been taught in school that the nuns were unselfish, perfect, and holy because they gave up their secular life to take a "vow of poverty." But I observed just the opposite: the nuns in New Market lived on top of the big hill by the church, in a nice, large, new brick house with central heating, a full bathroom with hot running water, a phone, and a live-in housekeeper (one of the nuns). Whereas my mother and I lived in a three-room apartment with no hot water, no indoor bathroom, no phone, and only a small heating stove, and my mother had to work five and a half days each week plus Friday nights at

New Market Produce just to make enough money for us to get by. Yet her contributions—those of an "unfit mother"—helped support the privileged lifestyle of nuns and priests.

Had the nuns all been kind and treated everyone with respect, I doubt I would have ever come to this feeling of resentment, but when the church deemed my mother unfit, I felt compelled to feel their opinions were no longer legitimate. I had become accustomed to the daily emphasis of a "proper" family having both a mother and a father, and although it made me feel like a freak, I understood and accepted the reality. However, when Mom was barred from the Christian Mother Society, my heart filled with anger and hurt.

Knights of Columbus

As I came to understand them, the Knights of Columbus can be partially described as a Catholic fraternal organization with a goal to promote and conduct events and programs that benefit the welfare of the parish and families of the organization. Employees of the Knights of Columbus are paid by the organization, which offers special benefits for families of the men who are members.

I was probably in the third grade when I first saw the Knights of Columbus parading through the church during a special service. I was too young to understand the scope or purpose of the organization, but seeing them for the first time had a lasting effect on me. Their aggressive, militaristic appearance and behavior frightened me as I sat next to my mother in church, and I snuggled closer to her for protection as they marched through the church dressed like soldiers of God—each wearing a black suit, a flowing black cape with red or white lining, a white sash, a ceremonial sword, and a black pointed hat straight out of 1776, complete with a flouncy feather.

I found their use of swords to be the most frightening aspect. Strapped to their hips, the swords clanked menacingly as the group of over a dozen men paraded through each and every aisle of the church, ensuring that everyone saw their presentation of power. At some point, they made a grand display of drawing their swords, waving them around, and then holding them out in front as they continued marching. Eventually, the leader barked the command for the men to sheathe their swords, which they did with showy flair and a short burst of metal-on-metal scraping noises before marching away from the seated congregation.

Although I was very young, I recognized some of the marching men as fathers of my classmates. Many were good men in the community, but I also recognized those who scorned my mother and me. In both subtle and blatant ways, these men and their families made sure Mom and I understood we were lower-class, beneath their status, and that I was a bastard. I took some comfort in knowing that most of the men I respected from the area were *not* marching with the Knights of Columbus, a fact that made me realize the majority of devout Catholic men in town were finding less showy ways to validate their faith and serve their church and community.

I expect the Knights of Columbus was involved in local events for the good of the church and community, but I was not made aware of anything in particular. Over the years, I came to understand that a few members of the local Knights of Columbus chapter were actually dishonest, arrogant men who liked to drive big, new cars—despite the fact they owed quite a bit of money to many of the local businesses.

The Move

I was nine in 1957 and would begin fourth grade in the fall. My mother was working eight to five at the Produce on weekdays as well as seven to nine on Friday evenings and nine to noon on Saturdays. Her job involved receiving and candling (quality check) eggs sold to the Produce by customers, selling feed, and butchering chickens for farmers who requested the service. She practically lived there.

Our actual home was a makeshift three-room apartment on the ground floor of a two-story building, which sported two storefront facades that reached for the sky, making the building seem much grander than it was. Our apartment shared an interior wall with a tavern, extending the entire length of the building, from the narrow sidewalk to the modest backyard, where Mom had a small vegetable garden. The front door opened directly onto the sidewalk in such proximity that when the door was open, a passerby would have to stop and wait for it to close before continuing. Our front room barely had space for a worn couch and an easy chair, as it had been split by a temporary wall constructed to create the tiny bedroom where Mom and

I slept together in a double bed. A chest of drawers, a cardboard closet, and an oil stove used for heating made the bedroom pretty crowded. Beyond the bedroom was a small kitchen with a two-burner cookstove, a water-stained single-compartment sink with cold running water, a table, four chairs, and a tiny refrigerator, the latter of which Mom told me was a luxury not found in every home. Like many of the homes in town, the toilet was a wooden structure located in the backyard.

Although our apartment was small and we hadn't lived there long, we were comfortable and happy there. The man who managed the tavern next door was a nice guy, and I especially liked that our little home was nearly equidistant from and located between the school I attended and Mom's workplace. Before going home after school, I always walked half a block past our building and on to the Produce to see Mom. I loved seeing her smile as she greeted me. She'd ask how school had gone and listen as I explained. I thought we had a good living arrangement, but things were about to change.

Shortly before school started that fall, Mom and I moved into a small two-story house built in the early 1900s and owned by Leo and Hilda Shea, who also owned Shea's Hardware, on Main Street, where they sold beer, pop, candy, and ice cream in addition to standard hardware stock. They were kind, honest people and ran a good business. Mom didn't explain to me how she could suddenly manage paying rent on a whole house, and I didn't ask, but I was happy to discover the house had a kitchen, a living room, and a dining room on the main floor and two bedrooms on the second floor. Although the house had cold running water and the toilet facilities were outside, I was thrilled to have my very own bedroom.

During the move, my main job had been to stay out of the way. I remember playing with Betty Simon, a classmate who lived across the street from our old apartment. She was the youngest of Joe and Bernice Simon's nine children. Betty's family lived upstairs in a large building and operated a tavern and a café on the main floor, below their living space. The large front porch that faced the street had benches set against the exterior wall and was often a gathering place for town kids looking for playmates. As customers entered or exited the tavern, many of them would say hello to the children playing outside.

I thought my life was predictable and often fun. While townspeople—both kids and adults—occasionally felt the need to remind me, in subtle ways, of my mother's unwed status, I handled it by sweeping the feelings to the back of my mind. Of course, I had no idea of the daily pain my mother faced being confronted about her divorced status by clergy or unkind peers. And I was oblivious to the effort it must have taken to get her first marriage annulled. I was ignorant of the scorn she overcame daily as she worked, attended church, and cared for me, the symbol of her pain.

CHAPTER 2

THE REIGN OF
SISTER X

Contrary to the learning atmosphere provided in Sister Mary Arthur's classroom, the next three years provided a totally different experience for me. Grades four, five, and six were ruled by a horrendous nun I'll call "Sister X."

Where Sister Mary Arthur clearly enjoyed nurturing children, Sister X—a tall, thin nun in her early thirties—seemed to think her position gave her the right to ridicule and embarrass children, ensuring they knew their place in the pecking order of the church's society. She openly favored children whose parents had money or whose fathers were in the Knights of Columbus. And she felt it was her duty to find ways to remind me of my fatherless status during class, with students in grades four, five, and six witnessing my embarrassment.

These classroom experiences motivated me to look up words in the dictionary Mom had purchased through my school; she wanted me to have the same dictionary the school used. In my copy of *Thorndike-Barnhart Dictionary*, labeled as an "advanced junior dictionary" (the copyright page is missing from my copy), definitions included the following:

> **bastard**, 1. child whose parents are not married to each other; illegitimate child. 2. born of parents who are not married to each other. 3. anything inferior or not genuine. 4. inferior; not genuine. 1,3 *n.*, 2,4 *adj.*

Truly, reading these definitions made my heart sink, but I tried to convince myself that the nun didn't dislike me personally but rather condemned the circumstances of my birth. Either way, the pressure on me as I mingled with other students dampened my spirits daily.

Although Sister X never made a direct reference to the fact that my mother had been denied membership to the Christian Mother Society, she and all the other nuns must've known about the issue because they worked with the mothers who were members. It is possible that Mom's exclusion is what compelled Sister X to repeatedly remind me I was a bastard.

Town Hierarchy

By this time, I had begun to understand the church-led pecking order of scorn in New Market. Clearly I was on the bottom. There was no one below a bastard where the church was concerned.

Of course, I understood that the town of New Market was founded around the establishment of St. Nicholas Catholic Church, and consequently, the church was rightfully the primary source of status in the town. A family could gain high status in the church if they had a daughter who became a nun, a son who became a brother or priest, a mother who was a leader in the Christian Mother Society, or a father who was in the Knights of Columbus. There was no strong secular social hierarchy asserting itself. Only the church empowered residents to elevate themselves above others—whether they were members of the church or not.

I found it interesting that as long as there was a father in the home, regardless of the family's situation, the kids received more pity than scorn from the church. For example, the father of one family spent the money he earned on booze and often beat his wife and his kids. As long as the wife stayed with him and took his beatings, the church seemed fine with the arrangement because there was a father in the family. Obviously, I did not envy those children, and I made a special effort to show them kindness, as did most of the townsfolk. But I realized that by encouraging the woman to stay, the church actually empowered the abusive man, thus becoming complicit in cursing the family with a life of abuse and trauma. The wife did eventually leave her husband, after more than three decades of marriage. I have no idea how church clergy reacted to her decision, but decades later, when my mother confessed to me that she had left her first husband due to his abusive behavior, I was not surprised that her local priest and some of her relatives hounded her to return to him despite her terror. She refused. The church seemed to have no regard for her safety or dignity.

Most of the townspeople respected my mother's ability to care for me while also working forty-five hours a week, paying her bills, attending Catholic mass every Sunday, donating regularly to the church, and trying to bring me up as a Catholic by sending me to St. Nicholas Catholic School. But none of it seemed to elevate me beyond bastard status in the eyes of Sister X or the church. Fortunately, New Market was a town of good businessmen and businesswomen, and how they treated their customers was not based on the church hierarchy. Businesses let you charge goods and services—à la "Put it on my bill"—as long as you made a payment when you could, and the townspeople generally seemed to respect Mom for her efforts to raise me on her own.

During and after the years I was under Sister X's reign, I absorbed some truths about life. Like many others, I knew of young girls who had gained weight and left town on "vacation," only to return weeks later, after having their baby in private. I heard stories about the church supposedly helping to arrange such trips and even putting children up for adoption. I have nothing but compassion for those young women, for their situation, and for their choice of action, but as I got older, I realized this bit of truth: Hypothetically, the mother of the fatherless child could return to her community to be embraced by the church, without the burden of having a baby out of wedlock. With luck, the child would be adopted into a "good" home—with both a father and mother—and would never be treated as a fatherless child. And the mother who adopted the out-of-wedlock child would be admired for taking in an orphan. I sincerely hope such ideal outcomes came to pass for everyone involved.

Yet my mom was scorned for embracing her responsibilities and caring for me on her own. Putting it bluntly, the church encouraged and rewarded child abandonment and eagerly punished the woman who kept and loved her own child. My mother could have given me up for adoption. She could have gotten her marriage annulled quietly and moved to a town as a single person and been respected. Instead, she chose to keep me and love me and raise me, bearing the scorn of the church. Why did the clergy and some church members think they were serving God when they held my mother and me up to such scorn? It would have been phenomenal if the church leaders, including the priest and nuns, had shown my mom love and compassion and led their congregation in that direction. The question I'd pose to church members of all faiths is *Why choose scorn over kindness?*

It was about this time, too, that I began understanding the subjection of women by the church and society. Women seemed to always have to bear burden and scorn. The wife of the aforementioned alcoholic abuser had to endure and suffer regardless of whether she stayed. My biological father, like the fathers of the children born to single girls, escaped from scorn or responsibility. Also, men escaped any negative nomenclature. For example, an unwed pregnant girl in those days might be called a *bitch* and the child a *bastard*, but there was no derisive name for the man who had sexual intercourse with the woman and subsequently fathered the child before leaving. Men seemed to escape all shame and responsibility because they were in power and in control of the laws and the writing of dictionaries.

Mom's Wedding

In November 1957, I was in the fourth grade and trying to get accustomed to Sister X and her ways. I had a lot to learn. Ironically, a happy event in Mom's life, one that eventually led to her acceptance into the Christian Mother Society, led to an instance where Sister X shamed me in front of the class.

Mom woke me one Saturday morning and told me to get dressed because we had company. I came downstairs to find Mom making breakfast for Ralph "Brass" Simon, his brother Ed Simon, and Ed's wife, Josie. Excitement was in the air, and everyone was dressed up. Mom wore her very best dress, and Josie wore a fine dress too. Brass and Ed were decked out in their Sunday clothes, each man dressed in a suit, white shirt, and tie. This was not normal attire for Saturday morning. There was something going on, but I had no clue. Then Mom told me she and Brass had just been married at St. Nicholas Catholic Church in New Market, with Ed and Josie as witnesses. It was a grand, happy breakfast, with everyone talking and laughing—except me.

Mom had told me nothing about the impending marriage, being in love, or a new future. Of course, I knew Brass and liked him. He was kind and would often babysit me while Mom worked on Friday nights. He had eaten dinner with us often, especially after we moved to the house a couple of months prior, but no one had prepared me for their marriage. I wasn't angry, but I was stunned that my mother had left me alone, sleeping, while she got married. I was happy for her, but I never felt more left out of Mom's life than I did during breakfast that morning.

I never told Mom of my feelings because I figured she had enough to worry about. Besides, I understood that marriage was a good thing for her and probably a good thing for me too. What I didn't realize at the time was that this was the beginning of a change in my mother's priorities. Over a period of years, she changed her role from that of the protective mother to the protective wife—more interested in proving herself worthy of her husband's faith-based expectations than she was in protecting her daughter from being harassed by the faithful. I'm actually glad it took years for me to realize that; otherwise, I might have resented my mother's change in loyalty and felt abandoned and depressed.

Ed and Josie left later in the morning, and Brass drove Mom and me to the cities, where we stopped at Sears. Mom bought an outfit for my doll, then used a pay phone to call her brother Chuck. After Mom finished her call, Brass drove us over to Uncle Chuck and Aunt Sally's home in St. Paul, where we spent the afternoon and early evening celebrating the wedding day. I played with my cousins Pat and Lynn, who were close to my age. Everyone there was happy for Mom, Brass, and me.

The following Monday morning at school, I reported the exciting news of Mom's marriage to everyone. My excitement grew when all the kids expressed their happiness for me and eagerly wanted to talk about it. My classmate Betty Simon and I were especially happy because Mom's new husband, Ralph "Brass" Simon, was Betty's dad's brother, or Betty's uncle, and his marriage to my mom made Betty and me cousins. Betty told me she already knew about the marriage because her family had talked about it at home. She explained that her entire family was happy about the marriage. Our enthusiasm at being cousins bubbled over as we jumped up and down, giggling like the silly schoolgirls we were.

Hearing our excitement, Sister X rushed over to discover what was going on. One of the kids told her that my mom had gotten married over the weekend. I told her I was so happy to have both a mother and a father in my family. But Sister X seemed eager to squelch my joy, as she quickly let me know—again, in front of the entire room of students—that my mother's marriage did not mean that Ralph Simon was my father. She emphasized that I was *not* a Simon or actually any part of the Simon family. She made sure I understood that I was still *not* in a "normal" family. "Your mother's last name may have changed, but *yours* has not!" she said. "Betty and you are not related. You are *not* cousins." The happy excitement in the room quickly died. Betty and I both bowed our heads in embarrassment and couldn't even look at anyone else in the room. The other students never spoke of it again.

Sister X knew how to stifle a little girl's moment of happiness and take away her joy. I felt especially bad because my friend Betty had been dragged into my shame. Neither of us would ever tell our parents about the shaming because we knew parents tended to blindly support anything the clergy or nuns did to children. Parents would somehow rationalize it, certain that the nuns knew what was best, dismissing their child's stories as mere exaggerations. And this is still happening today, even after hundreds of cases of documented abuse by priests have been exposed over the decades since. Why do parents and guardians not realize how their blind trust in church authority has enabled—and will likely continue to enable—the abuse of their children? Blind trust enables abuse, at least when humans are involved. This cannot be said often enough.

This was only one of many incidents during the year that Sister X made a special effort to humiliate students, especially those whose parents lacked money or influence. For example, a classmate came to school one day in a dress missing a couple top buttons in the back. The nun called her up front, scolded her for coming to school dressed raggedly, and told her to go home and not come back until her mother had fixed her dress. I remember the girl trying to explain about the buttons, but Sister X would not listen. Wrapping up her diatribe, Sister X told the child that her mother needed to dress her better. I wonder why she couldn't just have helped the girl without shaming her in front of the class. Why not just loan her a pin?

Sister X liked to praise some of her model students by holding one of their papers up in view of the entire class and then handing it to the owner. I think every student strived to get that recognition, but I never got that, even though I got good grades. One example of her ignoring my achievements was on a history test. The last question was "What is history?" I struggled to find the right words, and I can't remember my exact answer, but I think I wrote something like "History is telling what happened."

The next day, Sister X stood in front of our class and angrily scolded us—all of us—for not getting the correct answer to that question. "Only one student got the answer correct," she said, but she didn't name the student. When I got my test back, I discovered that I was that student. Yes, I was the only student awarded points for the answer to that question, but Sister X had no public praise for me, no holding up my test and announcing, "Nancy got the answer correct!" For me, the lack of praise was her way of saying I was not worthy of any approval from her. To this day, I cannot understand her motivation. Did she think she was doing God's work by stripping away the dignity of a child?

Soon after marrying Brass, Mom instructed me to start calling him "Dad," which was a bit awkward at first, but at least it cleared up any question I may have had regarding what I should call him. Up until that time, *Dad* was a word I had never been able to use. The awkwardness I felt when using the word had more to do with my feeling the word did not truly belong to me than with any lack of feeling toward my stepfather. He was not one to show emotion, but neither was I, nor was Mom, so I never regarded him as distant or cold, even though others may have thought he was. To me, he was always a man who truly cared for Mom and me.

As might be expected with any family, Dad's siblings, their children, and their grandchildren were divided on embracing Dad's new wife and child as part of their family. Dad had always been close to his brother Ed, who had served as best man at the wedding, and the brothers grew even closer as Mom and Ed's wife, Josie, became close friends. Ed and Josie's children always treated me like kin. Also, Joe and Bernice Simon's support never wavered, and my friendship with their youngest child, Betty, continued to grow through the years. Betty and I genuinely felt like kin, and her sister Bernice "Sis" Bergstrom (married name) became a close friend and cousin after we were older, when a few years' difference in age no longer seemed to matter. The same was true for the kids of Fred "Fritz" and Evelyn Simon—Richard "Bull" Simon and his two sisters, Kathy and Rosemary. Although Bull and Kathy have since passed away, Rosemary remains good friends with me to this day.

The Inquisition

I do not intend to imply that those not listed as friends necessarily treated me with disdain. Years and generations separated me from most of my new relatives. Understandably, several of them may have had difficulty getting past my bastard status, but only one seriously tried to do something about it.

A few months after Mom married Ralph Simon, one of his married nieces invited me to spend a Saturday morning playing with her daughter at her home. She was a couple of grades below me at school, and I didn't know her well enough to count her as a friend. Mom insisted that I accept the invitation, resulting in the bastard moment I now refer to as "the Inquisition."

The mother, Ralph's married adult niece, said she was glad I came, although I didn't get a feeling of warmth like I usually did from the mothers of my other friends. She sent her daughter and me upstairs to play in the daughter's room, where she showed me some of her toys. After a short time, one of her older brothers came to join us. That's when the Inquisition started.

To my astonishment, the girl demanded, "Brass is only your stepfather. What is your *real* father's name?"

Then her brother chimed, "Where is your *real* father? Why isn't he here?"

I was stunned. This was the first time any relative had ever asked me such questions. I gasped and tried to answer as best I could, but Mom had not revealed details to me about my father.

"I don't know his name," I admitted.

They didn't like that answer and turned more aggressive. Then I remembered Mom had once told me that he died.

Trying to satisfy them, I exclaimed, "He died!"

Suddenly, the girl knocked me down, hit my arm, and demanded I answer her question. "Where's your father?"

"He died!"

Rejecting my answer, the two siblings both jumped on me and held me down as they shouted, "Where's your father?" They kept asking the same question, and I kept giving the same answer. I asked them to let me up, but that only made them more aggressive. I struggled to get up—only to have them push me back down. I felt terrified as both of them sat on top of me, holding my arms down and yelling at me. What had I done to deserve their anger?

As their verbal and physical abuse continued, I felt pain in the many places I had been hit or held, and I became more frightened, not knowing when the ordeal would end. Finally, their mother called from downstairs, saying she had a snack for us in the kitchen. They released me immediately, and we went downstairs for our snack.

I hurried through the snack. I was afraid to say anything about the beating I had just received at the hands of my new cousins, and neither the mother nor her children brought it up. Explaining to the mother that Mom wanted me to come home immediately after the snack, I left, trying not to run.

When my mom got home from work, a few minutes after noon, she asked me how the visit had gone. All I told her was that I would *never* go back to that house again. She asked why, but I repeated, "I *never* want to play with that girl again, and I will *never* go back to that house again!" I'm sure Mom figured that something terrible had happened, but she didn't question me further. Decades later, I realized that Mom was no doubt a veteran of the kind of questioning I had experienced. I was not astounded to discover that the same family was socially close with Sister X, a relationship that may have empowered them to take any action necessary to expose my status.

Because that cousin lived in the same town as I did, we would see each other at school, church, and some family get-togethers. I was always civil to her, but I thought Mom knew I didn't like the girl. I was astounded when, years later, as I attended high school, Mom set up another horrible playdate with the same family. Incredible! Why did Mom continue to urge me to befriend this woman's daughter? It was probably part of Mom's never-ending attempts to get approval from Dad's (Ralph's) side of the family. Many years later, at Dad's mother's funeral, he and Mom learned what Dad's niece thought of us; she asserted that neither Dad nor his family had any right to any of Grandma Simon's heirlooms because Nancy was not a true Simon grandchild.

Sister X and Santa Claus

Sister X also felt obligated to destroy fun during the Christmas season. During my first three years of school, Christmastime was a happy and positive time in the classroom, but we soon discovered that fourth grade—taught by Sister X—would be different.

As the Christmas season approached, there was talk among my classmates about Santa Claus. When Sister X overheard a reference to the jolly elf, she furiously screamed "There is no such thing as Santa Claus!" Her rage continued as she lectured everyone in the classroom, making it extremely clear that we were *never* to believe in Santa Claus; we were to remember only our religion. Her outburst kept us too frightened to move. We tried not to stare at her as she screamed at us—trying desperately to convince a roomful of thirty or more fourth, fifth, and sixth graders to forget any seasonal magic related to a mythical man who spread cheer to everyone, rich or poor. She didn't care what our parents thought about the issue.

Most of us no longer believed in Santa anyway, but I wondered why she had made it her mission in life to squelch any belief in Santa Claus among children. For me, there was one positive aspect of her outburst: it wasn't aimed solely at me. Instead, Sister X had gotten angry with *all* her students, or maybe she was mad at the entire world, which was (and still is) full of people who liked to have fun at Christmastime.

Adoption

I'm not sure when the decision was made or when the process started, but after Mom married my stepfather, they decided to have him officially adopt me. I first realized this was in the works in early 1958, a few months after they were married. I was upstairs, in my room, after school, and my stepfather was home from work. He started work early, at about five in the morning, so he was often home before Mom, who worked until five in the evening. I came down the stairs to get something from the kitchen and discovered a strange lady sitting at the kitchen table with my stepfather. Although Dad was a kind man, he didn't normally smile much, unless he was nervous. But just then, as he answered the lady's questions, I could tell he was uncomfortable because he grinned way too wide and too often.

The strange lady told me her name and started asking me some questions. I felt rather uncomfortable around her too, but unlike Dad, I didn't know why she was there. After answering her questions, I went back up to my room. Later that evening, Mom explained that they were going through the adoption process. She said the lady had come to evaluate our home environment and that she may stop in other times without notice, so I should be on my best behavior. I honestly don't remember any of the questions or how many times she stopped by, but the visits went on for the next several months.

Finally, one morning in May of 1958, right after my tenth birthday, Mom announced I was not to go to school that day because we were to get dressed up and go to court. Dad drove us to Scott County Courthouse to have a judge finalize the adoption. We rode to the courthouse in silence.

The inside of the courthouse was huge and intimidating, with stone floors and high walls of varnished wood. The scene frightened me a little, and when I observed Mom talking too much and Dad smiling too much, I realized that they were nervous too. We met with several adults in the lobby, including the lady who had visited our home over the past year to ask questions. Others were probably lawyers. Then we went into a courtroom, where a judge was seated behind his high, intimidating desk. After some discussion with the lawyers, the judge said I was to meet with him in his office—without my parents. The visiting lady accompanied me and would be present during the entire private meeting.

The judge's office was huge and fancy, with polished wood from floor to ceiling. I sat in a big leather chair that made me feel small, and the judge sat in his chair on the other side of his huge desk. He asked me questions about how we lived, how they treated me, whether they were mean and hit me, and so on. He also asked whether I liked living with them and felt safe. I do not remember exactly how I answered all the questions, but I know I answered them honestly, which reflected positively on my mother and father. Then we all went back to the courtroom where my folks had been waiting. After the judge sat in his chair, he declared the adoption approved. My last name was now Simon, and I officially had a father.

I didn't start using my new name at school until I started the fifth grade, in the fall of 1958. Neither Sister X nor anyone else made any comment about the change. Perhaps Mom had registered my new name with the school and the church before school started in the fall. Not until 1960 did Mom request a copy of a new birth certificate reflecting the name change. The certificate, dated November 23, 1960, no longer listed my biological father's name—a last name I only vaguely remembered seeing on a couple of my children's books before my old name was mysteriously erased. In the years that followed, I had no access to my biological father's name, not even knowing how it was spelled.

Shortly after the adoption, Mom explained to me that Dad had wanted to adopt me because he wanted me to be his legal heir. She explained that if she and Dad were both killed in an accident, I would have no claim to any of his estate unless I had been legally adopted. She specifically said, "Dad was worried that some of his relatives would try to take his estate and leave Nancy with nothing." He knew adopting me was the right thing to do, even though it was a costly and difficult process that put him and Mom through strict scrutiny. First, although Mom was legally divorced, Catholic tradition stated she had to get her first marriage annulled before she could marry Dad.

I can only imagine how nerve-racking it must have been for Dad and Mom to work through all of this under the glaring eye of the church and its members in town, some of whom were eager to judge and condemn. Of course, marrying outside the Catholic Church would have been social suicide and a direct path to hell, according to Dad's beliefs. I know that most of Dad's relatives were supportive, and I am as sure he leaned on his brother Ed for support and encouragement as I am sure Mom leaned on her sister Tillie for support. The few relatives who didn't support the marriage were eager to judge Mom and declare "I told you so" to Dad if it didn't work out.

My mom was extremely happy about the adoption being finalized. My last name was finally the same as her new married last name. I think my mom thought the whole stigma of my being a bastard would be over. Although I loved writing *Nancy Ann Simon* instead of *Nancy Ann Schoenecker*, I seriously doubted my new last name would make a difference in my status with the nuns. And in fact, most things didn't change, especially at school, where I was still treated as a bastard by the same people.

Grades five and six dragged by, and Sister X continued treating me with disdain, but I found my subjects interesting and focused my energy on my studies and friends.

CHAPTER 3

PLEASANT MEMORIES

First Communion

Those early years at school were not without pleasant events. Although I had no father for most of that time, Mom had two sisters, Aunt Tillie and Aunt Caroline, who lived nearby, and they were incredibly supportive of Mom and me. Mom also had some good friends in town who had her back.

For example, for my first communion, Mom's good friend Francis Jandt made a beautiful dress especially for me. She and Mom picked out a special white dotted Swiss fabric. They discussed the pattern together, then Francis, an expert seamstress, described how she would make extra ruffles on the skirt. Her husband, Otto, had been gassed in World War I, rendering him unable to work. Although Otto received a small pension from the government, Francis helped support their household by taking in sewing, including altering suits for men, altering various garments for women, and designing and making clothes for adults and children. I was thrilled that Francis had volunteered to make me a special dress.

As I heard girls in my class eagerly discussing the new dresses and shoes their folks would buy them for First Communion, all I could think about was how little money Mom had to spend on my wardrobe. And I had grown. My white shoes from the previous year were too small, painful for me to wear. To ease my pain and save the expense of buying new shoes, Mom cut a hole at the toe of each to make them into sandals. They looked great. When

Communion Day came, my new dress was starched to perfection, all the accessories were sparkling new, and I felt like a princess. To celebrate my big day, Mom invited Aunt Caroline, Aunt Tillie, and their families. The next day at school, several classmates talked about their huge parties and all the gifted money they had received, but that didn't bother me; my Communion Day had felt special because I was surrounded by the love of my wonderful family. I didn't even notice I was the only girl with a homemade dress, which I have lovingly saved all these years. Presently, it hangs on the wall in my office, by my sewing machine.

My Doughnut Aunt

Mom's marriage to Ralph Simon in 1957 was good for all of us, but it was especially good for me because Ed and Josie Simon became my uncle and aunt. They were kind and fun. We spent many Sunday afternoons out at their farm, visiting with them and their children—Victor, Charlie, Dennis, Joyce, and Jan. Victor and Charlie were older and already dating. I thought their girlfriends were beautiful and friendly young women, and I was glad when these lovely girls later became their wives. They were always kind to me, and I admired them as role models. Dennis was about four years older than I was, and Joyce and Jan were younger, but I had fun visiting with all of them, as they each seemed to embrace me as a cousin.

I loved Sunday visits at Ed and Josie's house because it meant staying for supper, a warm and inviting family experience where everyone sat around the big kitchen table, talking, joking, and eating loads of home-cooked food. Whatever Aunt Josie served was delicious, and it was always accompanied by a large plate of her homemade bread, sliced thick and stacked high. She served many wonderful desserts over the years, but the dessert I loved most was her homemade cake doughnuts, which had no filling, sugar coating, or frosting. Even if there was another dessert, there was always a plate of those great doughnuts on the table. I praised the doughnuts often and ate as many as I could without being impolite. Aunt Josie definitely noticed my preference for her doughnuts. When we would leave for home after supper, we had to walk through their enclosed porch, where their big chest freezer stood. Walking just ahead of me on our way out, Aunt Josie would stop by the freezer, open the huge top, grab a bag of frozen doughnuts, and hand them to me. "For you," she would say. It's amazing how happy a bag of frozen doughnuts can make a little girl.

Aunt Josie always made me feel special. All her life, she continued to make her doughnuts and generously give them away. If you stopped at her house, she would have doughnuts ready to eat. If she came to visit, she sometimes brought a bag of doughnuts as a gift. When I got older, I asked for her doughnut recipe. She had to tell me the ingredients verbally, she said, because the recipe came from her mom's recipe book, which was written in Czech. Even now, I always use Aunt Josie's recipe to make doughnuts, and every time I do, I think of my wonderful "doughnut aunt."

My Favorite Chore

When I was growing up, Mom worked at the Produce Monday through Friday, Friday evening, and Saturday morning, which limited the time she had to do household chores. I wanted to help, and I did some of the easy housework on my own, like dusting, but since we had to heat water for cleaning on the stove, there weren't a lot of other chores Mom allowed me to do on my own. All I could do was watch and try to help her when I could.

My favorite chore was washing clothes. Our wringer washer sat in the corner of the kitchen. On washday, we would move the kitchen table back and roll the washer out toward the middle of the room. The rinse tub was set on a bench next to the washer. Mom would heat water on the stove and pour it into the washer, a task I was too small to manage. We would sort the dirty clothes into piles on the floor in the order they would be washed. Pile number one was whites. These were washed first, when the water was at its hottest. Next came the light-colored items. Then came the heavier items, like towels. After that came jeans and heavier slacks. Last came the dirtiest and heavy items, like floor rugs.

I paid close attention to Mom as she washed clothes, and I was particularly fascinated by the use of the wringer. Putting clothes through the wringer had to be done carefully. If you tried to stuff too many garments through at a time, it would jam and stop turning, forcing you to open the wringer, remove the excess clothing, start the wringer, and then reinsert the clothes in smaller amounts. Clothes with buttons needed to be run through with the buttons sitting flat, or the wringer would break the buttons. A wringer operator must take constant care to avoid getting her fingers or any of her clothing caught in the roller with the wet clothes.

Mom once got her finger caught in the wringer, and all I could do was watch helplessly. I saw the look of agony on her face as tears started to wet her cheeks, but she did not scream out. At that time, the wringer had no auto-release handle—a safety device added to later models—so she had to use her other hand to quickly stop the wringer and open the roller. Even in her haste, this procedure probably took almost a minute, but to me it seemed like hours. Her finger wasn't broken, but it did come out a bit flat. Almost no one went to a doctor in those days. Mom just bandaged the finger and finished washing clothes. Her finger was terribly bruised for a long time after.

I enjoyed helping to hang the washed clothes outside, on the clothesline. Mom would string our clotheslines between trees or from the house to a tree or a shed. Usually, the line was propped up high, with a post in the middle. To hang clothes, you removed the prop post, lowering the line for easier access. Once the clothes were hung, the prop post was replaced, raising the line high to keep the heavy, wet clothes from touching the ground as they dried.

We moved to the Shea house when I was nine years old, and Mom married a few months later. Soon, I took over washing all the clothes. Like our apartment, this house didn't have hot running water, but my stepfather purchased what we called "the donut," which was a round heating element attached to an electrical cord. When placed into a container of cold water and then plugged in, the donut would heat the water over the course of a few hours. Because the donut was submerged in water and connected directly to electricity, I had strict orders never to put my hands into the water while the donut was operating. During her lunch break on school days, Mom would fill the washing machine with water and plug in the donut. When I got home from school, the water would be hot. I would unplug and then remove the donut before starting to wash the clothes that were in piles on the kitchen floor. Because I was unable to handle the heavy pails of water, Mom or Dad would empty the washing machine when they got home from work.

Clothes were hung on outside clotheslines to dry no matter the season. Of course, hanging out clothes was a lot easier in the summer, when the warm breezes completely dried everything. Hanging clothes outside during winter was rough on my fingers, which always felt like ice afterward. I once tried to do it while wearing mittens but found it impossible to manipulate the clothespins. Using bare hands to quickly clip on the clothespins, I'd stop quite often to warm my hands in my pockets, but I couldn't waste too much time warming my hands because the wet clothes would start to freeze together in the basket. By the time all the clothes were washed and hung out during a winter washday, it was usually already time to take the first ones down and bring them inside—not because they were dry but because they were usually frozen hard as a board. I'd take the frozen clothes into the house and hang them on a wooden clothes rack or on a temporary clothesline strung up by the heat stove. Once inside, the clothes dried really fast, although they would drip excess water onto the floor, where I would place some newspapers to limit the mess. Washing clothes in those days took time, but they always smelled so good from being hung outside in the fresh air.

After washday came ironing day. There was no wrinkle-free cloth in those days. At age nine, I took over the ironing too. I loved to take a wrinkled piece of clothing and make it smooth and nice with the iron. I had a problem one summer day, though, when I was home alone, ironing clothes. There was a spark and a crackle, and the section of the iron's cord nearest the wall outlet burst into flames. For a moment, I didn't know what to do. Luckily, I didn't panic. I grabbed the cord at its midpoint and pulled the plug out of the outlet. Thank goodness, the flames disappeared. The cord's plug was melted, but no flames remained, and no house fire ensued. We didn't have a phone, so I couldn't call anyone, and I couldn't go for help because I didn't want to leave the house in case the outlet started on fire again. I pulled everything away from the wall outlet and watched it for over an hour before running down to the Produce to tell Mom what had happened. After hurrying home to make sure it was safe, she went back to work. When my stepfather got home, he replaced the melted plug with a new one, and I was back to ironing as usual the very next day.

I continued using a wringer washing machine for many years. When Gordy and I got married, in 1970, we moved into an apartment in Minneapolis. The building had a laundry room filled with automatic washing machines, but I had no idea how to use one. Lucky for me, being in the army had taught Gordy how to use an automatic washing machine, and he'd practiced further while living in apartments, so he taught me how to use the machines. During those first few years in an apartment, I learned to dislike using automatic washing machines, as it seemed to take forever; I had to either wait for each load in the small, depressing laundry room or keep running up and down the stairs between loads. I was happy when we moved to the farm, where I could once again use my wringer washing machine. I continued using that same wringer washer until we built our new house, in 1986. By that time, automatic washing machines had evolved for the better, allowing the operator to change settings based on the size of the load, the desired cycle length, and such. I readily transitioned to using an automatic washing machine.

Years later, when Mom was about ninety years old and living in her apartment at Mala Strana Assisted Living and Rehabilitation Center, she apologized for having me wash clothes when I was so young. I told her, "I liked to wash clothes. And I never felt like I was forced to do it." I added that I felt lucky to have a mother and a father that trusted me to do the work, because washing clothes helped build my confidence and self-esteem.

CHAPTER 4

BEYOND SISTER X

I was joyful when I finished the sixth grade, in the spring of 1960, and I looked forward to starting the seventh grade, where I would no longer have Sister X for a teacher. During that year, Mom finally got accepted into the Christian Mother Society due to her new status as a woman who had married a Catholic man in good standing with the church. She was ecstatic at the accomplishment, and she showed me her badge with pride. I knew she deserved credit for her years of patience and quiet effort. Although she worked at events with other members, some of them did not change their low opinion of her. I think it scarred her for life.

Sister Y

Sister Y, the nun who taught grades seven and eight, also served as principal. She was a short, energetic nun of about fifty years of age. She was an improvement over Sister X, and she had one quality we all enjoyed: she liked to have us sing Christmas carols during the season. Singing carols brought joy to most of us, I think. I wouldn't characterize the seventh and eighth grade, my last two years at St. Nicholas Catholic School, as especially good or bad, but it was just as well that I had not allowed myself high expectations for Sister Y. Although she never dwelled on my bastard status, she revealed her skill at shaming children whenever she felt the need.

I remember one instance in particular from the winter I was in the seventh grade. Most of the farm boys helped their parents with the chores in the morning, and although the boys cleaned up and changed clothes before being brought to school, chances are they had only one pair of overshoes to wear, both for chores and school. A quick rinse might remove most of the cow dung, but I think most of us can imagine a seventh-grade boy maybe missing a spot, especially if it had dried and stuck fast onto the rubber boot.

One morning, Sister Y spotted several dried clumps of dirt on the floor and easily determined the source was this boy's dirty boots. The boy may have deserved a one-on-one reprimand from the nun, but she instead chose to publicly shame him. She waited until all students in both grades, about twenty-five children, were seated before announcing the boy's name to the whole room. As the boy sat at his desk, Sister Y belittled him and his family for lack of cleanliness. As the merciless rant continued, he slumped in his desk, lowering his head in shame. At first, there were a few sneers and snickers from some of the students—most of whom *never* got their boots dirty—but their sense of superiority subsided as the nun continued haranguing the boy, until most of us became nearly as uncomfortable as the boy himself.

Bastards Can't Serve

One of my bastard moments—the one that most glaringly singled me out as a bastard to the entire St. Nicholas Catholic Church congregation—happened when I was about twelve years old, during the summer before I would enter the seventh grade. The hurt and embarrassment is still fresh in my memory.

The standard practice for weddings at St. Nicholas Catholic Church involved a sit-down meal for the wedding party and guests in the church basement following the ceremony. The young girls of the parish were invited to help serve food. Serving at a wedding was considered a great honor, and the parents of the bride awarded each girl a special apron for the occasion. Afterward, the girls would take every opportunity to show off their special aprons and talk about the wedding.

A wedding was planned for later that summer, and like all my friends, I was excited about the opportunity to serve. But when the girls in town began discussing their invitations to serve, I realized I still hadn't received one. I soon discovered that every girl in my grade, the grade above me, and the grade below me had been invited to serve—I was the *only* girl not invited. As the date came closer, I heard the other girls excitedly discussing when they needed to be there, what they were going to wear, and what the bridesmaids' dresses would be like. They didn't always realize I was listening, but when they did, they would stop talking. All I could do was walk away in shame.

By this time, Mom had remarried at St. Nicholas Catholic Church, I had been adopted, I was attending St. Nicholas Elementary School, and my last name was officially Simon—yet somehow, I was still not good enough. The bride's family knew Mom because they farmed outside of town and did business at the Produce, where Mom worked. We all attended the same church. But none of that mattered. The only thing that mattered, it seemed, was that I was a bastard and not worthy of being included in their family celebration or around "good" Catholics. Apparently, my presence would somehow stain their sacrament of marriage.

Although Mom and I talked about my exclusion, we never discussed it with that family or even talked about it aloud to anyone else. We dismissed the idea that it could have been an oversight because there was never any apology given to Mom or me. The experience is permanently seared into my soul, and those feelings of shame and embarrassment always come rushing back when I drive past that family farm. It is amazing how a childhood experience can affect a person's life forever.

I don't allow those old feelings of shame to overshadow the happiness in my present life, but as Gordy and I drove past that farm recently, I explained the experience to him for the first time. Gordy suggested an alternate explanation: "Maybe the family of the bride didn't choose which girls to invite—but used a list of eligible girls given to them by the church. From whom would that list originate?"

This was an aha moment for me! Of course the list of eligible girls came from someone at St. Nicholas—the ceremony and meal were hosted by the church, and all the girls attended the school. Had the nuns reviewed the list of girls and decided that a bastard had no place at a Catholic wedding? The discrimination I had suffered from Sister X seemed to validate this hypothesis. I began to view the experience in a different light. Although the memory still surfaces whenever I pass the farm, I no longer blame the bride or her parents.

Sister Y, the Priest, and the Report Cards

At the end of every grading period, the priest—I'll call him Father Job—came down to the school to personally hand out report cards. He always made a grand entrance and walked slowly up to Sister Y's desk, where they would chat briefly as she fawned over him, thanking him for taking time out of his busy schedule. Then he would borrow Sister Y's chair and sit at her desk as he straightened the pile of report cards by repeatedly tapping their sides on the hard surface, all the while making lame comments like "It's report card time again, boys and girls." After he got the stack as straight as he wanted it, the torture began. Father Job would pick up the top report card and call out the student's name. The student had to approach the side of the desk and wait as Father Job reviewed their report card and made comments loudly enough for the class to overhear, many of which were extremely cruel or embarrassing to the student.

If the priest's involvement in this ritual was meant to emphasize the importance of learning and grades, I can see how it could have been useful, but his comments and shaming failed to motivate anyone except through fear. My grades were good, and I don't specifically recall being shamed during this time. But like most kids, I never enjoyed the process, even though I looked forward to getting my grades. Knowing how clergy in the church felt about me, I was always terrified when he spoke to me, that he might say something about my bastard status, subjecting me to another bastard moment. Although that never happened, the experience was never positive.

I never once felt any warmth or compassion from that man, and his commenting on my report card felt like an invasion of privacy. Maybe that's not something most parents are worried about when they sign their kids up for Catholic school. Maybe I was more sensitive to the perceived intrusion than other students. But most of my classmates seemed noticeably uncomfortable as Father Job handed out the report cards. Maybe I would've believed he had our best interests in mind if he hadn't seemed to enjoy ridiculing us so much.

Of course, Father Job had a few pets he would regularly praise, and I'm sure they probably enjoyed the public attention, but not every student who received poor grades was singled out for his torture. If a student's father was in the Knights of Columbus, Father Job never said a negative word toward the child. I am definitely not suggesting he should have disparaged the student regardless of their parents' ranking in the church hierarchy, but I wondered why he only publicly put down those who were already down. If the priest honestly thought it would motivate them to do better, why wouldn't the public shaming work for every student, regardless of parental status?

After he handed out all the report cards, the priest would give us his blessing, which meant we would all pray and then exclaim, in unison, "Thank you, Father Job." After that, we would all stand up so he could leave.

May Day Celebration

A statue of the Virgin Mary adorned a space near the altar of St. Nicholas Catholic Church in New Market. During mass on the Sunday closest to the first of May, a procession of children from the congregation honored her with flowers. The child leading the parade crowned her "Queen of May" by placing a crown of flowers on her head. The other children placed the flowers they carried into the vases at Mary's feet. As the children participated in this spring event, their parents, along with the entire congregation, enjoyed seeing them dressed in their finest as they honored the Virgin Mary.

One day while I was in the eighth grade, Sister Y announced that I had been selected to crown the Virgin Mary at that year's May Day celebration. Sitting at my desk, shocked, I briefly envisioned myself reluctantly leading about eighty boys and girls, in grades one through eight, up to the statue of the Virgin Mary. No one was more surprised at the announcement than I was, but as I peeked out the corners of my eyes, I could see that some of my classmates were pretty shocked as well. After all, every one of them had experienced eight years of a nun-directed narrative in which I was not considered worthy. How could anyone expect these young people to drop their Catholic duty to scorn me and suddenly accept me as worthy? I didn't. I couldn't. And as I expected, I sensed some resentment from a few classmates who were favored by the nuns. I even remember overhearing some intentionally loud whispers among those same classmates during recess, expressing their disapproval at my being chosen.

Mom became ecstatic when I told her about my new duty. I'm sure she felt her little girl had been accepted by the nuns. Maybe she was right, but the nuns had never expressed any words of acceptance to me. My feelings about the event were irrelevant to anyone else. No one had asked me if I wanted to do it. I understood intuitively that I should feel pleased, but no one explained how or why I had been selected. No one seemed to understand that eight years of being shamed for my bastard status had not only killed my self-worth but also served to cement a negative sense of my worth in those classmates who had felt elevated by the way I was treated. That kind of learning sticks and cannot be reversed by a sudden gesture. I had felt mocked and foolish when Sister Y announced my selection, but I felt even more mocked and foolish during the May Day mass, trudging to the statue and placing the crown of flowers on Mary's head. I found myself wondering whether Sister X had agreed with the decision to have me lead. Maybe the selection was not really about me at all. I'll never know how or why I ended up leading the May Day procession.

Seventh and eighth grade at St. Nicholas Catholic School passed swiftly for me, if not painlessly. The school only went through grade eight, and honestly, I gave no thought to where I would go to high school.

CHAPTER 5

SCHOOL AWAY FROM HOME

My parents decided I would attend Bethlehem Academy (BA), a Catholic high school in Faribault, Minnesota, starting in the fall of 1962. Going to BA meant staying with relatives in Faribault from Monday through Friday each week and only being home on weekends. During my first year at BA, two of my cousins on my dad's side also attended the school, staying with my stepfather's older sister Grace. Her oldest son had been killed in action on January 21, 1945, as part of the Battle of Luzon during World War II—a tragedy she had to bear all her life.

Aunt Grace's house was small and dark, yet she was able to make money by taking care of two invalid men, who each had their own room. She worked hard at taking care of those men—making all the meals, cleaning up their messes, and doing some nursing chores. Betty and her older sister Mary Ann would also be staying at the house. Mary Ann, who was a senior at BA, slept in a tiny bedroom with just enough room for a single bed and a nightstand. Betty and I slept in a drafty enclosed porch that had only enough room for two single beds, which had to be jammed together to fit. At one end of the room was a rod for hanging a few clothes, but I mostly lived out of my suitcase all week. I was glad BA required uniforms, which eliminated pressure to buy and wear fashionable clothes.

I was careful not to say much about myself to potential new friends at BA, hoping the other students would not discover I was a bastard. Since Betty and I were close, I knew she wouldn't say anything to betray me, and although several older boys from New Market attended BA, I knew they wouldn't intentionally put me down. However, I still feared the subject would come up somehow.

Mary Ann had stayed with our aunt Grace throughout her high school years at BA, and the two of them had grown close. Sometimes on Wednesday nights during the winter, the two of them would go to bingo while Betty and I stayed at the house. One Wednesday night, one of the men our aunt was caring for decided to get up and go to the bathroom, which usually did not happen because they had commodes in their rooms. While Betty and I were doing our homework on the porch, a sudden, frantic call came from the bathroom. We went to the closed door and asked whether something was wrong. The man kept calling out for help, saying we had to enter the bathroom to help him. Despite our skepticism, we opened the door and there he was—half on and half off the bathroom stool, his long underwear wide open. Reluctantly, we entered to lend aid. Each of us taking one arm, we pulled him up and back onto the stool. He asked us to carry him to his room, but we told him to just use his walker, then we left the bathroom quickly. He called a few more times, but we did not respond. He eventually used his walker and managed to get back to his bedroom without any problem. We both thought he may have called for us just to make us come look at him. We reported the incident to our aunt when she got home. She was pretty mad at the man and told us it would never happen again. It didn't.

After that first year, Betty decided to go to New Prague High School (a public school), rather than continue at BA. Mary Ann had graduated, and except for the male boarders, I would've been the only one staying with my aunt. I really didn't want to stay there because the presence of the two boarders made the place seem creepy to me. Fortunately, Dad had another sister living in Faribault, and her youngest son would be leaving for college before school started. With large bedrooms upstairs, the house had plenty of room for me to stay.

Faribault in the 1960s

During my first year at BA, none of us girls—Mary Ann, Betty, and I— went to downtown Faribault very often. Mary Ann always wanted us to walk straight home from school, except during the holidays, when Betty and I sometimes convinced her to go shopping downtown after school. However, during my sophomore and junior years, my friends and I loved to walk the few extra blocks to visit downtown Faribault, which was considered a vibrant city in the 1960s. Although we seldom bought anything, we enjoyed seeing the variety of businesses, which included a department store, unique restaurants, and a movie theater. Downtown teemed with people and interesting places, giving us a free adventure after a day at school.

The variety and number of churches and both private and public schools made Faribault an exceptional city. Churches of various faiths flourished, but the fact that there were three different Catholic churches fascinated me. The Faribault students at BA always referred to the three Catholic churches as "the French church," "the German church," and "the Irish church." Those churches had official church names, of course, but the students rarely used them. Apparently, immigrants of those nationalities had settled in different areas of town and built their own churches. By the time I went to BA, this division of nationality was no longer strictly the case, but the labels for the churches still stuck.

Besides the public high school and the Catholic high school in Faribault, there were a number of other unique schools, including St. Mary's High School (a private Episcopal institution), Shattuck Military Academy, a school for the deaf, a school for the blind, and a hospital/school for the mentally challenged. As we walked the downtown streets, we'd see blind students training to navigate streets and stores, deaf students signing to each other on the street and in the stores, and mentally challenged individuals being trained to live in society while learning to shop. School uniforms identified which schools students attended, including uniforms from BA, St. Mary's, and Shattuck. Students without uniforms probably attended the public high school. With so much relative diversity in Faribault in the 1960s, downtown proved an exciting after-school experience for me.

An Old Friend

A bastard moment crept up on me one day early in my sophomore year, when I met a former classmate from New Market whose family had moved to Faribault when we were in the second grade.

We met by chance on the street near her house while I was walking back to my aunt's home after school. Delighted to see her, I greeted her enthusiastically, but she didn't seem as happy to see me. She talked about all her friends at the public school and bragged about living in a "big" town like Faribault, compared to living in New Market. We hadn't been talking for long when she said she had to get home. The conversation left me with that same old feeling of rejection and shame. I hoped I had misread her reaction.

The next spring, we again met by chance while both downtown with some of our school friends. I introduced my friends to her, but she again seemed disinterested, only stating how everything was so good with her and her friends. Then she said she was in a hurry, and she and her group walked on. This time I was sure I felt the same old bastard treatment I recalled from Sister X and some of the kids at school in New Market. Although I felt extremely hurt, I vowed not to let it dampen my spirits. I said nothing about it to my friends, and I told myself her behavior had more to do with her now being from the "big" town and my being from a "small" town.

Perhaps this was when I learned that my feeling like a bastard could grow from a variety of situations in which others assert their superiority or power to limit or control me. I didn't know it at the time, but this was something I was destined to experience from supervisors and coworkers many times throughout my career.

Riding to School

Spending weekends at home while attending BA meant that someone had to take me to Faribault on Monday mornings. During my freshman year, I rode along with Uncle Joe when he took his daughter Betty to school. Betty and I were close, and Uncle Joe was kind and often fun. But when Betty decided to go to public school for her sophomore year, my free ride dried up. However, Dad made an arrangement with a young man from New Market—an upperclassman at BA—to drive me to Faribault on Mondays and take me back to New Market on Fridays. I looked forward to riding with him and his friend because, although both were older than I, they were fun to be around, always friendly and kind.

On the first day of my sophomore year, however, I was not pleased to discover there would be another passenger—the boy who had held me down while he and his sister hit me and demanded to know my real father's name. Six years had passed since the horrible torture event, and neither he nor his sister had done or said anything to help heal my wounds. In fact, they both still behaved as though they were my superiors. I assured myself that I could handle riding with my "Inquisition cousin" in the back seat twice a week, thirty minutes each trip. I additionally rationalized that because he was a freshman and I was a sophomore, I wouldn't see him during the day.

Inquisition Déjà Vu

Although my assumption about not seeing my "Inquisition cousin" during the school day turned out to be true, his mother's reach still managed to find me. After school one day, my aunt informed me that Mom had called to suggest I go to a basketball game. Apparently, Dad's niece, the mother of the brother-sister team who tortured me, had called Mom to say they were picking up their son to take him to the game and that I was invited along—and Mom said I should go with them. I was speechless. How could Mom do this to me? How could she not understand how much their family scorned our family? How could she not remember how my last visit with that family had gone? I felt helpless. Like with the playdate six years earlier, I knew I couldn't get out of it.

Bethlehem Academy's basketball game that night was in Sleepy Eye, Minnesota. When they picked me up, I realized things were worse than I had anticipated. My dad's niece and her husband had brought their daughter along. Yikes! I would be sitting in the back seat with both of my "Inquisition cousins." I dreaded trying to talk to these people all the way to Sleepy Eye. As it turned out, I didn't have to worry about talking to them because, as soon as the car left town, the mother announced it was time to pray. We prayed the rosary and other prayers all the way to Sleepy Eye.

At the basketball game, my cousins talked with their friends, leaving me on my own to sit where I pleased, and on the entire trip home, we again had to pray, making conversation unnecessary. Praying on the way to basketball games was probably normal for them, but I wondered whether the mother thought she needed to pray to edify their bastard relative. I don't know why she believed in her own exalted status, but she had married an Irishman, and I understood from some of her children's comments that they felt being Irish was better than being German.

The German-Irish rift went back many generations in the New Market area and in nearby towns, with both sides claiming a higher pedigree. Mostly, though, they got along just fine, with only a few bad apples showing negative behavior on either side.

During the weekend, I confronted my mother about her part in arranging my trip to the basketball game. I told her I never wanted to go with them anywhere again.

Mom responded, "Wasn't it kind of nice that they wanted to take you with them?"

I didn't think Mom really believed this, but I didn't pursue it. I just replied, "These people think they are better than I am." I refrained from saying "better than *we are*" because I thought it might be hurtful to her, but I continued explaining, saying, "They just wanted to get me in the car and make me pray with them. They made us pray the rosary all the way there and back."

To this, Mom's only reply was "Oh."

I thought she understood my feelings at that point, but for insurance, I added, "If they call again, please tell them I have other plans."

If they ever called again, Mom never said so, and I didn't ask.

School Uniforms

Bethlehem Academy had a strict uniform for the girls but a rather lax dress code for the boys. The nuns aggressively enforced the rules for the girls' uniform—correct white blouse, regulation-height socks with no embellishments, plain shoes, and skirt hem landing below the knee. That last one was of particular concern to the nuns, as they did not approve of the emerging fashion trends involving shorter skirts.

Naturally, some of the girls found ways to resist—often rolling up the waistband of their skirt to raise the hem, then putting on a large belt to hide the waistband. I was no smarter than the other girls, and I was about to get a belt to do this, but during one of my classes, the nun-teacher suddenly called out one of the girls. She made the girl come up to the front of class and kneel on the floor. Of course, the girl's skirt did not touch the floor. The nun got angry, told the girl to remove her belt, and had her unroll the waistband of her skirt. The nun then took the girl's belt away from her. Many of the other students laughed at the girl as she hung her head in embarrassment and walked back to her seat. That girl's public shaming changed my plans—I would never get a belt or roll up the waistband of my skirt! Shortly after that, one of the new rules for the girls' uniform was "No belts allowed."

I remember the boys' dress code included no jeans, but other than that, there really didn't seem to be any issue with their choice of clothes. I never heard or saw a nun criticize a boy for what he was wearing, yet the nuns regularly called out girls for breaking the dress code. My observations reinforced my past experiences; the Catholic Church considered boys and men more important than girls and women. Men held all positions of supreme authority, and while women could play a part, as nuns, they seemed to always be under the authority of the priests.

Classroom Experiences

Although BA had a few lay teachers, most of the teachers were nuns. Religion was taught daily, just like English or history. I wanted to get good grades in my religion classes because they counted toward my grade point average.

Early on, our religion classes emphasized that, according to Catholic teachings, the pope spoke for God and was infallible when speaking of church doctrine—a "fact" that was drilled into us. During one class, the nun was going over many of the reforms implemented in the 1960s, during the Second Vatican Council, trying to explain some of the different opinions among the popes, past and current. My ears perked up when I heard that certain church decisions could be reversed.

This both confused and intrigued my young mind, and without considering any possible negative consequence, I raised my hand and innocently asked, "If the pope is infallible, how can one pope reverse what another pope has declared?" Seemed like a simple question to me.

The nun stared at me, put a huge frown on her face, stomped over to my front-row desk, and leaned over my desk in a way that made me sit back. She loudly pounded her finger on my desk, yelling, "You must have faith, young lady!"

Terrified by her aggressive response, I shriveled down low in my seat and said nothing. Satisfied with intimidating me and the entire class, the nun backed up, returned to the front of the room, and continued with the lesson.

The fact that she never really answered my question left me unsettled and, in a way, served to answer my question, though not in the way she intended. My takeaway from this moment was simply *popes are not infallible*. How could I think otherwise? I began believing that the idea of holy infallibility and the insistence that we "just have faith" were merely methods the Catholic Church used to control people. From then on, though, I refrained from asking questions.

As a follow-up note, reversals still happen. As recently as 2009, Pope Benedict XVI (2005–2013) revoked the excommunication of four bishops who had been cast out by Pope John Paul II (1978–2005) after having been made bishops—against the pope's wishes—by Archbishop Lefebvre in 1988. The reasons are beyond my understanding, and I might envy those who can "just have faith," but clearly, a pope's decisions are subject to change by a subsequent pope. It's interesting to note that one of the reinstated bishops, Richard Williamson, had said he did not believe the Holocaust happened, and in an interview, he said he believed the United States staged the terrorist attacks on September 11, 2001. Regardless of the degree of one's faith, it's hard not to conclude that no pope is infallible if their decrees can be reversed—but in saying so, I'm using reason, not faith.

One might think I would remember when to keep my mouth shut, but I had to relearn the same lesson again the next year, when I became overly curious in my class on world history, a subject I adored. As I paged through the textbook, I noticed that nearly every page highlighted a photograph and some deeds of a pope or an accomplished Catholic person from a particular era or place. After using this textbook for almost half a year, I wondered about this phenomenon, and during class discussion one day, I asked the nun about the highlighting of Catholic accomplishments.

"Are these events highlighted in the textbooks at public schools or other religious schools? Do those students learn a different history?" There was a silence, and I added, nearly whispering, "Would they?"

The nun's face became red with anger, and she loudly proclaimed, "History is history! It's all the same!"

46

I had to watch my back from that day on in history class. That nun was cold, almost rude, to me for the rest of the year, and I think I was lucky to get a passing grade. But just as before, her nonanswer was more of an answer than she probably would have liked.

Unlike public school students, BA students had to buy their own books. Many students sold their textbooks at the end of the year, but as a lover of history, I kept my world history text, and I can refresh my memory of the highlighted pieces whenever I like. History may be history, but much depends on what is emphasized and what is left out.

Libraries, Private and Public

The school librarian at BA was a tall, large, aggressive nun whom I found terrifying. She believed in teaching by humiliation and intimidation. If a student did anything incorrect, she would yell across the whole library to correct the behavior immediately. These bursts of vocal discipline did not create a good atmosphere for study, even for students who behaved.

During my sophomore and junior years, I found out that the friends with whom I walked to school were not fond of the school librarian either. When one of our classes assigned a paper that required some research in a library, the friends suggested we go to the public library instead, after school. Faribault had a huge, beautiful public library that was only a few blocks from BA, right on the main street of downtown Faribault. My friends had been to this library many times, but I had never before entered *any* public library. In New Market, we only had a county bookmobile that came every other week during the summer. In the Catholic elementary school I attended, we just had little library sections.

I had thought BA's school library was big, but it was nothing compared to Faribault Public Library, which was huge, spanning two floors and many different sections. I felt a bit intimidated when I went to use the card catalog, and my confusion must have shown, because one of the librarians came over to quietly ask if she could help. I told her what I was looking for, and she kindly explained how to find the information. She even helped me locate the books I needed. Then she told me she would be at her desk if I needed any more help. I was almost overwhelmed by her kindness. Here was someone who didn't know me, but she didn't judge me either. She just wanted to help me use the library, and she didn't yell. Over the next two years, I continued doing as much of my research as possible at the public library, where the kind, helpful librarians taught me more about the library than I ever learned from the nun librarians at BA.

The Art Teacher

An older nun at BA that I remember fondly was the art teacher. She was kind and especially enthusiastic about teaching art. My preference clear, I took art classes all three years at BA, loving to learn about the old masters and the types of art.

The old masters featured in the textbooks were those favored and hired by the Catholic Church. During his lifetime, Leonardo da Vinci was disliked by the popes and not favored by the Catholic Church. But this nun seemed to like Leonardo da Vinci, and she carefully suggested to certain students—including myself—that they read more about him. And I did, loving every minute.

During one of those years, our art class went on a field trip to the Minneapolis Institute of Art and the Walker Art Center, which was a fabulous learning experience for me. I had no idea that such wonderful places existed, and I have never forgotten that first exposure to the art world.

Working in the Cafeteria at BA

Another bright spot for me at BA was my working in the cafeteria during my sophomore and junior years. Going to BA was expensive, and to save money on school lunches, I applied to work in the cafeteria, where payment was a free lunch each day. As it turned out, this was probably the best experience of all three years at BA.

Another girl in my grade, Jan, worked in the cafeteria with me, and we became friends. Each day, we left our study hall early to walk down to the cafeteria. A total of three ladies worked in the kitchen—a head cook and two assistant cooks. These ladies were hard workers and extremely kind. They would greet us each day with giant smiles and treat us like the valuable workers we were. I learned not only how a high school cafeteria's kitchen worked but also how to serve food, smiling and treating every student with respect. Although their work kept the ladies busy, they always managed to smile and laugh.

Jan and I really liked the days when one of the food items was a peanut butter sandwich. Making hundreds of peanut butter sandwiches is extremely repetitive—lay down one slice of bread, pick up another slice of bread, and spread peanut butter on it before marrying the two slices, then repeat. One of the cooks would sometimes "accidentally" create a three-slice sandwich with two layers of peanut butter. Whenever this happened, the cooks would give the three-slice "mistake" to Jan and me to consume, and we always each ate half. After the cooks discovered how much we enjoyed eating these mistakes, it seemed there would often be at least two three-slice sandwiches for us to enjoy. Jan and I began to wonder whether they were really "mistakes" every time. These ladies were strong female role models for me. Although they did not earn big salaries or have glamorous jobs, they took pride in their work and made it enjoyable for themselves and their helpers.

My BA Experience

As I think back on those school days, I recall my parents' not consulting me before sending me to Bethlehem Academy. If they had, I would not have resisted. The school had a reputation for excellence, and it had been an all-girls school before it started accepting boys in 1935. I rather liked the idea of attending a renowned Catholic high school and living in Faribault, which was larger than New Market.

Local students who attended BA garnered prestige, and I thought maybe I would be part of that special group. My parents had both been working for years, affording them the extra expense of tuition, books, and transportation for my education. In fact, they were doing rather well. We lived in a decent house and had a kind landlord. Although I didn't think too much about it at the time, I later realized that our small family was no longer poor, having risen to one of the lower rungs on the middle-class ladder.

As a ninth-grade girl, I accepted their decision to send me to BA without much thought, and I am sure, to this day, that my parents had the best intentions for me. They wanted me to get a proper education, ensuring healthy spiritual and academic growth. What didn't occur to me at the time was that many of the children from New Market—those whose families had more money or higher status in the church—attended public school. And many of the children in my extended family went to public school too. Why would my folks think public school wasn't good enough for me?

Years later, I began wondering about other factors that influenced their decision to send me to BA. Had my parents felt compelled to give their only child a good Catholic education to appease some of the relatives on both Mom's and Dad's sides of the family? Was it an attempt to prove they were good Catholics, despite Mom's being a divorced woman who had a child out of wedlock and then got an annulment so she could marry a Catholic from their parish? Dad had always been obsessed with his religion, so he had a strong drive to please the church, to please the priest, and maybe to prove he'd done the right thing by marrying a woman previously condemned by his own church. None of these are necessarily bad reasons, and I love my parents for trying their best. Even then, as young as I was, I could have told them that no amount of good behavior after the fact would legitimize their station in the eyes of the few super-righteous people in town. There is no appeasement process for bastards or those who generate them.

Senior Year at Public School

I did not plan on going to college, because it was expensive. I knew my folks didn't have the money readily available. However, I knew that if I said I wanted to go, my folks would sacrifice and go into debt to send me there. I did not want that to happen, so instead of going to college, I planned to take business classes during my senior year to prepare myself for an office job after high school. After my junior year at BA, I discovered the school was eliminating the business classes I wanted to take in my senior year. That's when I decided to spend my senior year at New Prague High School, which offered the business classes I would need to take to apply for an office job after graduation.

Going to a new school my senior year was a bit intimidating, but I knew it was the right decision. I would be riding the school bus with many of my former classmates from elementary school in New Market, but that fact did not necessarily mean I would have friends in my classes. For example, my friend and cousin Betty also attended New Prague High School, but we didn't have any classes together, and my other close friend LaVonne was a grade behind me. Yet another good friend, Helen, lived in the Lakeville school district and attended school there. So I was nervous going into my senior year, made even worse by a few former New Market classmates' avoiding me like the plague. I wondered, *Will this be just like elementary school?* I was afraid that the "little bastard" label would come back strong.

To my relief, I discovered that the kids at New Prague welcomed me, and I made new friends quickly. Students who knew I was the new kid in school helped me find my classes, sat with me at lunch, and were generally kind. Although most of the students at New Prague were Catholic, they didn't seem to judge me like some of the Catholics I knew from my childhood. I ended up with a circle of friends that were Catholic, Protestant, or neither, and no one seemed to begrudge anyone else's religious preferences. Even if the high-ranking Catholics from New Market still considered me lower class, it didn't matter, because they had little to no influence over public schools, and their attitudes had no direct effect on me.

CHAPTER 6

BREAKING AWAY

Freedom

Attending public school was a good experience and gave me confidence. Not being surrounded by nuns who were constantly ready to pounce on my self-esteem allowed me to grow and feel freer. I learned that the rest of the world likely wouldn't judge me for being a bastard, at least not in the same way Catholic society did. I also learned that Catholics are less apt to judge harshly when they are either not in the majority or not led to said judgment by nuns and priests every day at school. It also proved I was right about studying history—there were no pictures of popes in the history textbooks in public school. However, living in New Market and attending St. Nicholas Catholic Church provided constant opportunities for the church to pull me back into their world of intimidation and shaming.

Religion Class

Because there were no religion classes for Catholics in the public school, St. Nicholas Catholic Church in New Market required teenage members who attended public high school to also attend religion class each Wednesday night during the school year, held in the church basement and taught not by a priest or nun but by an adult member of the congregation.

The church sent the class information to our house, indicating the time and place and emphasizing that attendance was mandatory. When I told my parents I wasn't going to attend, a heated discussion started. Dad said I had to attend and, of course, Mom agreed with him. I stated that I didn't think a religion class held only once a week could teach me any more than what I had already learned during three years of daily religion classes at BA. I also pointed out that the class was being taught by a relative of ours who was only a few years older than I was and had no more Catholic training than I did. What I didn't say—but what I knew—was that the instructor was the older brother of my "Inquisition cousins." I doubted he could teach me anything positive, and I questioned whether he would treat me decently in a religion class.

I also argued that my Wednesday evenings would be better spent doing the homework for my high school classes. Mom and Dad both asserted their usual arguments: *It will look bad if you don't attend. What will the neighbors say? All the other students are going. It's what the church expects.* But I stood my ground and emphatically insisted I would not attend. This was not the answer they wanted, but I never did go to those religion classes.

The Oath

The rating of movies by the Catholic Church goes back decades. The National Legion of Decency was formed in 1933 to identify and rate movies with objectionable content. If a movie was deemed objectionable by the Catholic Church, all Catholics were forbidden to view the film under pain of mortal sin.

The rating system and the pledge to obey by not seeing forbidden films became well known because the church distributed copies to congregations, and the National Legion had a strong lobbying influence in Congress. In the beginning, Protestant and Jewish leaders supported it as well, but the National Legion lost ground when, in 1952, the US Supreme Court ruled that sacrilege was not grounds for censorship for the general public. (Imagine how our world would be different if religions had the power to censor items for the general public!)

Although it was a national movement, it was up to local dioceses, usually priests, to enforce taking the oath. Aiming to expand their influence over the movie industry, the National League was reorganized, in 1965, into the National Catholic Office for Motion Pictures (NCOMP). When

I was a senior in high school, the Catholic leadership in New Market forbade local Catholic teenagers from attending the sinful B-rated, or partly objectionable, movies. (At the time, the C designation meant "condemned.") The church hierarchy demanded that all teenagers pledge or swear an oath that they would both not watch B-rated movies and not go to even A-rated, or morally unobjectionable, movies if shown in a movie theater that also showed B-rated movies—a rule that would make nearly every movie theater in the state of Minnesota off limits to oath-takers. When I shared this concern with my parents, they simply said I had to take the oath. "What will the neighbors think if you don't take it?" Mom asked.

A couple of weeks before the pledge date, the church started passing out the pledge to members, having the nuns discuss it in all schools where they taught, and having the priests explain the need for it during their sermons, all resulting in a highly anticipated event during the scheduled Sunday mass. During the priest's sermon that Sunday, he reminded everyone about the evils of these movies. I had read the pledge, and my parents knew my decision. Although I had explained my feelings to my mother, she still poked me with her elbow, encouraging me to participate, when the priest called for oath-takers to stand. She and I both knew the stakes: stand up and lie, or stay seated and face scorn. Well, I was pretty familiar with scorn already, and my religious upbringing had certainly taught me that lying was wrong. And yet Mom kept nudging me in the ribs, pushing me to stand along with every teenager taking the pledge that Sunday.

The priest repeated his call to stand and repeat the pledge after him. I stayed seated as I listened to the others pledge:

> I condemn all indecent and immoral motion pictures, and those which glorify crime or criminals. I promise to do all that I can to strengthen public opinion against the production of indecent and immoral films, and to unite with all who protest against them. I acknowledge my obligation to form a right conscience about pictures that are dangerous to my moral life. I pledge myself to remain away from them. I promise, further, to stay away altogether from places of amusement which show them as a matter of policy.

I knew that this was a pledge I could not possibly keep. I still wanted to go to movies with my friends, and taking the pledge would not allow me to go to the theater in New Prague, even if the movie was not B-rated. I knew if

I were to take the pledge, I wouldn't keep it, but I knew the same was true for almost every other teenager in church who was taking the pledge. As I continued listening, I felt the eyes of the congregation on me, the only teenager still seated, and I imagined the adults, nuns, and the priest thinking, *The little bastard continues defying God.* If looks could kill, I would've died that day in church, but no one ever said anything to me directly.

The following Saturday, I went out with my friends to see a movie in a theater that had shown a B-rated movie the previous weekend. As I suspected, teenage oath-takers were well represented, breaking their pledge, a mortal sin in the eyes of the Catholic Church. I guess they believed God would forgive them for breaking their oath if they went to confession the following week. Personally, I believe I did the right thing by not pledging, and although I won't judge others harshly for taking the oath and then breaking it, comments from friends let me know that my "sinful defiance" had been discussed in some homes.

The Workforce

After graduating from high school in 1966, I discovered that getting an office job was not a simple task. My folks had given me a used Chevy II after graduation, and during that summer, I drove to companies in Farmington, Northfield, and Faribault to apply for office jobs, thinking they were probably all similar. But an interview at a large national company headquartered in Northfield gave me a stark awakening—I needed to be picky about what job I accepted. Of course, I expected to start at the lowest rung of the ladder, but I also expected to be valued as an employee with clerical skills.

The supervisor who interviewed me oozed male superiority and projected an attitude toward me that lacked respect. He described the duties of the job, which included making and pouring coffee as well as passing out items at meetings, with no mention of actual clerical work. Because I knew people who *loved* working at this company, I assumed the way my interview proceeded—discussing the wrong job with, seemingly, whomever was available—was normal. When he went on to offer me the job, I turned it down, and he didn't ask me for a reason.

I mused over the fact that the supervisor had no idea I was a bastard, and yet he treated me like one. He probably treated everyone that way, especially women. Hoping this entry-level office job was not indicative of all of them—and especially hoping this supervisor's attitude was not the norm—I trudged on to apply at other companies.

I received no more offers for office jobs that summer, but I did have an opportunity to get a factory job. Fred and Loretta Mahowald from New Market worked at Frederick-Willys Pool Table Company in Farmington, where Fred was a supervisor. When he let people in New Market know the company was hiring, I applied along with several others from town—and got hired. My neighbor and Mom's good friend, Francis Jandt, was hired too, and she and I carpooled to work every day. I worked on two different assembly lines—one making small, toy pool tables and the other making the large, regular pool tables. The company treated employees well, and the work wasn't too hard. And even though the job also paid well, I stuck to my goal of working in an office.

In November, when Nutting Truck & Caster Company in Faribault contacted me to say they had an opening for an entry-level office worker, I jumped at the chance, even though the job paid much less per hour than what I was making.

Nutting Truck & Caster Company

I started my first office job in November 1966, at Nutting Truck & Caster Company, a family-owned business that had been in Faribault since 1891. They designed and manufactured floor trucks, which are two- or four-wheeled carts used to transport goods in factories, stores, railroad depots, and airports. If you visit a railroad depot museum, check the name on the carts displayed, because they are likely manufactured by Nutting Truck & Caster Company. My husband and I have seen our share at museums over the years, and we actually own two of the antiques.

I loved the new job, mainly because it required me to use many of the skills I had learned in high school and because the management especially appreciated my outstanding typing skills. I was disappointed, though, to discover that being in the working world did not mean freedom from persecution, for being a bastard or otherwise. For example, merely being female earned disdain from some of the men in positions of authority, and most of those positions were held by men anyway. Women were mostly hired for clerical positions—for example, receptionists, secretaries for male bosses, or assistants to male accountants.

The older, more experienced women usually tried to take the younger women under their wing for protection and guidance. Over time, my female coworkers delicately explained how things worked, giving advice along the lines of "Don't be in the break room alone with Mr. W," "Try to stand back from Mr. X when he's talking to you," "Never stand directly next to Mr. Y," and "Mr. Z likes to tell dirty jokes." The list of warnings was long, and I admit I was a bit discouraged that women in the office were subjected to this kind of harassment. On the other hand, I found it uplifting that the women stuck together and watched out for one another. Also, the vast majority of the men did not harass us, but it only takes a few bad apples to ruin the entire atmosphere in a workplace.

My direct supervisor was the most disgusting one. I worked in a large, open room with three rows of four single desks, spaced out to create aisles on all sides. My supervisor's desk was to the left of mine. Whenever he wanted to give me instructions or check what I was working on, he would get up and walk to the front of my desk, where he would face me and talk. He expected me to face him while he was talking, and he would rub his crotch the entire time, clearly visible just above the top of my desk—*disgusting!*

Luckily, growing up as a bastard in a Catholic school had trained me to stay silent and react as if it were all my fault—lowering my head, turning aside, and never looking up. One day, a female coworker confessed that my supervisor did the same thing to her, and it was then that I realized that being young and female was seemingly enough to qualify one to be treated with disdain—not dissimilar to my Catholic bastard upbringing—and there was no way to object. There was no support from management and no process to report sexual harassment, which included behavior that many considered a proper right of males at the time. The only advice given to the females was "Just stay away from him." The only recourse female coworkers had was to stick together.

Part of my job involved putting together special catalogs and flyers for customers, which meant I spent quite a bit of time alone in the basement, selecting the pages and assembling the catalogs. In an adjoining room, a man worked as a full-time printer, printing catalog pages, flyers, and so on. The girl who trained me took me down and introduced me to the printer, who was a really good man. He knew which of the men that worked upstairs were the bad apples. To help curb the harassment, he told me that whenever I came downstairs to work, I should come into the printshop to let him know I was there. He would then leave his door open, giving him full view of my work area. At first, I thought the precaution was probably unnecessary, but maybe the third time I went down to work alone, my supervisor showed up. Lucky for me, the printshop door was open, and when my supervisor planted his body directly in front of me, the printer stepped out of the shop, came over to me, and asked a question about the catalog on which I was working. He looked directly at my supervisor, who abandoned his mission and quickly went back upstairs. My supervisor never came down to the basement again while I worked in that position.

After a couple of years, I was promoted and given the new duty of fill-in receptionist and switchboard operator, which included routing incoming calls via a cord-operated switchboard. The operator would plug one side of a color-coded cord into the incoming-call port, greet the caller, and find out with whom they wished to speak. The operator would then plug the other side of the cord into the port corresponding to that person's phone. When the call ended, the ports would light up and beep, telling the operator it was all right to unplug both ends of the cord. This was usually quite easy and even fun, but when many calls came in simultaneously, routing phone activity via the board became challenging. Cords could become crossed, producing a tangled mess, sometimes causing the operator to accidentally pull out the wrong cords and cut off a call.

One time, I accidentally cut off an important long-distance call where I had our company's owner on the line. Right after I did it, panic set in. I thought, *Oh, man! What did I do? Will he come storming out and fire me?* Well, he didn't come out, but he did call the switchboard and ask about the call, sounding a bit upset.

I calmly answered, "Oh, did the call get cut off?"

He just answered yes and hung up, but immediately after he did, the caller I had cut off called back, saying his call had been disconnected, and he asked to be connected to the owner again. I reconnected the call, and nothing was ever said about it. I told the regular switchboard operator about the episode when she returned from break. She laughed loudly and explained, "Your response was perfect. It's the same response I use when I accidentally cut off a call. When you work switchboard, you will accidentally cut someone off sooner or later."

By the time I started working at Nutting Truck, some of the employees working in the factory and foundry were second- and third-generation employees. Even though I worked in the office, the engineers encouraged me to learn about the factory and foundry, even giving me tours of the factory floor.

One of the most fascinating tours for me was when I was allowed to view a "pour" at the foundry. Of course, I had seen the process depicted on television and in movies—foundry workers pouring molten metal from a big bucket into forms—but seeing it done live at Nutting Truck was awe-inspiring, even though the demonstration was small in comparison. From where I witnessed the demonstration, I felt the heat on my face; and as the molten metal poured into a form, I felt the resulting steam in the air moisten my nostrils and skin. I was eighteen and had never seen anything like it!

The men who worked in the foundry were not college educated, but as skilled craftsmen, they understood how to create quality molds and how to melt and pour metal safely. When designing the products, the engineers worked closely with the craftsmen in the foundry, depending on them to ensure a quality final product. I enjoyed getting to know these workers, and I felt privileged to learn about a foundry firsthand.

Working at Nutting Truck provided me with several great female role models in clerical careers. One lady in her forties had worked her way up to become a senior accountant. Another was the owner's personal secretary as well as the only one in the company who used shorthand, which proved me right about not taking a shorthand class in high school—I did *not* want to be a secretary.

Eva, another great role model for me, was the only person tasked with transcribing the Dictaphone (a brand of dictation machine) tapes recorded by all the salesmen, supervisors, and department heads. She was a cheerful, smart woman in her fifties, and I was thrilled to discover that my fast typing and my experience using a Dictaphone (from a class in high school) qualified me for the promotion that included becoming Eva's only backup. Eager to learn more about correspondence and sales, I embraced the opportunity. And she had the best typewriter in the office too—an IBM Selectric, a model introduced only six years earlier, in 1961. Eva was admired by all the women in the office, and I felt really fortunate when she decided to take me under her wing. She provided me with helpful, practical advice about being a woman in the workforce.

I was embraced by the young, unmarried women in the office, and because our budgets were tight, we normally brought our lunches from home. On payday Fridays, though, we treated ourselves to an inexpensive lunch at a small café downtown. This gave me regular experience in learning about other people's lives and worlds. I made friends with people who knew nothing of my small Catholic hometown nor the church members and townsfolk that looked down on me for being a bastard. The people at work simply decided my worth for themselves based on how I interacted with them.

After lunch one day in 1969, one of my female coworkers returned from her noon trip to the bank extremely excited, sharing that the bank had just installed new entryway doors that opened automatically. The rest of us could hardly believe her when she explained how the doors parted automatically, just like the interior doors of the starship *Enterprise* on the television show *Star Trek*. We were so intrigued that we had to check it out. The next day at lunch, everyone piled into a couple of cars and drove down to her bank. We took turns walking in and out of the bank just to experience the door opening for us. Yup, just like on *Star Trek*.

Nutting Truck & Caster Company was a good place to work, in part because the owner was a good person and business leader. He was always friendly and cheerful and treated each person like the valuable employee they were, talking to them as an equal. That respect garnered loyalty, which played no small part in earning the company a reputation for quality and dependable products.

I think it was sometime in 1969 when the owner's son graduated from college and started working in the office. His dad was set to retire, and the son would take over the company after a few years. The family had owned and operated the business in Faribault, Minnesota, since 1891, but in 1984, the company was sold to Faultless (a competitor) and relocated to Watertown, South Dakota.

The New Priest

A new priest—I'll call him Father Jack—came to New Market's St. Nicholas parish in June of 1967. I initially found him to be rather creepy, and as a young woman, I just did not want to stand anywhere close to him. However, one of the women I worked with at Nutting Truck & Caster Company considered him as a good family friend, saying that he'd once been the priest at her family's Catholic church and that her parents were disappointed when he moved on, as clergy often do. She'd even asked him to come back to Faribault to perform her marriage ceremony. Hearing her sparkling testimony about him, I thought I should revisit my feelings toward him and give him another chance.

I think it was late in the summer of 1968 when my mom told me this priest wanted me to run an errand for him: pick up some couch cushions from a store in Faribault and bring them to the priest's house in New Market, on the church grounds. After work one day, I picked up the three large cushions and put them into my little Ford Mustang, which I'd bought the previous year. Two of the cushions fit into the back seat, and the third had to sit in the front seat like a passenger. When I got to the priest's house, I drove around to the back, where four or five steps led up to the back door.

Father Jack came out the back door and asserted, "I'll hold the door while Ella brings in the cushions."

My stepfather's oldest sister, Aunt Ella Simon, was the housekeeper for the priest's house at that time. Ella was quite old and frail, but to earn a bit of money while living with her aged mother in New Market, she walked the three blocks to the priest's house, uphill, every day to do some housekeeping duties. Apparently, bringing in the cushions was part of that.

I was shocked that the priest planned to stand by and simply hold the door while an older, frail woman struggled to carry bulky cushions up steps and through a narrow doorway. I told Ella to stay where she was and that I would bring in the cushions, but Ella came down the steps and got one cushion anyway. I rushed up with the second cushion, then ran down to get the last from the front seat before Ella could. As I prepared to carry the last cushion into the house, I noticed how the priest had changed his stance. Father Jack was now partially blocking the doorway. Usually when someone holds a door open for another, they stand to the side, out of the way, so the other person can pass. Not this priest. He stood within the doorway, holding the door open with his back, his body blocking part of the opening. As I squeezed by him, I pushed the cushion in front of me and tried to rotate so I didn't have to touch him—not a pleasant experience.

After I left, I remained upset that he expected his aged housekeeper to carry the cushions. *What kind of person does that?* When I got home, I told my parents about his behavior. Although I was embarrassed to discuss it, I explained briefly how he had moved to hold the door open with his back, forcing me to squeeze past him. They just looked at me and expressed that the priest simply *couldn't* have meant anything by it, that the issue was all in my head—that I, not he, had nasty thoughts. I felt hurt but said no more. I didn't share the story at work the next day, because I did not want to anger the coworker who had expressed admiration for the priest, but I began to view her seeming obsession with him in a much different light. As the year went on, I found Father Jack's sermons and behavior even more discomforting, and I avoided communion and confession as often as I could.

The 1968 flu pandemic reached the US late in the year, and in January 1969, I came down with the virus. At that time, it was so widespread and dangerous that the doctors didn't even want anyone to come to the clinics. I phoned a local nurse to ask what I should do. She told me to stay home, and she gave Mom some instruction on what to watch for in case it became serious enough for me to be hospitalized. I was out of work for a full week. With no sick leave in those days, missing a week's wages was a hard financial hit, at least for me. By the time the weekend came, I thought I was getting better, but on Saturday I started to vomit. I was up all Saturday night, in the bathroom, so I stayed home from mass on Sunday morning. My folks were invited over to my aunt and uncle's house for an afternoon visit on Sunday, but I stayed home to get some rest, hoping to recover and return to work on Monday.

As I lay in bed, the phone rang. My folks only had the one wall phone in the kitchen, so I had to get out of bed to answer it. Although exhausted, I remained standing next to the phone as I spoke. It was Father Jack. He'd noticed I wasn't in church that morning. I told him I had been sick with the flu all week and spent the whole night throwing up.

After a short pause, Father Jack snidely remarked, "Oh, did someone forget to take her pill?"

I was a bit groggy, so I asked, "What?"

He repeated his nasty question. Then it dawned on me: he assumed I was sexually active and that I took birth control pills regularly, and now he was accusing me of being pregnant because I supposedly forgot to take a pill.

I got angry and exclaimed, "No, I didn't forget any pill! I have the flu! I was sick to my stomach all night, and standing here talking to you is making me weak and sick to my stomach again, and I may have to go throw up!" Then I slammed the receiver down to hang up on him. I was so mad that I was shaking, and as I continued to feel weaker from the flu, I staggered back to bed.

It was then that I decided the Catholic Church was not for me. I was twenty years old, with no regular boyfriend, and Father Jack assumed that I was having sex and that I was pregnant. *What the hell!* When my folks got home later that day, I told them what happened. As I watched their reaction, I became disappointed by their lack of outrage. Dad said nothing—absolutely nothing! And although I could sense that Mom disapproved of the priest's questions to me, she was careful, as always, not to offend Dad's extreme loyalty to the church. Neither of them became outwardly angry at the priest, but they did become visibly upset when I vehemently stated, "I never want to go to church again."

"You have to go to church!" Dad insisted.

I eventually agreed to continue going to mass on Sundays to keep up appearances. But I vowed never to go to communion or confession again. And I never did.

My takeaway from this is that my parents seemed to support the church regardless of what was done to their child. They were concerned about my not going to mass—but not about Father Jack's behavior toward me. This is an example of how, over the course of hundreds of years, Catholic parents have essentially empowered priests and nuns to abuse their children by ignoring reports of questionable behavior. Clergy can only do what the congregation empowers them to. Would I ever again share with my parents an improper thing a priest said or did? Never.

I said nothing about the phone call to the female coworker who adored this priest, but I tried to listen to her more closely to determine if my experience with him was unique to me, or if his behavior extended to others. If it did, how was her family overlooking such behavior? My folks seemed to think his behavior had been fine, even after I explained my experience to them. Was I the only one he'd offended?

Months later, I found out the priest had behaved inappropriately with others too. A couple of my close female friends, loyal Catholics, shared about things he had done that made them uncomfortable. They did not like him either, which was unusual for them because they came from families that always lauded the current priest. One friend even said her parents had become uncomfortable at a married-couples group formed by the priest. The purpose of the group was to discuss Catholic marriage, but the reason my friend's parents stopped going was because the priest kept talking about their sex life. Father Jack had told them that the wife should go to bed naked to entice her husband to have more sex. Although one might understand and even agree with that advice, what made her folks uncomfortable was when he pressured them to talk about their sexual encounters in front of the other couples in the group, couples who had been their neighbors and friends for years. I speculate that the only one in the room that wanted to hear those details was the priest, not the four or five couples who had farmed next to one another for a decade or more.

Pressure to Marry

In the spring of 1969, I was twenty-one and enjoying my life immensely. I was far from rich, but I was living at home with my folks and had few expenses. In 1967, they built a new rambler, which gave me my own bedroom on the ground floor. I was proud that I'd graduated high school with the skills to get my great office job, which I loved, at Nutting Truck & Caster Company in Faribault, only a twenty-five-mile drive from my folks' house in New Market. I had been promoted a couple of times and had learned even more office skills. By this time, I had taken several vacations, and my friend and I had another trip planned for July. Life, I decided, was good.

I enjoyed going out with my female friends and did not lament being single, but like most young women, I hoped to meet "Mr. Right." I did not spend time painting him in advance, however. I was of the mindset that I would know him when I met him.

Pressure to meet, date, and marry a man came in the form of subtle comments from older peers, cousins, aunts, uncles, and my mother, all who might ask, *Did you see anyone interesting at the dance?* One older cousin, who always treated me like her little sister, often gave me sound advice on many issues, but I didn't agree with one particular piece of advice she gave me about dating.

It was Christmas Day, and all the men were huddled around the television, watching football. The older cousin noticed I was uninterested in the game. She moved toward me, looked me in the eyes, and said, "If you want to get a man, you will have to learn to like football."

"No, I won't," I said bluntly. And I never did.

Mom often made comments indicating my goal should be to get married. These comments contradicted those she'd made to me when I was a little girl, when she'd often proclaim, "You don't need a man to be happy." With me having reached marrying age, though, she seemed to think I *did* need a man to be happy. I think she felt she needed me to marry a man so *she* could be happy. I wasn't angry about this, but I did try to see it from her point of view. For her, my marrying would complete the picture of her being a good mother. Maybe she felt my marrying would release her from the guilt of bringing a bastard into the world, a burden I think she carried to her grave.

This is the kind of gentle harassment singles put up with from relatives and friends. Generally, I didn't mind. Indeed, I believed they had my best interests at heart, and I never got any pressure from Aunt Tillie or Aunt Caroline, both experienced family women who knew the importance of picking a good mate, as they had done. However, there was one instance when Aunt Ella, one of Dad's sisters, went too far.

It began when my female cousin befriended a prison inmate by exchanging letters with him. Their relationship blossomed, and they soon married. Shortly after the wedding, Aunt Ella confronted me.

"Your cousin is the same age as you," she said, "but she married before you. It's time you find a man."

I couldn't believe what I was hearing, and I meant no disrespect to my cousin when I simply said, "I hope they make it work and live a happy life, but should I aspire to marry an inmate just so I am not single?"

"But he *is* a man!" barked Ella bluntly.

I did not judge my cousin's marrying an inmate, but wasn't it absurd to hold it up as an example meant to pressure me to find a man?

Meeting the Love of My Life

In June 1969, my world changed forever. My friend Corrine was a bridesmaid in her cousin's wedding, and she gave another friend and me free tickets to the wedding dance at Antlers Park in Lakeville, Minnesota. We had a great time dancing.

Toward the end of the event, my friend saw a guy whom she really liked, but she was too shy to go talk to him. I tried hard to convince her to just walk up to him and start talking.

"No," she said, "he is talking with another guy we don't even know."

I tried hard to convince her to go, but I became impatient and walked over to talk to him on my own. As it turned out, when he introduced me to the guy he was talking to, he introduced me as Betty Simon, my cousin. I turned to this guy and explained that I was Nancy, not my cousin Betty, and at that moment, I felt as if something hit me. Wow! We talked briefly, and I found out his name was Gordy Fredrickson and that he would be at the New Market baseball game on Sunday. By this time, the dance was over. I returned to my friend and we went home, but I knew the moment had changed my life forever. All I could think of was Gordy Fredrickson, and I knew I had to see him again—soon. After that, I became a real fan of the New Market baseball team and attended every game, where Gordy and I would meet and talk for a while.

The last game of the season was played on the historical Sunday when Neil Armstrong walked on the moon. Someone had brought a television to the ball game so people could view the walk on the moon without missing the baseball game. After the game, Gordy and I talked for quite a while. He asked me out, but when we tried to set a date, he told me that he was leaving the next day for a two-week vacation, driving down to visit army buddies in Tennessee and then Florida. The day he'd return was the same day I would be leaving on my trip to the Black Hills with my friend Clara. Over a month would pass before we could see each other again, delaying our first date until near the end of August.

There was a pause before he realized something aloud. "The State Fair will be starting by the time you return, and Johnny Cash will be doing a grandstand show on two nights during the week. It doesn't start until nine, but I'd like to pick you up soon after you get home from work so we can see as much of the fair as possible before the show starts."

I was ecstatic! He drove me the few short blocks from the baseball diamond to my house, and after he dropped me off, I went into the house, walking on clouds. I knew this was a pivotal moment in my life, and all I could think of for the next four weeks was the State Fair and going on a date with Gordy. Yes, it was a long wait for the right guy, but it was worth it.

Dusty Meets Gordy

My cat, Dusty, had been with us since the mid-1950s, when a farmer brought a kitten to the Produce, where Mom worked, saying the kitten needed a home. Mom fell in love with the kitten immediately, named her Dusty, and brought her home.

Dusty was a fun little kitten who quickly grew into a wonderful friend for me. By 1956, Dusty had matured to be patient, letting my friend Linda and me dress her in doll clothes and push her around in the doll buggy. Linda and I spent hours playing with Dusty, but Dusty picked her friends carefully and would run away when other kids would visit. Dusty lived to be over twenty years old, and although she continued liking Linda, she always made herself scarce when anyone else came over. In fact, Dusty hid whenever any relatives came to visit.

Neither my folks nor I had considered having Dusty as a house cat. She was an outside cat, and while she was allowed to come inside for a while, she always slept outdoors. Dad had made her a little house out of a wooden beer case. He cut a hole in the side for a door and filled the box with fresh straw regularly. During the winter, the cat house was placed close to our house, surrounded by bales of straw and situated so the snow would not blow in. Dusty usually had two litters of kittens every year, and because there was always a farmer looking for weaned kittens, we had no trouble giving them away.

Dusty was still with us when I had my first date with Gordy, in 1969. By this time, my folks and I were living in a new rambler house with an attached garage. When Gordy pulled into the driveway, I came out to meet him immediately, but as he got out of the car, Dusty ran out from the open garage to meet him too. She rubbed against his legs and purred, letting him know she liked him right away. He knelt to pet her and scratch under her chin. The scene of the two of them bonding was a signal to me that he was special. From then on, nearly every time Gordy came to pick me up, Dusty would hear his car coming and run out front to greet him. Because Gordy was the only person Dusty ever greeted, I figured it was a sign I should marry the guy.

Dating Gordy

My date with Gordy at the fair went great, except for a tense experience in the midway that revealed an important characteristic about Gordy, one that would make me like him even more than I already did.

We arrived early so we could enjoy the rest of the State Fair before the evening show. Things were going well, and I didn't want to mess it up. When Gordy said he liked going on rides, I said I liked rides too, even though rides were not my favorite thing. As we strolled through the midway, he suggested we go on one of the tamer rides. The Ferris wheel was right there, and I stared at it in awe. This was no ordinary Ferris wheel—but a *double* Ferris wheel. Its two wheels rotated at opposite ends of shared support arms located on both sides of the wheels. The entire apparatus rotated on a center drive wheel, which powered the two larger wheels, so when riders were on top, they were as high or higher than the diameter of two small Ferris wheels!

As we stood in line for tickets, I thought I should maybe mention my serious fear of heights, but because I didn't want to mess up the date, I kept silent. Besides, my early-childhood lessons from my mother had taught me to keep my fears to myself because, supposedly, no one else cared about them. I kept hoping the ride would be quick and that we would only briefly be at the very top as the Ferris wheel turned. I hid my nervousness when the operator locked us into the carriage, and I braced myself for the ride.

After the first round, we were at the bottom and the operator was stopping to let people off. I was relieved that I had made it this far. I continued to be nervous and uncomfortable as the ride continued and we moved toward the top of the wheel. As we approached the very top, Gordy mentioned that the view of the fairgrounds was spectacular, but I was thinking, *Oh, please keep going!* Then, when we were positioned at the very top of the double Ferris wheel, it stopped! The seat gently rocked back and forth. I was terrified! Even with my eyes closed, I was holding on to the handle so hard, my fingers hurt. Gordy realized I was frightened and tried to take my hand, but I grabbed on to his forearm without realizing how hard I was digging in. I'd nearly drawn blood before the Ferris wheel started moving again, rotating down toward the loading deck. The ride operator must've noticed the look of terror on my face, because he soon let us off. Gordy was extremely comforting to me and said he wouldn't have proposed the idea if I had said I was afraid of heights. He agreed that the operator had probably seen my fear and wanted to get me off quickly.

"That was the shortest Ferris wheel ride I've ever been on," he said, winking at me, "but still the best."

I explained to him that the Ferris wheel ride had triggered some memories and that my fear of heights traced back to when I was very young. I added that Mom never showed any sympathy for my fears. Then I told Gordy more about myself than I'd ever told anyone . . .

Mom never showed much understanding for my fears, small or large. There are pictures of me when I was three, during the winter, where I am with my older cousin Jack Schmitz and Mom. Both photos show Jack and me on the top of huge snowbanks, with Jack holding me. Mom had insisted I pose on Jack's shoulders for the photographs, but I cried because it was so high up. She made me feel like I ruined the photos because I wouldn't be on Jack's shoulders.

When I was about eight years old, someone staked a horse out in the open lot between the Produce and Simon's Place, a local bar and café. Some of the local children wanted to sit on the horse, so Mom got the idea to bring out her camera and take a picture of each of the kids on the horse, including me. But I refused—it seemed so high up and scary. Mom got angry at me for being afraid, and I walked away crying. As she made a big deal out of taking photos of the other kids, she also made sure no one comforted me or even came near me. I walked home in shame. The lesson I learned was that I had to hide my fears and get over myself if I were to ever deserve affection, because no one is going to care about my fears—tough lessons for a little girl.

Gordy and I headed to the grandstand to claim our seats. The show was wonderful, with Johnny Cash singing all his hits. His song "A Boy Named

Sue" was a chart topper in 1969, but there was one line in the song that all the radio stations bleeped out. The crowd got quiet as the line approached in the song. I think the entire grandstand was holding their breath in anticipation. When the moment came, we all heard Johnny Cash sing, "'Cause I'm the *bleep* that named you Sue." He'd literally said the word *bleep*, garnering groans from the crowd. It was fortunate that I cut my groan short, because Cash then leaned into the microphone and said, "Well, you can't say *son of a bitch* up here," which about half the audience missed due to the groans. Even Gordy leaned over and asked what Cash had said. Well, as soon as all the people who'd missed it got the information from the people next to them, the entire crowd cheered. It was a great show.

I love how writing encourages reflection. For example, as I write this memoir, over fifty years after sharing my fears with Gordy and then seeing Johnny Cash perform, I see a clear juxtaposition: In the song "A Boy Named Sue," the father named his son Sue to ensure he learned how to be tough enough to endure life in the cruel world. Was Mom's refusal to show sympathy for my fears her attempt at preparing me for the cruel world? I have to admit that it may have helped. Her "training" kicked in on a most important first date, and maybe it was for the best, because the situation allowed me to discover I was with a guy who listened and was wonderfully understanding and supportive. Contrary to Mom's statement, I found someone who cared about my fears. The Ferris wheel ride was quite a lesson in love.

After the concert, Gordy and I were in no hurry as we made the long, quiet walk back to his car in the cool darkness. He took my hand—it was magic! All I felt was love. I knew in that instant that he was the man for me. I don't remember many details after that, but I do remember being extremely happy, and from that night on, I only had eyes for Gordy.

On one of our other early dates, we ended up eating at Shakey's Pizza. The restaurant's dining area was one big room with tables and benches, and there was no table service. Customers lined up at the counter to order and prepay for their pizza, then take a numbered ticket for pickup. Our order placed, we picked up a pitcher of beer, then sat down to wait for our number to be called. To this day, I can still see Gordy's back and his sexy tush as he walked up to get our order. I smiled with satisfaction, knowing that this guy was mine.

After many dates, Gordy broached the topic of our future together, and after a discussion about religion, he basically asked me to marry him. I said yes—no hesitation. We knew we still had some dating to do to get to know each other.

After several more dates with Gordy, I was surprised to discover that two local boys I'd known most of my life were interested in asking me out. I turned them down by simply saying I was dating someone else, and I am sure there were no hard feelings. As I thought about it later, though, I wondered why they had waited so long to ask. I was twenty-one years old and had been around town most of my life. Could it be, I thought, that my status as a bastard had held them back? I knew their Catholic families may have felt I was below them. But had my dating Gordy, perhaps, suggested to those boys that it was okay to date a bastard, at least *this* bastard? I dismissed the thought, deciding I was just happy they hadn't asked me out before I met Gordy. Had I been dating anyone else at the time, Gordy and I may have never met at that dance in June.

The upcoming holidays offered opportunities for Gordy to meet my extended family, and in December, Gordy agreed to have Christmas dinner with Mom, Dad, and me at the home of the Schmitzes, my aunt Tillie's family. I explained to Gordy that Aunt Tillie's entire family would be there—Ron, Jack, Gene, Mitz, and their spouses. I also told him the men would all be gathered around the television to watch football. Gordy explained that he didn't care to watch football when visiting people, adding, "I'll hang out in the kitchen and talk with the women."

When the football game started on Christmas Day, the separation between the men and women in the house unfolded as I'd predicted, and Gordy and I found ourselves in the kitchen, enjoying the company of my mom, my aunts, and the other wives. After a bit, Tillie's oldest son, Ron, came into the kitchen to visit with us too. As I expected, Gordy passed everyone's inspection with flying colors. Aunt Tillie really liked him. Ron and Jack gave me a silent nod of approval. Mitz was more verbal, telling me he was a keeper. I smiled to myself as I thought, *I didn't even have to fake an interest in football to find a man.*

Approval from another of my favorite aunts was even easier. Aunt Caroline owned The St. Patrick Store, which doubled as a tavern, and Gordy's folks frequented with his mom's brothers and their wives. They all knew Aunt Caroline, and Aunt Caroline had known Gordy since he was a little boy. She let me know how happy she was that I was with him, and Gordy said he was happy that he would soon call her "Aunt Caroline."

Many questions weighed heavily on my mind early in our relationship: Did Gordy know about my being a bastard? How would he react to finding out? Luckily, I never had to explain my circumstances to him, because I soon became aware that he already knew and that it didn't matter to him. I had no desire to deny my past, but I felt relieved to be free of the stigma. All my life, the bastard label had hung on my being. Yes, I had many relatives on both my mother's and my stepfather's sides who loved me and never judged me for that label, but growing up and continuing to live in a Catholic environment meant the label was always near the surface, if not right on top.

As my relationship with Gordy progressed, I discovered his parents, too, knew about my background, and they didn't judge me for it either. At first, this phenomenon was hard for me to grasp, but I eventually started to look at myself and the world around me in a more positive way. I began to judge myself less harshly. Even though I had already given up on the Catholic religion by that time, this new view gave me a better perspective on religions and people.

CHAPTER 7

SEEKING A
NEW IDENTITY

The Pledge

I had every reason to be happy. My fiancé and I were in love and therefore thought everything possible. We planned to marry in the fall. Although Gordy and I were of different religions, we were sure we had worked out every possible issue of conflict. And even though I had undergone eleven years of Catholic schooling and Gordy had been baptized and confirmed as a Lutheran, neither of us was devout—for a number of reasons based on experiences during our young lives. Consequently, we thought we were flexible on where to have the ceremony.

My stepfather, who had been raised Catholic, was always concerned about offending the church. Gordy and I respected his concern, which was why we were intent on having our wedding ceremony at St. Nicholas Church in New Market, the church Dad had attended all his life. The only snag Gordy foresaw to getting married in a Catholic church concerned a long-standing rule that had recently been relaxed; the *Catholic Bulletin* had published an article stating the church no longer required a non-Catholic to sign a paper promising to raise their children Catholic. With that out of the way, I called Father Crane for an appointment. The phone call was brief, and he told me we should meet him at his office the following Saturday.

During the days prior to our scheduled meeting with the priest, I pondered my relationship with my hometown of New Market, the school, and the church. For you to begin to understand the town as a whole, get rid of all your generalizations of "sleepy small towns." Really, no towns like that exist anyway. Even the fictional town of Mayberry, depicted in *The Andy Griffith Show* in the 1960s, defies its own stereotype. Towns with one Catholic church—or a single church of any denomination—are influenced or even controlled by said church to varying degrees, and people of all faiths and philosophies often cherry-pick their topics of support or rebellion. Even my devout stepfather, who was both generous and practical, wondered aloud things like "Why can't we buy the priest a Ford or Chevy, instead of an expensive car?"

Mom and I had attended St. Nicholas Catholic Church in New Market ever since we moved from Minneapolis to New Market, when I was three years old, and except for baptism, I experienced all the sacraments at St. Nicholas. I had been baptized as a baby at Holy Rosary Catholic Church in Minneapolis, and like most people baptized as babies, I have no recollection of the event. However, Aunt Tillie, one of Mom's older sisters, took great delight in reminding me of a particular aspect of the day.

On a Sunday in May of 1948, Aunt Tillie and her husband, Ewald Schmitz, had to miss mass at St. Nicholas Catholic Church in their hometown of New Market so they could drive the thirty-plus miles to Minneapolis to witness my baptism and become my godparents. As I grew older, I learned what wonderfully generous people they were, and I knew I had the best godparents in the world. Tillie loved to joke and laugh, and when I was growing up, she would enjoy telling one particular story about a visit from the New Market priest on the Monday after my baptism.

In the story, Aunt Tillie's husband was at work and their boys were at school when the priest came knocking at their door. After Tillie let him in, he blurted out something she already knew: "None of the Schmitz family was at mass on Sunday."

Tillie took no offense at what might have seemed like an accusation of neglect. She just chirped, "We stood up as godparents for my sister's baby girl at Holy Rosary Church in Minneapolis on Sunday."

The priest calmed down and smiled. "Well, that's wonderful! What did they name the baby?"

"They named her Nancy Ann."

The priest immediately became incensed and started to scold her. "How could you have let them give the child a horse's name?"

At that point in the retelling, Tillie would inevitably burst out laughing, abruptly ending the story without disclosing the practical details those listening needed to understand fully. When *not* overcome with laughter, she would explain that the priest who performed the baptism had said he thought "Nancy Ann" was a nice name, a kind comment that courteous people often make to doting parents and godparents. And apparently, Tillie had a hard time getting over—to the point of laughter—how absurd and unkind it was for a priest to make a serious value judgment about the name someone chose for their precious little baby. Aunt Tillie told me this story many times over the following decades—not to be mean but because she thought it was funny. I knew she wasn't making fun of me.

I later realized that the priest's remark about my name was the first of many unkind comments aimed at me by the clergy in New Market. The particular priest visiting Tillie that day hadn't known of my bastard status, but his visit may have foreshadowed how my being a bastard would define me when Mom and I moved to New Market four years later.

I was skeptical about the meeting Gordy and I were scheduled to have with Father Crane. If I had learned only one thing for sure about the church and the school during my time in New Market, it was that they treated some families better than others—that is, they praised some families, regardless of their deeds, while scorning others, sometimes even publicly. I knew I fell squarely into the scorned category.

On the Saturday of our meeting with Father Crane, Gordy and I held hands as we stood at the base of the long stairs that led upward to St. Nicholas Catholic Church, positioned majestically on a hill rising nearly fifty feet above the east end of New Market. When I was a child, Mom and I would climb these never-ending stairs together, our hands running along the black pipe-like railing, and the climb always reminded me that the road to heaven was not wide and easy. The church itself, a beautiful brick structure, faced west, as did the priest's house, located north of the church, as well as the nuns' house, located to the south. A sidewalk connected the buildings' fronts, giving the scene a tidy, respectable appearance.

Continuing to hold hands, Gordy and I began our climb. During our ascent, I reflected on Father Crane's reputation: he was liked by most of the townspeople and even adored by some. A few had criticized him for spending too many evenings at one of several taverns in town, saying a bar was no place for a priest to spend his free time. Others, eager to defend anything done by the clergy, said that frequenting bars put him in touch with his congregation. Dad neither defended nor condemned Father Crane's actions, just accepting that the priest could do whatever he wanted to. He was, after all, the priest.

As we approached the priest's house, I wondered if my history would come up during this meeting. With that thought heavy on my mind, I knocked on the door. The housekeeper opened the door a moment later.

"Hello," I said flatly. "We have an appointment to see Father Crane."

"Go right into his office. He is expecting you."

Father Crane was a tall, confident, middle-aged man with dark hair. Lacking the pasty whiteness of many clergy, his complexion had taken on a ruddy look, and he appeared robust and healthy. Father Crane already knew me, but I started the conversation by reintroducing myself and then, using my best etiquette, introducing Gordy. Hoping to gain some acceptance for my Lutheran fiancé, I added that Gordy had played baseball for New Market and was a member of Highview Christiania Lutheran Church, south of Farmington. Although the priest followed the town baseball team, like most of the townsfolk, he did not comment on Gordy's baseball connection. He did, however, add that he was familiar with Gordy's church. The two men briefly exchanged greetings.

With no further pleasantries, Father Crane pointed to a form on his desk, which he had prepared for Gordy to sign, a form pledging to raise any children as Catholic.

I immediately jumped in to say, "But I thought the church no longer required a non-Catholic to sign the form?"

"Where did you get that idea?" asked Father Crane.

"I read it in the paper."

"Well, you can't believe everything you read in the paper," he said with authority. "What paper did you read it in?"

"The *Catholic Bulletin*," I replied carefully, "the official paper of the Archdiocese of St. Paul and Minneapolis, of which this parish is a part."

Father Crane tilted his head slightly, seeming to indicate that he did not like my response. His demeanor darkened as he asserted, "That may be the case in some places—but *not* in New Market. Besides, I've never heard of anyone not willing to sign the form."

Gordy gingerly said, "I would prefer not to sign a form promising anything other than my vows to my wife. We came here with the understanding that signing the pledge was no longer required. I guess we were wrong."

"We will not be signing the form," I summarized, expressionless. Then I asked, "Could I please get a copy of my baptismal certificate?"

At this point, Father Crane actually turned his back on us as he asked, "Were you baptized in this church?"

I was pretty sure he already knew the answer to his question, although I may have overestimated his knowledge of my background. I told him I was not baptized at St. Nicholas but that my mother had given the church a copy of my baptismal certificate before my First Communion.

"When I was confirmed," I added, "the priest told me that the certificate was still on file."

Without turning to face us, Father Crane flatly said, "We don't keep copies of *such things* on file."

I was pretty sure he was lying about that, and his reference to my baptismal certificate as "such things" burned in my ears. There was no more to be said. Gordy and I waited only a moment before leaving.

Hand in hand, we marched down the long steps leading toward the car. We didn't need to say anything to support each other because we knew this would not stop us from getting married.

As Gordy opened the car door for me, he joked, "Well, that went well." We both laughed lightly.

After he got into the car, I asserted, "Now I have to break the news to Mom and Dad. I'll do that tomorrow."

The next day, I told my mother we would not be getting married in St. Nicholas Catholic Church, briefly explaining what had happened. She did not seem surprised at my news, though she was clearly disappointed. I told her I knew I'd been baptized at Holy Rosary Church in Minneapolis and that I needed to go there to get a copy of my baptismal certificate. Mom told me she was certain they would have a copy on file. She asked when Gordy and I would go to pick up the copy. I told her I would call the church ahead of time and that we would try to go up on Saturday.

When Gordy arrived to pick me up on Saturday, Mom stopped me just as I was about to go out the door. She handed a folded note to me, adding, "Here is the name you were baptized under." Then she quickly left the room.

I knew it was a painful moment for her, but only later would I understand why she had been so secretive about the matter. When I got to the car, Gordy and I read the name: Nancy Ann Guillaume. This was the first time I saw my last name as written on my baptismal certificate.

The Certificate

Gordy parked his red 1968 Ford Mustang Fastback on the street about fifty yards from Holy Rosary Catholic Church in South Minneapolis, and from that short distance, we could see the spires of the church poking into the sunny sky. The grand brick structure glorified God and intimidated mankind, but as we crossed the quiet street and followed the narrow sidewalk toward the entry, I felt only the intimidation. Scattered grass clippings lined the edge of the walkway, and a few round-leafed weeds clustered in the cracks, detracting only slightly from the manicured appearance of the grounds.

As we approached the grand door, Gordy said, "It's a beautiful structure, but it's only a building. Remember, you said he seemed kind on the phone."

I smiled, though I felt my hand sweating, but rather than release my grip on his hand, I held on to him more tightly. Holding his hand had always given me strength and courage. With his free hand, Gordy opened the door, and we mustered the courage to face another priest—the second in as many weeks—to ask for a copy of my baptismal certificate so we could get married in a church. I repeated to myself what Gordy had reminded me of earlier: *He seemed kind on the phone.*

I was glad when a man appeared, interrupting my thoughts and saving me from reliving the meeting with Father Crane. The man was not dressed as a priest, which was almost a relief for me; he may have been a clerk for the priest of the church. After all, the church had a big congregation, and I am sure there were records to keep and other matters that needed tending.

"Hello," the clerk said gently.

"Hello," I replied. "I talked to someone on the telephone to request a copy of my baptismal certificate. Thanks for seeing us so soon."

He just smiled and asked the name and approximate date.

"Nancy A. Guillaume. I was baptized in May 1948." I had only known the last name I was baptized with for a little over an hour. I felt strange saying it aloud, claiming it as mine as I tripped over the pronunciation.

The kind clerk left and came back with a folded copy within a few minutes. I unfolded the document immediately and read silently:

This is to Certify
that *Nancy Ann Guillaume,*
the daughter of *Charles Guillaume*
and *Rita Schoenecker,*
born in Minneapolis on April 30, 1948,
was baptized on *May 16, 1948,*
in the Church of *Holy Rosary, Minneapolis,*
according to the Rite of the Roman Catholic Church.

Astonished, I stared at the document, which answered a question that Mom had never volunteered to answer: Had she been married to my father? Clearly, the answer was no, proving that I really was a bastard. I recalled that as a young child, I had seen a photograph of my father, but the photo and any record of his existence had mysteriously disappeared around the time Mom remarried, nearly a decade prior to my trip to Holy Rosary Church with Gordy.

I continued staring at the document. Earlier that day, I had seen my father's last name in my mother's own handwriting, but that copy of my baptismal certificate was the first time I'd seen my father's entire name in print—*Charles Guillaume*. That had been *my* last name for a few months, long ago. I felt a familiar pain in my stomach, a pain I associated with memories.

Some memories are easily and readily revisited, but others need to be sought out, fished for and hooked, before being brought to the surface. And then there are those memories just slightly below the surface, which to me are less memories and more gut feelings. When a word or phrase jolts one of my bastard moments to life, I feel physical pain in my stomach. And as I stared at the certificate, I relived the pain of "the Inquisition," when two younger cousins pushed me to the floor, sat on me, and hit me repeatedly, demanding I reveal my father's real name.

The moment became awkward as I continued staring at the paper, the clerk and Gordy standing silently nearby, awaiting my next move. I looked at the clerk and uttered, "Thank you very much!"

Gordy added, "Thank you," then dug his wallet out to pay the small fee required for the copy. Then he moved to open the door for me.

On the walk back to our car, my stomach continued hurting, and my mind flashed once again to the "Inquisition" I had experienced at the hands of my stepfather's grandniece and grandnephew. I could feel their weight on me as I struggled to stand up, their questions repeating in my mind—*Where is your real father? Why isn't he here?*

Gordy seemed to know something was wrong, and he cautiously tried to be positive. "Well, you got the certificate."

Still in the midst of my horrible bastard moment, I made light of it. "If I'd known my father's name back when I was in school, I could've saved myself a few bruises."

"Bruises?" asked Gordy.

I had told no one the details of the experience, and although I was not eager to recall them all now, I recited the memory for Gordy as we walked back to the car, punctuating the story by confessing he was the only person I'd told it to in the ten years since.

Gordy said nothing at first, but I could see on his face that the story had upset him. Once we settled into the Mustang's black vinyl interior, we buckled our seat belts slowly. Instead of starting the engine, he paused. "Those kids, those cousins of yours—I'll bet they were told to ask those questions. Blame that on the mother more than on the kids."

"I agree." My stomach still hurt a little, so I tried to make light of it again. "Oh well, I suppose no one can blame her for not wanting her uncle to adopt a bastard into the family."

Gordy turned the ignition key, and the Mustang's engine roared to attention. "Yes, we can," he said dryly. "Yes, we can."

The Break

The week following our visit to Holy Rosary Church, Gordy called the pastor at Highview Christiania Lutheran Church, where he had been confirmed eleven years earlier, and asked to meet with him to discuss our getting married there. Pastor Almquist said we should meet with him the next Saturday.

Highview Christiania Lutheran Church was a twenty-minute drive from New Market, and Gordy took the opportunity to share with me a few details about the church. First, he admitted he was no expert on his church's history, but he did know it had been founded in the mid-1800s by a group of Norwegians and had been called Christiania Lutheran Free Church until the mid-1960s, when the name was changed to Highview Christiania Lutheran Church.

Gordy seemed enthusiastic about the church as he explained. "It's a simple but beautiful building. And there are a lot of good people there, like there are in any church. When I was in the eighth grade and attending catechism, I took things pretty seriously and considered the ministry for a while." He looked at me for a reaction.

"Really?" was the only thing I could think of to say.

"Really, but it didn't last long. The more I got into it, the more I realized how different the clergy were compared to me, or even to my expectations. Anyway," he continued, "when I was little, all the ministers for our church had heavy Norwegian accents. I adored listening to the accents, but I often found it a bit hard to understand. We lived in a farm community where my family members were the only non-Catholics. When I was in the second and third grade, I was the only non-Catholic in the country school. I thought the whole world was Catholic except for our little church in the country, where we had to drive twenty-five miles of dirt or gravel roads to attend, and where it seemed everyone had a Norwegian brogue. Honestly, when I was a kid, I thought the way to tell a Lutheran from a Catholic was that all Lutherans had a Norwegian accent."

After his last statement, Gordy laughed aloud at his own folly. I still love it when he does this.

"The church rules were strict. When my sisters attended catechism, the pastor regularly told them they were going to hell. When my oldest sister got married, nearly a decade later, a different pastor told her that if she had a wedding dance, she and her husband would go to hell. They had a dance anyway, of course. I quit going to church before I joined the army."

Maybe Gordy started to see me squirming in the seat. "Hey, don't worry. *The pastor sounded kind on the phone.*" We were laughing as we pulled into the gravel parking lot of Highview Christiania Lutheran Church—a good sign, I thought at the time.

Without knocking, we entered the small addition to the church. Gordy shared how he loved the way they'd made a functional addition to the old church without messing up the classic, beautiful design. Pastor Almquist waited in his office. This time, Gordy did the introductions. The pastor shook hands with each of us, then motioned for us to sit down in the chairs across from him.

Gordy and I had agreed beforehand that he would explain our situation and I would add anything he omitted. We were prepared to tell the pastor what I knew of my entire background—but would let details unfold as necessary, not lead with them. Gordy began by explaining what had happened at our meeting with Father Crane and how we had to go to Holy Rosary to get my baptismal certificate. I explained that we had wanted to marry in Dad's church to appease my parents.

Pastor Almquist listened with an almost scary intensity. Then he addressed me directly.

"This is a difficult time for you and your folks. I know the priest at All Saints Catholic Church, in Lakeville. I will speak to him about your situation if you want me to. I am sure he would marry you without requiring you to sign the pledge. Maybe that would ease your parents' concerns."

I was overwhelmed by his kindness and understanding, but I considered his idea for a moment. Did I really want to regress after taking this big step away? Speaking with care, I tried to convey my meaning without sounding mean.

"Thank you for the suggestion. But I think that after going this far, I may as well continue to break from the Catholic Church. If I pull back now, I would have to start all over again if we have children because my folks would be intent on having them baptized Catholic."

Pastor Almquist nodded his understanding.

"If we can," I added, "we would like to get married in this church."

"Yes," answered Pastor Almquist after a short hesitation, "but you would need to attend a marriage class together at Fairview South Hospital. I require the class for all marriages I perform." He explained how the classes met several times and consisted of discussions covering marriage vows, practical issues, and living together as man and wife—all based on a small paperback text titled *Your Life Together,* which would serve as our guide to the class.

As Gordy and I exchanged glances, we nodded our agreement to each other and then to the pastor.

"I need to bring up a couple of things," Gordy said reluctantly. "I hope it doesn't change your mind, but if it does, we understand. I want to be transparent in explaining the type of wedding we are planning."

Pastor Almquist sat back in his chair, indicating he was ready to listen.

"First," Gordy began, "this church has a lot of history for me. My great-grandparents, my grandparents, and my folks got married here. I was baptized and confirmed here. My dad's father and my dad each married a Catholic woman from New Market. The women did not remain Catholic, changing to Lutheran. So if you think about it, more than three-fourths of my relatives are Catholic. Add that to the fact that nearly all of Nancy's relatives are Catholic, and you may realize that there will not be many Lutherans at the wedding."

Pastor Almquist just nodded, as if to say, *What's the problem?*

"Not that I'm saying that's a problem in itself," Gordy continued, "but I need to explain that although we want to get married in this Lutheran church, the reception will look more like one of the many Catholic wedding receptions I've attended with my parents throughout my life. There will be alcohol and dancing. And yet I want to invite you, and I'm inviting you to say grace before we eat. Waiting for silence to say grace after the crowd has had almost two hours of free alcohol . . . it's a lot to ask."

The pastor smiled humbly before explaining, in some detail, his training and experience. He said he'd ministered in a number of places where alcohol was central to the culture and that he felt comfortable with the reception scene as Gordy had described it. (Gordy later told me he'd been shocked by the pastor's positive response; he'd thought the pastor would tell us, then and there, we were going straight to hell.)

When Pastor Almquist went on to explain he had worked closely with several local priests to resolve issues regarding mixed marriages, I realized he was not on a mission to convert me. In fact, he seemed to understand the trauma of changing religions, especially regarding the scorn that would be handed to me by some of my relatives. Doing more than just being sympathetic, though, he had suggestions and gave options, unlike the other priests I knew, who always wanted to handle matters in their way or not at all. Pastor Almquist actually listened to what Gordy and I had to say and responded thoughtfully—an experience I had never had with a priest or nun while growing up Catholic.

After Pastor Almquist scheduled us to attend a series of marriage classes at Fairview South Hospital, Gordy and I drove to New Market. Gordy told me he'd been totally shocked by the pastor's experience with alcohol and willingness to be at our reception.

"I'm not saying it is either good or bad that he didn't tell us we would be going straight to hell," he explained, "but I think his understanding of the world as it is goes a long way to successfully ministering to his congregation. As I told you before, I do not totally disagree with those who defend your priest for spending time in the local taverns."

"How *much* time should he spend there? That's the key," I mused, not expecting an answer. Then I launched into what I knew I needed to say before we got to New Market. I told Gordy I would tell my folks immediately once I got home and that I wanted to do it alone.

"I know they're going to hate me for a while, or maybe longer, because they think I've failed them, but there have been so many episodes with the church where they have failed me too. I don't know how Mom hasn't become fed up with the church. They condemned her for the divorce and for bearing a bastard, they denied her acceptance into the Christian Mother Society, and they made her wait years for an annulment when those who had money could buy one easily. I knew she did it all to try to win approval from Dad, his relatives, and some of the snooty church members and townspeople. I also know she wanted the Catholic Church's approval for my sake, but approval from those people was denied and always will be. Nothing will change just because their out-of-wedlock daughter had a nice Catholic wedding. I'm done playing the game."

Gordy agreed and then cautioned me. "Don't let all that out to your folks, though. Show no anger."

"Agreed. I'm good at hiding my real feelings. I've had to do it all my life, just as Mom has."

After Gordy dropped me off at home, I wondered whether Dad would kick me out after I told him the news. As I entered the kitchen through the door from the garage, Mom was in the kitchen, and Dad was in the living room, watching a baseball game. Determined to get the confrontation over with, I stood in the archway between the two rooms and began saying what I knew I had to say. I told them we were not getting married in the New

Market church. I told them we were getting married in Gordy's church by a Lutheran minister and that he would be giving us marriage classes soon.

As I delivered this information, I saw their shoulders sink and their demeanors grow dark. I saw pain and fear on Mom's face and growing anger on Dad's. After only a brief silence, Dad rose from his easy chair.

"I wash my hands of the whole thing!" he exclaimed, then stomped out of the living room and into the bedroom, abruptly closing the door.

I had expected worse.

I thought Mom's first response showed a shallow concern for appearances.

"You were going to have such a beautiful wedding!" she exclaimed with disappointment.

"It will still be a beautiful wedding," I shot back.

"What are people going to say?" she bemoaned. "What are the *neighbors* going to say?"

"I don't give a damn what the neighbors say!" I fumed.

We were both silent for a moment.

Then Mom asked, almost softly, "Who will pay for the wedding?"

"We will pay for it ourselves," I replied.

"Who will walk you down the aisle?" She was persistent.

I wanted to ask her why I supposedly needed a father to walk me down the aisle when I had been denied one for much of my life, but I knew it would have been too cruel to say. I couldn't help thinking it, though. I knew Mom was in enough pain as it was. Instead, I asserted, "I can do it myself. I'll walk alone."

"Maybe you can ask one of your older cousins, like Ron or Jack."

"No, I don't want to put them in a situation where they have to make a tough choice. I can do it myself. I'll walk alone."

We had no further conversation on the topic that day, nor did we speak much about anything for the remaining months I lived at home with my parents. All I could hope for was that, with time, the tensions would relax and the wounds would heal, but it didn't appear likely. At that moment, I knew there was no turning back for me.

Support from Friends

Although my situation at home put extreme stress on me, I had good friends at work who helped me keep my balance. At first, though, I told no one about the difficulty of my homelife, not even my good friend Jenny Billings, whom I had been close with since starting work at Nutting Truck four years prior.

Our friendship deepened further after I introduced Gordy to Jenny and her husband, Craig. The four of us became friends. When we visited them at their home, we discussed theater and movies, shared stories, drank wine, and laughed a lot. One time, we packed a lunch of wine and cheese and spread a blanket in a grove of trees by a lake. We had a wonderful picnic.

One day at work, the stress seemed to hit me hard, and I needed to cry. I rushed to the restroom and hid in a stall as I let the tears come, unaware that my friend Jenny had followed me into the restroom and heard my stifled sobs. Jenny waited a few moments before softly encouraging me to come out and tell her what was wrong. Just looking into her eyes made me feel that Jenny was someone in whom I could confide and trust. The whole story tumbled out of me. I don't remember what she said to me exactly, but it seemed to calm me down. The tears stopped, and I was able to take control of myself again. Returning to my desk, I felt as if a weight had been taken off my shoulders.

A few minutes later, Jenny came up to my desk and told me I was coming home with her for lunch. Craig worked nearby, and they always went home for lunch together. Craig picked up both of us at noon and took us to their apartment. Jenny quickly explained to Craig what was going on, and they both provided much-needed emotional support to me. When Gordy called me that night, I told him about the lunch, and he was happy to hear I was getting the additional support. He told me to thank Jenny for him.

The next day at work, Jenny told me to come home with her and Craig for lunch again. I quickly agreed, knowing that it was good to talk with people who knew exactly what was going on with me. The lunch discussion took a turn that truly surprised me when Jenny's tone turned extremely serious.

"Craig and I have decided to tell you about the religion issues we had to face before we married. No one else at work knows, but we decided to trust you and Gordy with the story."

Craig began by looking at me directly and holding his gaze for an unusually long moment before saying, "I used to be a Roman Catholic priest."

I don't remember the exact words that spilled out of my mouth—maybe something like "Wow!" or "Really?" I remained shocked as they explained.

Craig was a practicing Roman Catholic priest when he met Jenny. They would see each other at the church's social events, and they felt a powerful attraction between them. Craig knew he could no longer live without Jenny. They were in love and felt they must be together. Because staying in the priesthood was no longer an option for Craig, as the Roman Catholic Church expected all priests to be celibate, Craig left the priesthood and married Jenny.

In the 1960s, leaving the priesthood meant being condemned by the Catholic Church, Catholic society, and, of course, all your Catholic relatives. Jenny was condemned as someone who wrongly enticed a priest to sin. As the two of them explained to me the tension and anger among their families, I realized that my and Gordy's experience paled in comparison.

I was home alone when Gordy called that night, so I could tell him the entire story without my folks hearing. He was as shocked as I had been. Talking about Craig and Jenny's situation helped ease our feelings. I continued having lunch with Craig and Jenny whenever I was invited in the following weeks. Their emotional support was invaluable to me at the time.

I had enjoyed working at Nutting Truck & Caster Company, but I decided to leave to seek employment closer to where Gordy and I would be living, in Minneapolis, after we married. Although I felt sad to leave my friends and coworkers, I looked forward to the adventure of marriage as well as searching for a new job in the cities.

On my last day at Nutting Truck, my coworkers threw me a going-away party, where we shared food and friendship during lunchtime and into the afternoon. As a parting gift, they gave me two cutting boards—one the shape of a pig and the other a more standard rectangle—each with the words "Nutting Truck & Caster Company, Faribault, Minnesota" burned into the surface. These were both quality, standard items given to vendors as promotional gifts, but the rectangle was extra special because it was signed by everyone in the office.

Marriage Class

Gordy and I thought the classes were excellent. We did our reading and filled out a small workbook. Instead of lecture, the class was more of a discussion among the group, with the leader going over conflict resolution, the handling of money, and a whole list of practical matters that might be considered simple, but they are only simple if both members of the marriage are on the same page.

Gordy and I discovered that we had already discussed most of the areas of possible conflict on our own. However, we were surprised to learn that many of the couples had not. For those couples, the homework may have comprised new challenges, but that was really the point of the class—to uncover potential areas of conflict and resolve them before the marriage.

There would be one session remaining for us after we were married, but Pastor Almquist said that finishing the course before the wedding ceremony was not necessary. He said many couples attended for several months after getting married. For us, the classes mostly served to reinforce things we had already discussed—budgeting money and having only a limited time to spend together because we both worked and Gordy attended the University of Minnesota full-time. It seemed we already had a strong start.

Wedding Dress and Veil

After we announced we were getting married in a Lutheran church, Mom told me she and Dad would not pay for any part of our wedding. When Dad had declared he would "wash his hands of the whole thing," I guess he truly meant keeping his hands off everything, including his wallet. Gordy and I didn't blink. We'd decided we would pay for our own wedding, and we went ahead with plans for a large reception and dance.

I also decided I would make my own wedding dress and veil—not to save money but because I wanted my dress to feel special to me. I selected a design similar to my maternal grandmother's dress, visible in a black-and-white photo I had. Although the dress in the photo was clearly not white, neither I nor Mom could determine the color. And her sisters disagreed on the color: Aunt Caroline said she remembered their mother saying it was blue. Aunt Tillie insisted that their mother said it was green. I decided mine would be white. I used the pattern I'd selected for the basic design and created the rest of the pieces to make it special for me.

I remembered loving the veil my cousin Betty Simon wore at her wedding, the year before. I called her to find out where she'd gotten it, and she told me she'd made it herself. She volunteered to bring her veil over so I could see the details and figure out how to make a similar one. Betty and I spent a fun afternoon talking veils, sequins, lace, and weddings. That afternoon brought back many happy childhood memories of the two of us playing together.

Bridesmaids

Getting married in a Lutheran church complicated choosing my bridesmaids because Catholic rules prohibited any Catholic from partaking in non-Catholic services or sacraments. In 1970, my two best friends were both members of St. Nicholas Catholic Church in New Market. We had attended elementary school together, remained friends during high school, and become even closer friends after high school. I wanted to ask both of them to be bridesmaids and one of them to be my maid of honor, but I knew being in a Lutheran wedding could be a problem for them.

Although only the maid of honor had to sign as an official witness to the marriage, I feared the New Market priest would make an issue of their being attendants in a non-Catholic wedding ceremony. Other Catholics would be in the wedding, though, but they belonged to churches outside New Market, and I knew they would have no issue with being in my wedding.

I didn't want to put my friends in a difficult position, having to choose between me and their church. And I didn't want them to feel they had to be in my wedding just to honor our friendship while, at the same time, compromising their faith and risking scorn from the priest and members of the Catholic Church in New Market. I knew, all too well, how cruel some people could be. Yet I wanted them to know I would love having them in my wedding. I wanted to give them an easy way out should they choose not to participate in the ceremony.

Before I broached the topic with them, I told them about my wedding plans at Highview Christiania Lutheran Church because I knew they would be genuinely happy for me. They were, and we shared the moment of joy together. Then I explained how I would love to have them in my bridal party—but also understood that the Catholic Church prohibited them from partaking in any non-Catholic religious services. As I paused, their silence told me they'd realized they should not partake in the ceremony itself, so I suggested they participate in other ways. When I asked whether they would like to open the gifts, their faces brightened as they both said yes.

No matter their role, I just hoped they understood how much they meant to me and that our friendships would remain solid. Both of them went on to throw me a wedding shower, be my personal attendants on the wedding day, and open gifts at the reception—great friends!

Booking on Short Notice

Planning the wedding was mostly up to me, as I'd expected, but Gordy and I worked together on some of the planning. It was late summer, and when we tried to book a hall for the reception, all the convenient places were booked through the following spring and into the summer. What rescued us from this dilemma was that we were flexible on the date because Pastor Almquist had several Saturdays open.

When we discovered that the Knights of Columbus Hall (KC Hall) in New Prague was not booked on October 31, 1970, we jumped on it. We did not care that the wedding would be on Halloween, and neither did Pastor Almquist. Although we were not oblivious to the irony of our celebrating our wedding in the Knights of Columbus Hall, we thought it might make my parents a bit more comfortable. I actually think it did. The KC Hall wasn't fancy, but they were known for good food. The facility had ample seating for three hundred and a bar over which to serve our own alcohol, served by the venue's staff.

Booking a band on short notice was another challenge. All the bands were either booked or would not work on Halloween, but Gordy's cousin Ben had a friend who had a small band that would be just perfect for the KC Hall, which had a smaller dance floor than the bigger venues. At first, the bandleader was reluctant to ask his band to play on Halloween, but when they decided to accept the job, Gordy and I were thrilled.

Bridal Showers for the Bastard—Yes and No

Like any bride-to-be who had attended showers for relatives and friends, I looked forward to my turn being the center of attention, the one "showered" with gifts before my wedding. At twenty-one years old, I was maybe too old to feel giddy about the prospect, but I confess to feeling really excited—and I was thrilled when two of my best friends, LaVonne and Helen, told me they would host a shower for me. I knew many of my old friends would be there and that it would be a fun get-together. Similarly, I was delighted when Gordy's sisters, Joyce and Judy, told me they would host a shower for his relatives to attend. I knew the event would be a great opportunity for me to meet his female relatives and neighbors, whom he had fondly described to me.

In those days, family bridal showers were often given for the bride-to-be by her aunts or siblings. I had no siblings, but I had many aunts, and I knew that Mom had attended showers for her nieces on her side of the family as well as for Dad's nieces on the Simon side of the family. The customary protocol of the times called for a shower from the aunts on my mother's side and another from the aunts on my father's side. I didn't even think to consider how the location of the wedding ceremony could affect that tradition.

When I got home from work at Nutting Truck one day, there was a gift and small card for me sitting on the table. Mom said that Dad's older sister Ella had delivered it earlier. It was a nice gift: a set of ceramic bowls and a bath towel. Mom told me Ella had said I deserved a bridal shower gift even if the Simons didn't throw me a traditional bridal shower. My first reaction was to acknowledge Ella's thoughtfulness—then Mom explained, a little too readily, a detail I had not yet considered.

"If you're not getting married at St. Nicholas, you can't expect them to host your bridal shower in their basement."

I confess I was blindsided by the news and hurt by the direct way Mom had delivered it, as if to say, *That's what you get for not being married in the church.* She hadn't said that, and maybe it's unfair to attribute the attitude to her, but I could've used a little comfort from my mother at the time. Instead, I received more of an *I told you so.*

After a moment, I turned to Mom and said, "Guess that means none of my Simon aunts in the parish could give me a bridal shower in their home either."

I can try to understand Mom's loyalty to Dad, comforting him and his fellow Catholics about my lost soul, but with his family having rejected her so many times, I expected a little more empathy. Honestly, the lack of initial support from Mom and from some on Dad's side of the family nearly broke my heart, but I resolved not to let it do so. Like so many other slights before this, I just blocked it out.

On the Schoenecker side, my godmother, Aunt Tillie (Schmitz), made it quite clear she wanted to give me a bridal shower, and she offered as much as soon as she found out I was engaged. But her house was tiny, so her daughter-in-law, Stella Schmitz, stepped up and offered to host at her house in Bloomington.

Stella was married to Tillie's oldest son, Ron Schmitz, and had always been extremely kind to me. Mom and I had stayed with Tillie and her husband, and Ron was like a big brother to me. I had also stayed with Ron and Stella at their home in Bloomington a few times during the summers to help with their kids. Even though Stella was an experienced cook and hostess, she always felt extremely nervous about hosting and usually avoided it, including for anyone on her side of the family. When Stella announced she was hosting the family bridal shower for me, I was honored that she would make a special effort to overcome her anxiety.

The shower was great. All of Mom's side of the family came, and I was grateful for their support and gifts. Aunt Peggy surprised me with a crystal bud vase and relish dish, each engraved with the letter *F*, which in 1970 was considered an expensive, thoughtful, and personal gift. She also brought our wedding present, which she thought was better given before the wedding, but I waited until after the shower to open it so I could do so more privately and with Aunt Peggy by my side.

Inside the box were a dozen long-stemmed crystal wineglasses that matched the bud vase, again each with the letter *F* etched on it. I tried to express my thanks for such an expensive gift, but Aunt Peggy told me that she and Uncle Cyril had talked it over, and since I was an only child, they wanted to spend the same amount on me as they spent on the other families. I felt truly honored. Over fifty years later, whenever Gordy and I use those glasses, on both routine and special occasions, we always drink a toast to Aunt Peggy and Uncle Cyril.

Aunt Peggy was a kind, sweet, and fun woman who was especially good to me as I grew up. I still have the typed letter she sent me for First Communion; they were not able to come down for the celebration. The letter was written to me, not to my mom, and that made me feel so grown-up and special. And yet I didn't fully realize just how innate her kindness was until a family get-together with some of Gordy's relatives shortly after we were married.

I was visiting with Gordy's aunt Anna, who was married to Ed Cervenka—a brother of Helen, Gordy's mom. When it was mentioned that Anna had attended school for a time in Prior Lake, Minnesota, I added that Aunt Peggy had grown up in Prior Lake, too, and that the two women were of similar age. Anna was thrilled to find out my aunt Peggy (by then a Schoenecker) was Peggy Simones from Prior Lake, all grown up. Anna explained that she and her sister, Helen, were the "poor Bohemian girls" among the predominantly Irish and German kids at school in Prior Lake. Most students were not friendly to them, and no one ever invited them to birthday parties. But when their classmate Peggy Simones had a birthday party, she invited the two Bohemian girls, and they were delighted. Both Anna and Helen told me how wonderful my aunt Peggy was and how happy it made them to know their nephew married Peggy's niece.

The next time I saw Aunt Peggy, I told her the story and how happy she had made those "poor Bohemian girls."

"They were my classmates," responded Aunt Peggy. "Of course I would invite them." Excluding any one of her classmates, for whatever reason, was an option Aunt Peggy hadn't considered. The memory of that one act of kindness lasted a lifetime.

A Dispiriting RSVP

After my dad's side of the family refused to throw me a bridal shower, I began to understand and even accept their feelings about the union, but I sent them all invitations to the wedding anyway. If they chose not to come, that would be their choice, but I was not about to leave anyone out.

When the RSVPs started to come back, one included a special letter to Dad. Mom showed me the letter and waited as I read it. It was from Dad's sister, the married aunt I stayed with in Faribault during my sophomore and junior years at Bethlehem Academy. Maybe they had worked past my being a bastard, but my getting married outside the Catholic Church seemed to reaffirm their feelings about Dad's marrying Mom and adopting me.

The tone of the letter was one of *I told you so*, of *She isn't worthy*. They were disappointed that "Nancy has turned her back on God." The letter went on to say they would come to the wedding only for Dad's sake, to give him support for "what Nancy was doing to him." I'm not sure of Mom's reasons for showing me the letter, as her feelings seemed to be all over the place. Maybe she thought it would make me come to my senses and move the wedding to the Catholic church. She probably felt the letter was a rebuke to Dad for marrying her and adopting her bastard daughter. I did not like being seen as a daughter who had wronged her father, but I was powerless to change the feelings of others.

"If that's how my aunt feels," I said, handing the letter back to Mom, "she and her family could always stay home."

The Wedding

The wedding went as planned, with the packed church offering a beautiful setting for our ceremony. Pastor Almquist attended the reception as promised and managed to say a fine prayer before the meal. Gordy and I were especially pleased that our wedding was well attended by both sides of the family, which we took to mean that the bridal-shower drama was not a sign of outright rejection by Dad's family. And perhaps only Gordy and I realized the irony of the large picture of the pope hanging on the far wall, watching as people ate, drank, danced, and generally celebrated for hours, well into the night, even after Gordy and I left.

When Gordy and I went to settle up with the KC Hall, we discovered Mom and Dad had paid the bill, which left us with some much-needed cash and a sense of reconciliation with my folks. I was excited about the prospect of moving beyond my bastard identity, a journey that is the subject of part 2 of this memoir.

CHAPTER 8

MOM'S STORY

Although my bastard moments were largely a result of my mom's actions, she brought me into this world, and the joy in my life is only possible because of her. I have no interest in judging her behavior. And although her silence about her past sometimes made things more difficult for me, her circumstances are not only important to consider but also fascinating. Consequently, the story of my bastard moments needs to include a view into Mom's family history, a journey through the first half of the 1900s—following Mom's path to becoming a single mother and subsequently doing what she thought best, even if that meant keeping truths from me for decades.

Many details about Mom's story were mysteries to me as I grew up, and they continued being mysteries even as I began writing this memoir. Although my research uncovered facts that surprised and sometimes angered me, I wrote the preceding chapters without exposing newfound facts, limiting my readers' knowledge to what I knew at the time. Thus, as I try to piece together her story in this chapter, readers will discover her motivations and secrets in context. See if you can spot any "there but for the grace of God go I" moments, as certain aspects of my mother's story are common enough.

The Schoeneckers

My mom, Rita Katherine Schoenecker, was born on July 6, 1914, and was the seventh of eleven children born to Joseph and Helena (Witt) Schoenecker.

All the children were born at home. Mom's elder siblings included Edward, Caroline, Tillie (Mathilda), Ben (Benno), Emil, and Laura. Her younger siblings were Cyril, Charles, Florian, and Ralph. Ralph passed away less than a month after he was born, in 1923.

Married in May 1903, Joseph and Helena farmed the eighty-acre farm where Joseph grew up for the first twenty-four years of their marriage. Located in Section 24, Belle Plaine Township, Scott County, Minnesota, their farm was north of Union Hill—a town with a store, a school, a church, a cemetery, and a few houses, situated along both sides of Minnesota State Highway 19—and about five miles west of New Prague. Because no roads bordered the farm, the Schoeneckers had to drive through the yard of their neighbor and relative, Virgil Schoenecker, to enter their farmstead.

In the early 1900s, many roads were merely buggy trails, not improved to accommodate automobiles. Clearing snow on buggy trails was not a priority because people got around on sleighs. Some families owned a cutter, a lightweight open sleigh meant to be pulled by one horse and carry only two passengers. Although built for speed, they could be quite fancy and decorative. If freight or more than two people had to be carried, families used a large sleigh pulled by a team of horses.

Because long-distance travel was slow and often impossible in spring and winter, people hesitated to travel beyond their hometown. Consequently, regardless of how small a town was in those days, it was the necessary center of social activity for the area. For example, Union Hill had a community band that performed at functions, a community theater that put on plays regularly, and an all-male choir, directed by Joe Busch.

My grandfather Joseph Schoenecker was a faithful member of the choir, and according to his son Cyril, regardless of how cold the weather, his dad would harness the team to the sleigh and drive over two miles into town to rehearse. Choir practice offered some freedom from the daily grind, and the men enjoyed gathering for drinks after rehearsal. Music played an important role in the church-centered community, and Cyril took his brief turn at pumping the handle on the church organ as the organist played.

The flu pandemic in 1918 kept people close to their homes, as well. Of course, schools were closed, and families kept to themselves as much as they could. Although Cyril, who was born March 1, 1918, had no memory of the flu pandemic, the stories his parents told him described a time when entire families would become sick, rendering them unable to care for themselves or their animals. Neighbors would have to care for sick families and their farm animals until the family recovered. If the sick family survived, they often needed to care for other families struck with the deadly influenza. His dad, Joseph, told him of a time when he struggled not to pass out as he drove horses to town to get medicine for his family.

According to Mom, who was born four years before Cyril, their dad was not the best of farmers. Mom loved her dad a great deal, as did the rest of the kids, and her explanation for his farm failure was that his heart wasn't in it; he had wanted to become a butcher, not a farmer.

As a young man, Joseph moved to Eden Valley—a town located over ninety miles north of Union Hill—where he stayed with his older brother Henry, who had married in 1895 and owned a hardware store in town. Joseph started working at his brother's store, but he also learned the butchering trade while working in town for a butcher named Ruhland, who trained him as an apprentice. Joseph liked the butchering trade, but Eden Valley was far away from Union Hill, and the woman Joseph was courting, Helena Witt, lived on a farm near Union Hill.

When Joseph and Helena planned to marry, Joseph was offered a partnership in the butchering business where he had trained. Joseph wanted to move to Eden Valley to take advantage of the offer, but Helena was reluctant to move so far away from her own family. Instead, she desired that her husband farm land near to her family, as did several of her brothers, working the land north of Union Hill. Joseph eventually succumbed to her wishes—against his own ambitions—and the two of them took over his parents' farm, his parents continuing to live with them.

Losing the Homeplace

Joseph's failure at farming was due to more than just not liking the work. His handling of the business during harder times led to losing the homeplace.

For many who owned farms, lived in rural areas, and/or worked for a living, the Great Depression started years earlier than the famous stock market crash in 1929. As the rich became richer, the poor became poorer, and finally, when the greed of the rich had sucked the production of our country dry, the inevitable crash occurred. It was, according to many rural folks, a matter of "the chickens coming home to roost." The low farm prices during the 1920s devastated the finances of farm after farm, and feeding a large family became more difficult for Joseph and Helena, who would become one of many couples to lose their farm before the crash.

I was unaware of their losing the farm until 2006, when my husband and I recorded an interview with Uncle Cyril, in which he shared some details. Although he was only nine at the time the farm was lost, he'd already been working closely with his dad, becoming his right-hand helper on some farm-connected escapades, which are the subjects of later paragraphs. Working closely with his dad gave Uncle Cyril an understanding of the times and the way the world operated for the poor—or to phrase it more accurately, *against* the poor.

It is generally true that unscrupulous businessmen and con men flourished during the 1920s and 1930s. These men preyed on the weaknesses of their customers: poverty, alcohol, and gambling, with some people checking all three boxes. Of course, there are at least two sides to every story, but I can only give you Uncle Cyril's version, which is probably somewhat biased, but using information from my interview with him, I pieced together a short narrative of the events leading up to my grandfather's losing the farm.

Although Grandpa owned the eighty-acre farm, the family ran it at a loss for many years. Grandpa borrowed money to keep it going, but he may have irresponsibly spent money on alcohol and gambling. In a nearby town, a businessman—I'll call him Farley—readily loaned Grandpa money while also supplying the family with groceries and other needs. As the debt piled up, Farley may have convinced Grandpa to "trade up" for a larger farm. Farley ended up owning the eighty-acre farm on which Grandpa had been raised, but the deal completely paid off Grandpa's debt to the businessman, and in fairness to Farley, how else could he have gotten reimbursed for what Grandpa owed him? The deal allowed Grandpa to start fresh on a new, larger farm owned by Farley. I'm sure the deal sounded good to a farmer burdened by debt, especially one with lots of children and a (possible) penchant for alcohol.

Mom was about thirteen when a man came to the farm with the piece of paper saying that her dad no longer owned the homeplace where he had grown up. The family would have to move to Farley's farm, ten miles east, in Cedar Lake Township, west of New Market. Although probably no one used the term *bastard moment* as I do in this memoir, I am sure the moment when Grandpa and the family were essentially kicked off the family farm would have qualified as such a moment, especially for Grandpa. And yet there would be worse times to come.

Aftermath of the Loss

The Schoenecker family made the big move to Farley's farm on a weekday in the fall of 1927. Lacking the money to have their possessions hauled, they loaded them into their field wagons, hitched up their horses, and made the journey, also driving their livestock the entire ten miles to the new farm. The journey led them down miles of gravel roads, many of which had little to no traffic, but the middle of their route followed the nearly mile-long main street of New Prague, a town of about fifteen hundred people at the time.

New Prague was established in the mid-1800s and settled mostly by people who emigrated from the former Austrian colonies of Bohemia, Moravia, and Slovakia. After the nation of Czechoslovakia was established in 1919, its people began calling themselves "Czechs," but at the time and well into the mid-1900s, most of them called themselves "Bohemians," because they had emigrated from Bohemia decades before there even was a Czechoslovakia. Many German-speaking immigrants settled in the town as well.

According to the 1856 census, Le Sueur County, which includes the southern half of New Prague, had more Bohemians (Czechs) at the time than any other county in the state. And the neighboring Rice County and Scott County, the latter of which included the northern half of New Prague, each had large Czech populations too.

Due to the proximity of their home countries, the Bohemians and Germans in New Prague developed a sense of kinship and competition, but the period during World War I was tense. Mom told me that, when she was a child, the Czechs and Germans in New Prague often verbally abused one another and that she and her siblings did not always feel welcome in town. In 1927, when the Schoeneckers drove their cattle and loaded wagons down Main Street, a few townspeople made some negative comments about the family's German ethnicity, but most just berated them for using their city's streets to drive cattle.

Once the move was completed, the Schoeneckers settled into their home, west of New Market—the same town Mom would return to decades later as a single mother, with me in tow. Some things didn't change much for the children. They continued cutting across their neighbors' farmland on their walk to school, but they had new neighbors with different farmland. However, their new school was District Number 48 School, a one-room country school west of New Market, which was less than a mile from their house. Back in Union Hill, they'd had to walk over two miles to school, but all their neighbors had been either German relatives or old friends of the family.

Uncle Cyril remembers studying German in first grade at Union Hill, but nearly all the families at the new school were Czech and spoke Czech at home. Tensions between the two nationalities had been high during World War I but eased after the war. Although some animosity might have remained, Uncle Cyril said the children got along fine in school. He even explained that one of the older students told his classmates they needed to quit speaking Czech at recess and speak only English so the new students could understand them.

Leaving the farm and moving to a new place was hardest on their father, Joseph, who alone carried the burdens of his failures; he and his family had to work on a rented farm with no real hope of winning ownership. He didn't even have a plan for feeding his large family through the winter. There were no jobs available that paid enough to make a living for a married man with a family. He owed money for rent and would have to continue running up his account with Farley for groceries. And he felt the sting of being a loser. He alone was at fault for letting his family down, and he was ashamed beyond what he could bear.

One afternoon in the fall of 1927, Joseph loaded his shotgun and took a solemn walk out to the pasture. He sat on the ground, leaned against a tree, and turned the long weapon around, placing the wide barrel into his mouth. As he struggled to assume the difficult position, he paused just long enough to appreciate the world around him for the last time—then his youngest son, Florian, just six years old, entered his peripheral vision. Did this enable him to see that his life meant something? I don't know, but he removed the gun from his mouth, stood up, and told his son he'd set out hunting for pheasant or squirrel but found none. "Let's go home," he said as he reached for the boy's small hand. Then Joseph led the way back to the house.

This is the story as Grandpa told it to my mother when he was living with her, about a decade later. Florian died in his late teens, and neither Mom nor I knew how much he would have remembered of the episode. Grandpa said he didn't tell the story to anyone else during all those years, and as far as I know, Mom hasn't told anyone but me. The story is relevant to my memoir because the deep despair that leads one to end it all is often the result of far more than one "bastard moment." It is, instead, the culmination of many, leaving them feeling powerless to put themselves right.

The suicide rate among farmers is exceeded only by those for mining and certain construction jobs, but historically, the rate for farmers has soared during hard times—as during the 1920s, 1930s, 1980s, and the era before and during the COVID-19 pandemic, which started in 2020.

Hearing this story about Grandpa led me to review my bastard moments and consider how fortunate I was to always feel as if I could climb beyond those moments, although I did often feel alone.

Apparently, Grandpa somehow buckled down and came up with some ideas to earn money. He saw that the farmstead bordered a large creek and a huge slough with tall grass that had not been cut all summer. Grandpa had the foresight to cut the tall, dry grass, even though it would make poor feed. The following spring, Scott County began building a road nearby, and the construction company needed feed for their mules. With most farmers having fed their store of hay to their own stock over the winter, Joseph was in position to get a good price for his slough hay, and he sorely needed the cash.

Cooking Moon

The lead-up to the 1929 stock market crash continued squeezing farmers and other rural folks financially, and many had no options. Without a job or any means of income, many turned to illegally making and selling moonshine, a high-proof corn whiskey produced by distilling, or "cooking," cornmeal, yeast, sugar, and water—also called "cooking moon." The noun *moonshine* comes from the verb (to) *moonshine*, a British slang term referring to any illegal activity done at night, as if "by the light of the moon." This illegal high-proof liquor also came to be called *hooch*, *home brew*, and *moon*.

The National Prohibition Act, which Congress passed in 1919, over President Woodrow Wilson's veto, forbade the "manufacture, sale, and transportation of intoxicating liquors." However, even though it was illegal to home-brew liquor or beer, consuming it was not illegal, and those who made it for their own use were rarely prosecuted. Citizens of various professions embraced the country's demand for alcohol by making moonshine and selling it. Called "bootleggers" because they hid flasks of moonshine in their boots, most of these local entrepreneurs were small-time operators and sold only to locals. But if their product earned a good reputation, they could find themselves cooking moonshine for distributors, who had the means to transport it to the speakeasies in cities.

My mother did not tell me the details of how her dad got started cooking moon; it is likely she did not know. But in 2006, when Gordy and I interviewed Mom's younger brother Cyril, he was able to tell us the story and give some details of the operation.

Although Cyril was only eleven years old when Grandpa started cooking moon, he was Grandpa's main helper, gaining firsthand knowledge of every detail. Uncle Cyril told us that Grandpa got started when his friend from Jordan, Minnesota—whom I'll call "Fred"—visited the farm. Fred noticed two qualities that made Grandpa's farm ideal for making moon: First, Porter Creek (Mom always called it Plum Creek) flowed through the west end of the farm, and both sides of the creek had acres of lowland and thick willow trees—perfect terrain for hiding a still. Second, a spring supplied a steady flow of clear water, which they would need as well. Within a few days, Fred had set up a copper still near the spring and made it invisible from all directions. Access could be gained through a gate of cut trees, made to look like a pile of brush. The brush-wall illusion even fooled Farley, the owner of the land, whenever he hunted in the slough, forty feet or less from the still's location.

To ensure that paths to the still did not become obvious through wear, they approached from four different routes. Heating the water and special mash took a lot of fuel. To ensure their seemingly excessive fuel usage did not draw attention, they purchased the fuel from three different suppliers, who delivered it to the fuel barrel on the farm. Uncle Cyril also told of Fred making a deal with one of the suppliers to fill his truck with fuel and let Fred deliver it at night, with no questions asked as to where he delivered it. Fred would pay the bill.

After the finished moonshine was collected via the copper tubing, it was put into large wooden kegs and stacked onto a stoneboat, or heavy sled, near the still. Oak chips were added to the kegs to give the brew additional flavor, and molasses was added to give it color. Young Cyril would collect the kegs, use a team of horses to pull the full stoneboat of liquor to a small brooder house—also on skids, able to be pulled to any part of the farm—and stack them inside for storage. Fred would pick the kegs up from the brooder house at night, driving a souped-up car with the back seat removed and replaced with planks, providing space for up to six kegs. Uncle Cyril said local people and even federal agents sometimes tried to follow Fred from Jordan, but he always lost them by taking different routes, probably including some buggy trails through thickly wooded areas.

The operation ran smoothly in the summer, but the high risk of getting caught should not be underestimated. At any time, the operation could have been discovered and subsequently reported by Farley, the men who delivered fuel, neighbors who noticed Fred picking up or returning the barrels, or a random hunter searching the slough for pheasants or other game. Everyone had to be careful, and in the winter, they couldn't cook because the willows lost the leaves that otherwise hid the still, and paths in the snow would reveal their routes.

One story that Uncle Cyril related to us happened during the early years when Grandpa was cooking moon. Cyril's older sisters and older brother Emil would go to dances, most of which were free, but they had no spending money. Emil came up with the idea to take a bit of moonshine out of his dad's kegs, sitting in the shed, awaiting pickup by Fred. Emil would uncork each barrel and siphon a little of the precious fluid into a jug, then carefully replace each cork. At the dance, he could sell swigs of the stuff to others and have a few swigs for himself. Apparently, his dad got wise to the scheme and marked the corks so he'd know if they were tampered with again. Cyril didn't explain to me how Grandpa dealt with Emil, but he did say that Emil assured his dad he would never pinch moonshine again.

I do not know if Grandpa fell behind on rent or if other problems arose, but at the end of the summer in 1931, Farley decided he wanted to rent the farm to someone else. He gave Grandpa notice that he had to leave the next spring. Farley built a new chicken barn for his new renter and allowed Grandpa to use it until he left. Desperate for money, Grandpa listened to

Fred's plan to build a false wall at one end of the new barn so they could cook moonshine in the winter. The wall ran floor to ceiling and was hinged on one side so it could be opened like a door. It held nests for laying hens, disguising its true purpose. Behind the wall sat Fred's copper still. It must have been a nightmare getting water to the still, keeping it fired, and transporting kegs in and out, but they didn't get to use it for long anyway.

That winter, Farley's new renter decided to snoop around the place that would be his new home come spring. He perceived the difference in dimensions between the outside and inside of the new chicken barn and discovered both the false wall and the still behind it. He reported it to the authorities, Cyril said, but when Grandpa and Fred found out they'd been discovered, they removed the still before the authorities came to investigate. After this close call, for which an arrest would have meant jail time, one might think that Grandpa and Fred would have learned a lesson and quit their illegal activities. But their need for money had not diminished, nor had the demand for their product.

Joseph and Helena moved their family to New Prague in April of 1932, leaving the machinery and stock on the farm because it was owned by Farley. Fred continued to hire Grandpa to cook for him, driving him to his still, on a farm near Jordan, every Monday. Grandpa would stay at the farm until Friday evening, when Fred would drive him back to New Prague. The Schoeneckers did not stay long in New Prague before moving to Jordan in the fall of the same year. Grandpa continued cooking moon, and Cyril lied to his schoolmates in Jordan when asked what his dad did for a living. "He's a carpenter," Cyril would assert boldly.

Because he did not attend school in New Prague during the short time the family lived there, Cyril had to start the seventh grade again in the fall of 1932. He told of a nun-teacher who was constantly on his case. "You're skinny because you smoke all the time," she often proclaimed. But Cyril never smoked as a child or as an adult. The other students knew the nun's feelings toward Cyril, and to irritate her, they voted him into a student leadership position. Cyril said that after the election, the nun, angry, declared the election void. "So much for democracy," Cyril later commented.

New to Jordan, the Schoeneckers first moved into the larger of two houses on the Levi Morlock farmstead, bordering Sand Creek, right on the edge of town. Soon after, they moved to a smaller house by the railroad tracks. During this time, Mom and Laura worked as maids in Minneapolis. Mom's older sister Laura met her future husband, George Stockinger, during that time, and after marrying, they lived in Jordan, where George got a job driving trucks for Morlock.

Helena liked Jordan because she could manage walking to the Catholic church. According to Uncle Cyril, she walked the near three-quarters of a mile, along State Highway 169, to attend mass every day. Both Uncle Cyril and my mother had the same answers when I asked them what they remember most about their mother: she was kind, devoutly religious, and prayed often during the day. And they both also indicated she was that way as long as they knew her, from when they were children on the farm to when she died.

Grandpa continued cooking moon through 1932 and much of 1933, and Fred continued driving Grandpa to the still and boarding him all week before taking him home on Friday night. However, their luck soon ran out, and federal agents discovered the operation. They arrested the entire group, including Grandpa, Fred, his boss, the drivers, and the distributors.

Many people whose only crime was cooking moon went to federal prison, sometimes for years. Moonshine stills behind false chicken coop walls were almost as common as chickens, and it wasn't uncommon for children who grew up during the 1940s and 1950s to be able to name several adults they associated with daily who had done jail time for bootlegging. In New Market, for instance, a respected local businessman was arrested for it and did time. And one of the janitors at Gordy's high school became known as "Bootlegger Bill" among the students who knew his past, and they even admired him for it. In some cases, doing time became a badge of honor, reflecting that the man had disobeyed an unpopular law and done what was needed to feed his family.

Of course, not all the bootlegging lawlessness was that simple, and much of it was a result of greed. Beyond that, the illegal brew helped finance crime and create criminal organizations that ruled cities and destroyed lives. But the poor who went to prison for bootlegging, having done it just to feed their families, were not generally scorned. Most of the people I knew saw Prohibition as a big mistake for the country—one that was finally rectified by repeal on December 5, 1933.

Shortly after Grandpa was arrested for cooking moonshine, the judge released him. According to my mother, the judge felt sorry for an old man who was trying to make a living for his wife and children in the hard times that were the 1930s. Although he was freed, there was no work for him anywhere. How the family scraped by over the next few years is something only those who lived through the era can explain. By this time, the four eldest of Joseph and Helena's children—Ed, Caroline, Tillie, and Laura—were married. Benno and Emil worked at nearby farms, and my mom, Rita, worked as a housemaid for well-to-do people in the cities. Cyril, Charles, and Florian were still in school. And Grandpa was working at the WPA (Works Progress Administration), a New Deal agency that employed millions of jobless, usually unskilled men, to work on public projects, including roads and public buildings.

For Joseph, being head of the family became even more challenging when Helena, his wife of thirty-two years, died on June 27, 1935, following a long illness. The family took the loss hard. Mom's sister Laura, who was only thirteen months older than Mom and had been married since 1932, was living with her husband and child in Jordan when Helena died. No doubt it was a comfort to Mom and Laura to live close to each other in those difficult times of grief.

However, tragedy pulls no punches, and before long, Laura was stricken with tuberculosis and had to be sent to a state treatment center in western Minnesota. Laura's husband, George, struggled to provide and care for their son, driving a truck that picked up milk from farms in the Jordan area. Mom told me she often helped out by making their son, Roger, a meal or watching him while George was gone, but sometimes the situation seemed to be more than George could handle. Mom didn't elaborate on the situation, but I am sure it put a lot of pressure on her and that there was little she could do except try to pitch in when she could.

Meanwhile, Laura's tuberculosis had caused one of her lungs to collapse, making her recovery slow and difficult. Over a year later, she returned to her family, her health restored, but she would live the rest of her life with only one lung. A year or so later, in May of 1937, Laura had her second child, a boy they named Tommy.

Dissolving a Family

My grandfather's decision to send his children to stay with friends and relatives after their mother's death probably had as much to do with housekeeping as with poverty. When her mother died, Mom was twenty-one and working in the cities as a maid, probably enjoying an independent life, with some time off once in a while. I am sure she felt some pressure to marry, but it's no surprise she didn't share her dating history with me. As I grew up, though, she recounted to me the extent of her dad's grief over the loss of his wife, which encouraged her to dutifully quit her job and return to Jordan to help out.

Mom worked hard to do the housekeeping and care for her father and her three younger brothers—Cyril, Chuck, and Florian. Caring for a household with four men when short on income—especially in an era long before wash-and-wear clothing and automatic washers and dryers—Mom may have felt frustrated that her labor earned her no money.

Her youngest brother, Florian, was the first child to be placed into the care of others. Grandpa sent Florian to live with his adult sister Tillie and her husband, Ewald, in New Market. A year or so later, when Florian turned seventeen, in July of 1938, he joined the CCC (Civilian Conservation Corps), a volunteer public works program for young, unmarried men, expanded to include ages seventeen through twenty-five. Records show that Florian's work group, CCC Company 3709, helped build the Gunflint Trail (near Grand Marais, Minnesota), which was constructed during the winter of 1938 and over the following year.

Because Florian was a ward of Tillie, his CCC wages—about thirty dollars a month—went directly to her and her family. Years later, Aunt Tillie told me those wages helped get her family through the winter. After being honorably discharged from the CCC on March 25, 1939, Florian returned to New Market, where he worked grinding feed for Clarence Wagner. Sadly, Florian was killed on June 3, 1940, when the car in which he was riding left New Market via County Road 2 and accidentally hit a horse about a quarter mile west of town. The three friends he'd been riding with were injured to varying degrees, but they all recovered fully.

Cyril and Charles were both in high school when their mother died, in 1935. Cyril was eager to complete high school and continue playing sports, an area where he excelled. In fact, it was his teammates who gave him the nickname "Slim." He said his brother Charles, who was a year younger, wanted to join the CCC once he turned seventeen, in 1936. Cyril worked at an oil station in town and eventually moved to stay with the family who owned it as he completed his junior year. Then he moved in with his sister Laura and her husband, George, who lived in Jordan.

George worked for a man named Morlock, who had several truck routes. One delivered milk in town, another picked up cans of cream from farmers, and yet another hauled cattle from farms to the stockyards in South St. Paul. Cyril drove George's cream route on Wednesdays and Fridays. Apparently, the school administrators were understanding and allowed him to play sports even if he missed school two mornings each week. He also had a job working for the shop teacher one hour each day, earning him six dollars each month. He considered himself pretty lucky to have the jobs.

Like most women, Mom probably dreamed of having her own home, which, perhaps, helped motivate her to marry when she did. On August 14, 1937, she married Paul H. Juergens in a church in Remer, Minnesota, less than a month after his twenty-first birthday, when he no longer needed anyone to sign for him. I'm not claiming that permission was an issue, but why did they marry in Remer, a town about two hundred miles north of Jordan? Why not marry in Jordan, where the parents of both couples lived? The place and date of their wedding were unknown to me when I started writing this memoir—until a friend discovered the information in 2021, when he found a note in the margin of the New Market church's official book, on the page documenting her second marriage, in 1957. There was a handwritten note on the side of the page:

July 25, 1953: declared attempted marriage of
Rita [K]. Schoenecker to Paul Juergens Aug. 14, 1937,
at Remer Minn. before Rev. M. Thompson Null and Void
(The writer assumed my mom spelled her middle name, Katherine, with a C.)

I was shocked. These facts led me to believe they had eloped. Of course, they were both twenty-one or older, giving them the freedom to do as they pleased, but they clearly wanted to leave their present circumstances and get far enough away that the distance would prohibit easy contact with relatives. The drive to Remer had to be over four hours in those days.

An additional shock for me was the discovery that the Juergens family was not Catholic, leading me to believe that Mom and Paul were not married in a Catholic church. I quickly dug out an old cookbook Mom had saved from her days in Remer, entitled *"The Reliable" Cook Book*..... (title as it appears on the cover, including the quote marks and long ellipsis), published by the Ladies Guild of the Mason Memorial Congregational Church, in Remer, Minnesota. I reached out to all five churches in Remer via email and letter, but I received responses from only two—the Catholic church and Bethany Lutheran Church—neither of which had any records from before 1940. However, a friend of ours found an article in the *Jordan Independent*, dated August 26, 1937, that describes the Schoenecker-Juergens nuptials of August 15, 1937, as taking place at Bethany Lutheran Church. (The date in the article differs by one day from the note on the second marriage listing on the New Market church's record.)

After reading the newspaper article, I was astounded to discover Mom's first marriage had taken place in a Lutheran church, not a Catholic one. I immediately thought back to the day I told my folks that Gordy and I were not going to be married in a Catholic church, and I began to smile at the irony of Mom's apparent hypocrisy. But I also wondered if Dad had known at the time, and I understood how careful she had to be to not shake up her relationship with him. As I recalled her bemoaning, "You were going to have such a beautiful wedding," I wondered if she had been picturing a big wedding in a Catholic church—the kind I had assumed she once had but now know she never experienced.

Grandpa's family had all been relocated by the time Mom married Paul, in August 1937, and Grandpa moved in with Laura and George the following spring, when he was working for the City of Jordan.

It is possible that Grandpa had known Paul Juergens's parents for some time, even before the wedding, and Cyril said he had a friend named *Ray* Juergens, but he did not explain any relationship between Ray and Paul. Uncle Cyril told no stories about Paul courting Mom, and Gordy and I failed to ask during the interview with him. No one volunteered information regarding Mom's mysteries.

After their marriage, Mom and Paul remained in Remer for a short time. Mom said they rented a farm near Remer and that Grandpa stayed with them sometimes. I doubt they farmed long. Mom never mentioned a planting, a harvest, a garden, any birthday or anniversary celebrations, Christmas, or any other kind of socializing or special event as happening during the time she and Paul lived in Remer. But she did mention having to do much of the work on the farm, including milking the cows twice a day.

When Grandpa visited her in Remer, he would occasionally go fishing with a friend at a nearby lake. In 1938, during one such routine fishing outing, Grandpa and his friend died. The subsequent articles in the *New Prague Times* and the *Jordan Independent* said the men were both found dead that Sunday morning in a boat on Spring Lake, near Remer, Minnesota, where they had been fishing. The cause of death was listed as unknown. Mom speculated the boat may have capsized and that both men exhausted themselves righting it and then climbing aboard. She gave me no other details and never talked about the funeral or whether there was an investigation. Joseph Schoenecker (1878–1938) was buried in the church cemetery at Union Hill, the town where Mom first attended grade school.

Shortly after Grandpa's death, Mom and Paul moved back to live with his folks, Fred and Sylvia Juergens. The 1940s census lists the four of them as well as Mom's brother Charles living at the Juergenses' farm, with Charles listed as a farmworker, not a dependent. Mom never gave me any details about the time living with her in-laws, but her sister Laura's oldest son, Roger Stockinger, wrote the following in the memory book at Mom's surprise eighty-fifth birthday party:

I remember . . . [at] the Juergenses' farm, sitting on the picnic table singing 'You Are My Sunshine.' The time the jersey bull was loose in the field by where the chicken house was. He was mean. Got after me. I threw chunks of wood at it till Rita got me out of there. . . . I recall one hot day they were putting hay up in the barn. They took a break and I filled Fred Juergens's beer bottle with water from the stock tank. He was not happy. Lucky for me he didn't know I was the culprit!

Roger's notes to my mother at her party serve to place Mom at her in-laws' farm at a time when Roger was young and mischievous, probably around 1940, when Laura, George, and their two children, Roger and Tommy, ages six and two, respectively, visited the Juergenses' farm.

Tragedy struck the Stockinger family the day before Christmas in 1940. Mom was visiting Laura that day. The two sisters were busy baking cookies and making other holiday preparations. Tommy, three years old, wanted a toy barn for Christmas, and he knew there was a wrapped, barn-shaped gift with his name on it under the tree. Nothing can match the excitement of a child expecting the perfect gift for Christmas, and Tommy was rightly excited.

According to Mom, Tommy's enthusiasm led George to take him along on his milk route, ostensibly to take his young son's mind off the gift and give his wife a break. Once Tommy and his brother, Roger, were in the truck, Tommy wanted to sit by the door. Roger complied with his little brother's wishes, moving to sit in the middle, next to his dad. At one of George's stops, he was backing the truck up in a farmer's yard when the passenger door opened and Tommy fell to the ground. Before George could stop the truck, the front wheel rolled over the child.

Tommy's wake was at his parents' home, which was customary at the time. Mom explained that Laura unwrapped Tommy's gift and displayed the toy barn near his small casket, creating an image that stuck in the minds of all who were present.

Traveling West

Mom and Paul left his parents' farm in the early years of World War II, and in 1941, they set out to find work in the war plants on the West Coast. First, they traveled to Oregon to stay with some of Paul's relatives.

Mom soon got a job in the Portland area at one of the three Kaiser Shipyards facilities located there. The Kaiser Shipyards—seven in total, all on the West Coast—built ships between 1941 and 1945 under the Emergency Shipbuilding Program. The shipbuilders there took pride in their fast pace and high-quality workmanship. Mom assisted one such shipbuilder, and to facilitate his fast pace, she carried his toolbox as she followed closely behind him, handing him tools as needed. To increase his efficiency further, the shipbuilder would simply drop each tool immediately after use, and Mom would pick them up.

Henry J. Kaiser is credited with devising the production techniques that enabled shipyards to build ships quickly for the war effort. He recommended welding seams instead of riveting because it took less strength and was easier to teach to thousands of unskilled laborers. Mom's fast-paced job was highly valued by the government. She always related this story to me with pride, a pride that can only be gained by doing a useful job and feeling needed.

During the fall of 1942, Mom and Paul moved to Los Angeles, where Mom got a job in a big department store as a gift wrapper during the holidays. She enjoyed her job and her stay in Los Angeles, she said, but when they'd initially searched for housing, some landlords were reluctant to rent to them because of their German surname (Mom had taken Paul's: Juergens). Obviously, they succeeded in renting a place to live, and Mom got a job despite her German name, but I think this part of the story is a reminder to all of us of the tense atmosphere during World War II. She didn't elaborate.

Mom also never mentioned that her younger brother Cyril visited her while she was living in LA. Cyril made a passing comment about the visit during my 2006 interview with him, also explaining, in great detail, his army desert maneuvers from when he was stationed somewhere in California. I was pleased to learn that Cyril also took the time to visit Mom and Paul, but now I wish I had asked him more questions about that visit.

Mom and Paul left California late in December of 1942 and came home by way of the Grand Canyon, where Paul took her picture at Yavapai Point on January 1, 1943. Even though she is not smiling in the photograph, Mom looks like a pretty young woman with a good future ahead of her. Out of the many photos she must have thrown away—either to block painful memories or to avoid explaining them to me or her second husband—this was one of the photos she kept, and she always showed it to me proudly. Was this a happy moment for her? I think she tried to remember it as one.

During my time living at home with Mom, she would characterize her years traveling west with Paul as a fun adventure. But she later revealed to me that it was more of a traveling nightmare. And only during her last few years before dying did she begin to tell a deeper, more tragic story.

It seems that Mom worked during those years, but Paul did not. He acquired a male traveling companion, and the two men spent a lot of time together. Mom said Paul was constantly verbally abusing her and that he would drive fast to scare her, even threatening to drive the car over a cliff. He once drove fast through a field of tall corn, where they couldn't see where they were going. She had begged him to slow down, but he seemed to enjoy terrorizing her. Finally, she admitted to us that he would hit her often, breaking her nose at least once, but she did not say where they were living at the time. If he did break her nose more than once, she didn't know because she never went to a doctor to check. When she confessed these things to Gordy and me, she seemed remorseful, ashamed that it had ever happened, as if it were her fault for failing as a wife. She seemed to think she had to keep all the terror to herself.

Many of those who didn't know the details of Mom's past assumed I was Paul's daughter. She let people think it sometimes just so she didn't have to explain. I feel sad when I consider all the secrets Mom thought she had to keep to herself. Was she keeping them from me? From her second husband? From her relatives? Or was she just trying to block them from her memory? Probably all of the above.

Return to Minnesota

When they returned to Minnesota a few months later, Mom abruptly left Paul and moved to Jordan, Minnesota, where she stayed with her sister Laura and her husband, George. The priest at Jordan insisted Mom should go back to her husband, even though she was terribly afraid of him by that time. The priest was adamant that even a battered woman has an obligation to stay with her husband if she wants to remain in the Catholic Church. It seems that according to the Catholic Church, "love, honor, and obey" were vows that only women had to follow. Nothing a man did, even violence, freed the woman from her vows; whereas the man was allowed to dishonor her and behave in ways that proved he had abandoned his vows.

Mom's siblings mostly supported her leaving Paul, but they also emphasized her duty to her marriage and her Catholic faith. Years later, when Mom's oldest brother, Ed, divorced his wife and then married a divorced woman, his actions may have cast Mom's divorce in a better light, at least in the eyes of her siblings; such a light shines less harshly on men than it does on women. Bitterness between Mom and those who judged her harshly for her actions lingered for years and never totally diminished, even into the decade before Mom died.

Now, after recently discovering that her first marriage did not take place in a Catholic church, I realize the rift between Mom and her relatives took on additional dimensions. I had thought her leaving Paul was the main issue, but perhaps Mom's abandoning her faith, when she married outside the church, was the greater disappointment for them—and the greater shame for Mom.

Freedom

As a young woman having left a husband she feared, Mom may not have felt free to express to anyone the true joy she felt, but she must have felt a newfound freedom and independence. Soon after she returned to Jordan in 1943, her brother Ed and his wife, Betty, reached out to her from Buffalo, New York, where Ed worked for a battery manufacturer. Ed said all the factories there were looking for workers and that the pay was good, and Mom's experience working in the Oregon shipyards made her a viable candidate.

Mom moved to Buffalo, found a rooming house, and got a job at the Buffalo Arms Corporation, which made machine guns, among other things. She and several other women were tasked with inspecting the covers for the newly assembled machine guns, which led to her claim of being a "cover girl," the actual title of the job. Mom loved to tell this story, and it was one of many happy references to the period of time she worked at Buffalo Arms. She was young, she was free, and, for the first time in her twenty-nine years, she was independent and making good money. Also, after nearly a decade spent with a husband who showed her no love, she now had the support and friendship of family members around her.

Soon her younger brother Charles and his wife, Sally, moved to Buffalo and secured jobs there too. Charles had lived with Mom and her husband for a while after the family broke up, so they had always been close. And in a short time, Sally and Mom became good friends.

When Cyril and his girlfriend, Peggy, came to visit Mom, her brothers, and their wives in Buffalo in the summer of 1944, they took a short trip to Niagara Falls. Mom cherished the photo of Chuck, Cyril, Peggy, and her dressed in their waterproof outfits, which were required apparel to visit Cave of the Winds. Mom had only good things to say about her experiences in Buffalo, but it only lasted as long as the war. Everyone celebrated the end of the war, and no one begrudged that returning veterans would impact employment opportunities, especially for women.

Mom's divorce was finalized before she moved back to Minneapolis—a fact that must have given her a spike of joy. With some money saved and a background with solid work experiences, she must have felt independent and confident as she sought employment as domestic help. Soon she got a housekeeping position, working for Bernard and Helen Baskin, in Minneapolis. The Jewish family lived in a large, comfortable home and was well off enough to afford a live-in housekeeper.

Mom loved the job and the family. She described them as kind, thoughtful, and forgiving. *Kind* and *thoughtful* because they treated her like one of the family, and *forgiving* because they didn't mind her taking a while to raise her cooking skills up to their expectations. Not that Mom couldn't cook; she could, having gained experience cooking for her brothers, father, and husband, each of whom had seemed satisfied with her skills. The way she explained it, she'd been taught how to cook like all women who descended from German farmers; the basic meat and potatoes she cooked were always well done, but she knew nothing about lamb, veal, or fancy vegetables.

Her employers, of a wealthier class of people, may not have been keen on the way Mom cooked, but they gave her time to adapt. For example, one day, the lady of the house brought some asparagus back from the store and told Mom to fix it for dinner—which was their evening meal. Well, Mom had never seen or cooked asparagus before, but she figured she would treat it like other vegetables. She cut off and discarded the top part, washed the remaining stems, and cooked them in water. When Mom brought the serving plate to the table, the family was pretty disappointed to see that their special vegetable was missing its delectable top. Mom said everyone had a good laugh about it then and many times afterward.

With a good job and newly single, Mom was ready to kick up her heels and enjoy her freedom, which included some shopping. In photos with relatives taken in December 1945 and January 1946, she's proudly wearing a mink coat she'd bought for herself. She also brought gifts for some of her nieces and nephews that year.

Mom enjoyed spending time with Laura and her family whenever they would pick her up and bring her to their home in Minneapolis. Roger, Laura's oldest son, wrote in Mom's memory book at her surprise eighty-fifth birthday party: "I remember sitting in the back seat with Rita singing songs on the way back to [the Baskins'], where she worked. I think 'Across the Alley from the Alamo' was one we sang. Her fur coat, boy was she proud." Because the song was a 1947 hit for the Mills Brothers, reaching number two on the national jukebox charts, we can infer Mom worked for the Baskin family for several years, including 1947.

In the summer of 1946, it appears Mom was dating Ray, a man from Jordan, whom she'd known before the war. Her photo album displayed pictures of Ray in uniform, from 1942, and scenes from a 1946 outing to Bemidji, Minnesota, for which she was joined by Ray, Ann (his sister), and Ann's husband. In one of the Bemidji photos, Mom is wearing a bathing suit, and the scene clearly looks like everyone is having a good time. Mom kept these photos all her life, treasuring them beyond any concern over erasing a record of her past.

My guess is she was truly interested in Ray, but if he was from a strict Catholic family, he would not have married a divorced woman, and an annulment through the church would take time and money. Many strict Catholic families did not approve of annulment anyway. Although Mom never explained it in detail, her fondness for the photos and her appearance in the outing indicate she had not wanted to break with Ray at the time. Maybe he broke it off with her because she was divorced. She never did share the reason for their breakup, but she proudly showed me the photos several times.

Jilted

Neither Mom nor any of her siblings told stories about where or how she came to meet Charles Guillaume, the man who would become my biological father. It remains a mystery to me, their daughter, even to this day.

It's not at all a surprise she met someone. She was young and attractive and liked to talk to people and have fun. Did she meet him at a private social function? A dance? A wedding? A nightclub? Through friends? Not one of her relatives could tell me, or maybe they just knew that talking about it was taboo. But if they were serious about each other, why not get married? One likely possibility is that Charles wanted to be able to break off the relationship easily.

Clearly, Mom was in love and enjoying being treated like she was special, especially after the horrible experience with her first husband and a possible recent breakup with Ray. She was thirty-three when she became pregnant with me. Years later, she told me he had promised to care for her and her child. Then, suddenly, he was gone. Mom remained bitter about it for the rest of her life.

Although Mom was silent or vague about most of her past, I remember her repeating certain phrases to me about my father. She'd lament that he "ran out on her" or "ran out on us." I remember her telling me more than once, "He always said he'd marry me, but then I got pregnant with you, so he left." For me, this explanation was hurtful because it put the blame on me, but I can understand it may have been a true expression of how she initially felt at the time. "He promised to marry me and care for us" is another statement she repeated often, revealing that he made promises before *and* after she became pregnant.

Mom repeated those claims to me many times when I was a child, probably to justify her behavior to herself and to me. She had felt happy with Charles, believing he was committed because she wanted it, not necessarily because it was logical to believe it; love seldom leaves room for logic, and economic demands are used to justify many decisions. Also, I wonder whether she suspected she was infertile. I remember her telling me, after my first period, that there were times in her life when she would not have a period for several months, with only four or five periods a year, which could help explain why she didn't become pregnant until she was thirty-three.

As scary as parenthood can be, Charles did not leave immediately after Mom became pregnant. He stayed on and continued to make promises, saying they would marry. I do not know when exactly he left Minnesota, but soon after he did, Mom—pregnant and single—left the job with the Baskin family and had to move in with her sister Laura and her husband. Laura was kind, but she probably let Mom know of her disapproval. Why wouldn't she? Mom had once again broken the rules of Laura's faith as well as her own. I can only imagine how difficult it must have been for Mom to accept being taken in by Laura, when, months earlier, she had brought gifts for Laura's children. If Laura offered Mom refuge, it was indeed an act of sisterly kindness.

My Birth and Early Life with Mom

My bastard identity has stayed with me like a birthmark, but I was unaware of it until the episode with the chanting boys, as told in part 1, chapter 1. Before that, I was privileged to be sheltered and surrounded by people who treated me special, despite the fact that my mom had no money and no husband.

My mother gave birth to me on April 30, 1948, at Minneapolis City Hospital, which became Hennepin County General Hospital in 1964 and Hennepin County Medical Center in 1974. When I was an adult, Mom told me the hospital was known to care for the poor and penniless.

As a thirty-three-year-old single mother, Mom may not have been the ideal candidate for employment, yet she had uncanny luck in landing the right job at the right time. During the first three and a half years of our lives together, she worked as a live-in housekeeper and nanny in Minneapolis for Leon and Elsie Charrier and their two children, Lorraine, about age ten, and Charley, age four. The house was in a well-kept neighborhood a few blocks off Nicollet Avenue in South Minneapolis, an area eventually displaced by Interstate 35 in the 1960s. Although Mom had no money, we lived with the Charriers in their fine, roomy house, giving me the privileged experience of being in the care of my mother all day and having two playmates as well.

Lorraine and Charley were like siblings to me, and their parents were kind, generous, and loving. Charley cared for me as if I were his little sister, playing games with me and helping me learn while his parents were working away from their home. Mom was a special nanny to all of us, and we provided both an outlet for her love and an opportunity for her to feel loved and needed. The job was a perfect fit for the needs of a penniless single mother and a kind family in need of a loving nanny.

Mom and I spent every holiday with the Charriers as if we were one family. Although I was too young to remember many details, Mom later related stories of those happy times to me, and I recall a few special events. I have dozens of photos of me with this family, many during Christmas, including my first Christmas. One shows the three of us children playing together by the tree, and in another, we're playing with their dog.

Our next-door neighbors, the DeShanes, consisted of a father, mother, children, and Mr. DeShane's father, whom everyone in the neighborhood called "Grandpa DeShane." That entire family was friendly to us, and they gave me one of my first books, *The Three Bears Visit Goldilocks*. At the top of the first page, Mom wrote, in pencil, "Nancy, from DeShanes, March 1, 1951." And on the inside of the back cover, she placed stickers spelling out my name.

Grandpa DeShane may have been retired, and he may have been fairly old, but I think he earned the term *Grandpa* because he treated youngsters in the neighborhood as if they were his grandchildren. For example, Charley, Lorraine, and I played in a small sandbox in the yard, but Grandpa DeShane worried about me, the little girl, sitting in the hot sun, so he built a roof over the sandbox to protect me.

During the time we lived there (1948–1951), Grandpa DeShane would often go to the Minneapolis City Dump, where people were allowed to enter and walk around to search for items that were thrown away but still fixable. He would bring back items, repair them, and give them to people. For example, he found a small sled that just needed a couple of new boards. He replaced the boards, painted the sled bright red, and gave it to Mom for me. Because the sled was so short, he thought it would be perfect for Mom's little girl. I loved it, and it was the only sled I ever had.

I enjoyed using that sled throughout my childhood and even into my teens. After I moved away from home, my parents saved the sled. My stepfather later repainted it, and they gave it back to me in 1986. Even now, after all these years, when I decorate for Christmas on the Friday after Thanksgiving, my little red sled is among the first Christmas decorations I place by the tree. The sled, Grandpa DeShane, the book, and all the other happy memories from those years living with the Charriers—I cherish them all.

While we were living with the Charriers, I never realized that Lorraine was considered different by society. She had an intellectual disability. I remember her as a sweet person, and growing up with her for the first three years of my life provided me with an understanding of love beyond what I would have otherwise had. My association with her—and her disability—was part of my privileged early childhood. Mom's nanny job came to an end just as Lorraine was starting to need care and teaching beyond what the Charriers and Mom could provide at home. The family made the inevitable but difficult decision to send her to a group home at the special needs school in Faribault.

Elsie and Mom kept in touch until Mom passed away, and Charley continued to stay in touch with Mom and me until he passed away. I last saw him at Mom's surprise eighty-fifth birthday party, where we shared some memories. When Mom died, in 2009, Charley was too ill to attend the funeral. He called me from the hospital the next day, and we talked for a time, crying and sharing memories of Mom. He passed away shortly after that. His mother, Elsie Charrier Russell Spillman, lived to be one hundred, outliving three husbands and both her children. She passed away in 2013.

Our Small-Town Family

For the first few years of my life, I was extremely lucky to have my mother's guiding hand close to me at all times, but that changed abruptly when the job with the Charriers ended.

I wasn't yet four years old when we moved to New Market, Minnesota, in the fall of 1951. We joined the family of Mom's sister Tillie Schmitz, which included her husband, Ewald, as well as their four children—Ron (17), Jack (14), Gene (10), and Mary Jo, or "Mitz" (8). Mom's older brother Ben Schoenecker lived with them too. The house had three bedrooms upstairs—a small one, where Mom, Mitz, and I slept; a larger one, where Tillie and Uncle Ewald slept; and, at the top of the stairs, a walk-through bedroom, where the three boys and Uncle Ben slept. Typical of most houses in town at the time, the kitchen had cold running water, and the toilet was a standard outhouse, located in the backyard.

Their oldest son, Ron, was in high school and stayed at St. John's University, near St. Cloud. Jack attended the public high school in New Prague and rode the bus to and from school daily. Gene and Mitz walked the couple of blocks to St. Nicholas Catholic School in New Market, where I would not start first grade for another three years (in 1954).

Mom and I lived at the Schmitzes' for less than a year, but during that time, I was treated as one of the family. Our time there was an extension of my privileged childhood, and I was loved and nurtured by everyone in their home. I recall sitting close to Uncle Ewald on the couch as he held his arm around me while we watched programs together on a small black-and-white television. Mitz and I played together like sisters, and Jack patiently read to me. Cousin Jack insisted I call him "*Uncle* Jack" because one of his friends was an uncle, and he wanted to be an uncle too.

Leaving me in Aunt Tillie's loving care during the day, Mom was lucky to get a job nearby, at New Market Produce, which I've already covered. The building was less than a hundred yards from the Schmitzes' house, giving her the convenience of a short walk to work.

One of Mom's coworkers was named Rosie, and they became good friends while having fun working together. There was a lot of good-natured kidding between the two of them and the customers, most of whom were farmers.

Often, women and their daughters would come to the Produce to buy cloth feed sacks, out of which they would make clothing. Living on farms, they needed to purchase feed anyway, so their selections were purely based on the sacks themselves, which sported beautiful colors and designs, purposely appealing to the fashion-minded women who made clothes for their families. Feed-sack dresses were pretty common, especially for school, because the cotton material was both durable and attractive. In those days, girls had to wear dresses to school, and only on cold winter days were they permitted to wear jeans under their dresses. Once the schoolhouse warmed up, usually by midmorning, they had to remove their jeans and rely on long stockings to keep their legs warm.

The front window display at the Produce featured full sacks of feed, allowing passersby to admire the latest patterns—a kind of window shopping never seen at fancy city stores. After making a selection, a woman would come inside with her husband and tell Mom which sacks she wanted, and in this way, Mom got to know many of the farm women as well as the men. Sometimes, Mom had to move the sacks around to access a preferred print, and because she was thin and not especially strong, she found lifting the sacks difficult. Customers would often help her carry the feed sacks to their car or just do it by themselves. Rosie, who had been at the job for a while, could handle the sacks better than Mom, but Mom was many times left trying to lug the sacks on her own.

Events Force Change

Hard tragedies ensued for Aunt Tillie's family. Uncle Ben died in 1952, and Tillie's husband, Ewald, died June 28, 1953. Ron, who had enlisted in the air force after high school, took a leave from the service to come home for his dad's funeral. Uncle Ewald had been a loving father and husband, and he was liked and respected by the townsfolk, who had elected him town constable. He'd had a good job working for the county transportation department, but when he died, Aunt Tillie had to face things alone. In 1954, she sold the house to buy a Jack Sprat Food Store owned by a family named Thomas.

There was room enough in the back of the store for her to live there, and the building was next to the small ground-floor apartment into which Mom and I had moved.

Three of Aunt Tillie's children were at home and could help their mother with the grocery store, but with an established, popular general store and a butcher shop already in town, Tillie's Jack Sprat store struggled. Aunt Tillie's second-oldest son, Jack, graduated from New Prague High School in 1955, and in January of 1956, Tillie sold the store and its inventory. She moved her family to Prior Lake, where she secured a job cooking at the only public school in town, which served grades one through twelve. On the weekends, she cleaned houses in town and worked in the kitchen at The Embassy, an upscale restaurant located on State Highway 65, south of the Minnesota River, in the area called the "River Bottoms." Jack got a job to help out, Gene got a basketball scholarship after his air force service, and Mitz married soon after high school.

Tillie and Mom were especially close, and I am sure Mom felt quite alone after Tillie left town; I felt like I had lost part of my family too. Indeed, Mom and I were alone in town, without any family support. Although Mom had made friends at work and through the church, there was no friend in town who could provide support like her sister Tillie—support she would sorely need in the years to come.

Up to this point in my life, I had never felt any hint of scorn from anyone for being the child of an unwed mother; no one used or referred to the word *bastard*. All that would change when I started at St. Nicholas Catholic School in the fall of 1954.

Lingering Mysteries

As I grew up, neither Mom nor any one of her relatives talked about her first marriage. I have no idea whether she was happy as a newlywed, and I don't know when the relationship started to sour. But when it did, there was no one to whom she could turn for help. I suppose she felt it was up to her to make it all work out. To be fair, Paul Juergens may have become displeased with the marriage, as well, but it was Mom who had to bear the disapproval of relatives for marrying outside of her religion, and she no longer had her parents to turn to for help or guidance.

Decades later, after Mom remarried, I came to understand that she did not welcome questions about her past. But after her second husband passed away, in 1991, I hoped she would reconsider my desire to get some answers.

From 2001 until she passed away, in 2009, Mom lived in a comfortable studio apartment at Mala Strana Assisted Living, in New Prague. Gordy and I visited her every Sunday and sometimes during the week. She liked it there. She could read or watch television, and there were always plenty of other residents with whom she could play cards or visit.

I figured the comfortable, secure setting of Mala Strana was an ideal place to bring up her brother Cyril's 2006 interview and the family breakup. I thought it might elicit a response from her. Maybe she would volunteer something about her dating, her marriage, or anything at all, really. Instead, she showed no interest in watching the taped interview with Cyril, and whenever I brought it up, she would nervously move on to something else or simply say, "I don't want to talk about it," in a way that indicated the conversation was over.

I am not proclaiming my mother was a totally innocent victim of circumstances, but I can only wonder what terrible memories she had of those times. Did she blame others for pushing her into marriage, or did she herself feel guilty for wanting the marriage to happen? In any case, the wounds were deep, and it seems that not talking about it was her only way to cope. She took her secrets from that critical time of her life to the grave.

Charles Guillaume's mother, my paternal grandmother, sent a baby gift, which was listed in a baby book that Mom had at one time. The book contained a list of other gift givers, pictures of me, my footprint, and a lock of my hair. I remember seeing my baby book when I was a child, but I was too young at the time to remember details. Besides, I expected the book to always be available to me and never disappear. Although I do not remember exactly when the book vanished, I recall that a few years before my stepfather, Ralph Simon, died, Mom phrased a question to me in a manner fraught with uncertainty: "You took your baby book with you when you got married, didn't you?" I told her I hadn't. She said nothing more. At the time, I surmised she had searched for it in vain. I wondered if Mom had destroyed the book herself and only asked me about it as a way to avoid explaining its disappearance.

If she did destroy my baby book in a moment of remorse or fear, it would not have been her first attempt at covering up records of her past. For example, I had two beloved children's books—one Mom had given to me on Christmas Day in 1949 and the Goldilocks one the DeShanes had given to me in 1951—that were inexplicably defaced, which was especially upsetting because I took good care of them. Mom had written my name inside the cover of each, my first and middle names on the top line and my last name below that. I don't know how old I was when I discovered that something had changed, but I was shocked to see that, in both books, *Nancy Ann* was still clearly printed on the page, but below it, the entire area had been erased with such force that the surface of the page was peeled and torn, totally eradicating any trace of my last name.

I always cherished those books, but as I grew older, I seldom looked at them. I still can't recall the last name written in those books. Was it *Guillaume?* Did Mom erase the name to hide something about her past from me or her second husband, Ralph? Did seeing the name cause her distress? When she asked me about the missing baby book, I wondered whether she suspected Ralph of destroying it. But in the end, I am totally unsure which one of them—presuming it was one or the other—destroyed the book or whether it was merely misplaced. Mom and Dad each may have had their reasons to want the book gone. I knew Dad and Mom cared for each other and had a pleasant life together, but I also knew Mom's past haunted both of them.

On Father's Day, Dad always took Mom, Gordy, and me to the church dinner in New Market, where the young fathers cooked chicken on huge outdoor grills. Dad seemed proud and happy in his role as a father as the four of us sat on benches behind the church while his friends came over to visit. Yet something about the past gnawed on him. The Saturday before one Father's Day, we had my folks and Gordy's folks over for noon dinner, and we gave each father a blue cap embroidered with the words "#1 Dad." Both fathers donned their caps immediately and wore them the whole day. However, weeks later, when Dad was wearing his cap, Gordy and I noticed he had picked apart the threads on the "#1" so the cap just read "Dad." I know he didn't do this to hurt Mom or me, though it may have briefly had that effect. I think it was his way to humbly express that he was not the total father he wished to be, even though we tried to tell him he was.

As he aged, Dad also became more obsessed with having "everything right with the Catholic Church," as he stated it to Mom. His anxiety about his state of grace increased to a point where it sometimes led him to lose control of his reason and behave strangely. For example, one weeknight in the late 1980s, Dad had an anxiety attack, prompting Mom to call Gordy and me at one in the morning, insisting we come over immediately. Gordy and I lived only five miles away at the time, and when we arrived at their house, within half an hour, Dad was fidgeting in his chair and mumbling something about a shovel and going to hell.

Mom explained that back in the 1930s, Dad had been working on some farmland that bordered the railroad tracks. Next to the tracks, he found a shovel that the railroad workers must have accidentally left behind. Dad took the shovel home with him. Decades later, approaching the end of his life, he was worried that God would not forgive him for stealing the shovel.

I asked Dad whether he confessed to the priest about it. He said he had and that the priest had given him absolution. I told him that if he confessed and the priest absolved him, then God had forgiven him too. But Dad would not accept that answer. He was still afraid God had not forgiven him. Mom explained that weeks earlier, in an attempt to calm Dad, she had tried calling the railroad to report the incident about the shovel, but the original railroad company didn't exist anymore. She persisted and called the only existing railroad company in the area to find someone that Dad could pay for the shovel. Fortunately, she found an understanding employee, who said sending a check to the railroad company would be too complicated for their present accounting system. He suggested Dad write a check to any charity for the amount of the shovel and said that the railroad company would consider that full payment for the shovel. Mom sent a check to a charity the next day, but Dad continued panicking about the shovel.

That night, as we continued trying to convince Dad that full repayment had been made, Mom asked us to help convince Dad to take the medication the doctor had prescribed for these panic attacks. I wanted to ask Mom, "Why the heck didn't you start by telling us he had medication that he was not taking?" But, of course, I said nothing. Gordy and I had no idea Dad was under a doctor's care for panic attacks. We finally got Dad to calm down a little, and he began to agree that the shovel situation was cleared up. After a few more minutes, we convinced him to take his medication, and the medication took effect a short time later. After we got him to bed and ensured that Mom was fine, Gordy and I drove home.

On the way home, Gordy and I discussed Dad's situation. Neither of us could say for sure whether Dad's fears were extreme and unusual for a man of faith, but we were surprised that his faith seemed to fail to provide him comfort. Dad was an honest and kind man, but his record of panic attacks and his concern for his state of grace may help explain a few other irrational acts.

Once I asked Mom what my biological father had done for a living, and she said he'd been a clerk at J.C. Penney, which may explain Mom's access to discounts on jewelry and clothes. It may also explain why he was in Minneapolis, even though he was from the Chicago area, a huge retail center. Did his family have money? Why didn't he take her with him when he left Minnesota? Did he think she was not good enough for his family? Obviously, it wouldn't have been the first time that one partner's love for the other died, if that was the case, or maybe he was ashamed to have impregnated a woman before marrying her. He wouldn't have been the first guy to get too righteous for his lover after the deed was done.

All of this is speculation, of course, but there is one thing I recently discovered that suggests there was more to the story than his simply leaving. Shortly after Mom's death, in 2009, I found an old life insurance policy, which she had sold for cash many years earlier. She had taken it out in November of 1948, seven months *after* I was born, when we were living with her sister Laura, who was the beneficiary of the policy. The name on the policy was "Rita K. Guillaume," and yet she and my father had never married! Did she use the name for convenience? Or was it really her name? Wouldn't using a false name on an insurance policy have made it difficult—maybe impossible—for any benefactor to collect on it? Was she still receiving some promise of commitment from my father nearly seven months after my birth? Or was she merely fantasizing about a future with him? There is no way for me to discover the answers, but I always come back to this fact: there is nothing I needed to know about my biological father that my mom couldn't have told me if she had wanted to. Yet she chose to say nothing or lie to me, which were both worse.

Shortly after graduating from high school, I remember asking her directly, "Was your first husband, Juergens, my father?" (We referred to him by his last name the few times we talked about him.) I was eighteen at the time, and because of other discussions we'd had about my real father, I thought my question was more or less rhetorical. I expected her answer would be *No, Juergens was not your father.* I had hoped that my query might spark a conversation leading to some facts about my real father and maybe some facts about Juergens.

I was shocked when Mom snapped back a quick "Yes!" She said no more and walked away. I knew her answer was not true, and it left me confused. Was it just too difficult for her to state the truth directly, even though our previous discussions had revealed she had left Juergens nearly four years before I was born? I remained hopeful that she might voluntarily provide the answers to all my questions one day, but it never happened.

I have an early memory—from when Mom and I would spend evenings together in our small apartment—of Mom talking about my father. Perhaps it was during the time when I believed her story about his dying in a car accident, a time when she could feel a bit freer to talk about him. Mom had always told me her ethnicity was purely German, and when I asked her about my father's ethnicity, she didn't hesitate. "French and Irish," she answered. This made sense to me because Mom's complexion was darker than mine and her eyes were dark brown. My eyes are hazel, with a hint of green. I knew I didn't get my fair skin and hazel eyes from Mom's side of the family.

Recently, I submitted a saliva sample to 23andMe, a company that traces ancestry using DNA. Results confirmed German, French, and Irish DNA in the percentages I expected, and the results also listed several relatives of mine with the last name *Guillaume*, which I had not entered on any of the forms when registering with 23andMe.

CONCLUSION

My mother's love was dear to me during her lifetime, and her memory will remain dear to me as long as I live. I came to understand that by locking her memories inside, she empowered them to control her, making her fearful and causing her to behave irrationally, in ways that were sometimes hurtful to Dad and me. Although writing this memoir has helped me understand her refusal to discuss her past with me, it has also convinced me to not follow her path but, instead, free myself of the burden of holding memories inside me, where they can fester.

Letting the memories go is not an attempt at any kind of revenge but more a matter of purging myself of the memories and any residual anger I may have had toward people or places. However, I hope my stories may also serve to enlighten those who follow the rules of their religion that could lead them to shaming and scorning others, especially young children. My decision to leave the Catholic Church was mine and mine alone, but I hope people from every religion everywhere can grow to see that unkind deeds serve to lead people away from religion, not motivate them to emulate those who scorned them.

DEFINITIONS

Some pictures may be worth a thousand words, but there are some words for which there are no pictures. The use of the term *bastard* has changed dramatically since the 1800s—but especially so over the past fifty years. The dilemma of the bastard was tied to the subjugation of women; scorn for a woman was expressed in the name *bitch*, and scorn for her offspring—a "son of a bitch"—was expressed in the name *bastard*. That there was no name of scorn assigned to the man involved reflected that men controlled the power.

Women who were "safely" married, without a bastard child, were often ready to condemn another woman as a "bitch" because it reinforced their status of being married, which was a woman's only path to status in many societies. Also, although a fatherless female was technically a bastard, there was no curse word for the daughter of a bitch, probably because it was the male, not the female, who inherited an estate, and only the bastard son, not the daughter, needed to be discredited to ensure the legitimate son would inherit the estate.

When I was a child, I looked up the word *bastard* in my copy of *Thorndike-Barnhart Dictionary*. The first two meanings emphasized a child born of unmarried parents, and the second and third meanings emphasized inferiority:

> **bastard**, 1. child whose parents are not married to each other; illegitimate child. 2. born of parents who are not married to each other. 3. anything inferior or not genuine. 4. inferior; not genuine. 1,3 *n.*, 2,4 *adj.*

More-current dictionaries, however, emphasize the general negative denotation of the word. The legal definition of *bastard* that was once used to disinherit children is now listed as "archaic or derogatory":

1 *informal* an unpleasant or despicable person: *he lied to me, the bastard!*

• *[with adjective] British informal* a person of a specified kind: *he was a lucky bastard.*

• *British informal* a difficult or awkward undertaking, situation, or device: *it's been a bastard of a week.*

2 *archaic or derogatory* a person born of parents not married to each other.

(*New Oxford American Dictionary*, "bastard," accessed March 27, 2021, via the Dictionary app on macOS.)

The Old Testament is clear on its condemnation of a bastard. Although there is no Hebrew word that translates exactly to the English word *bastard,* many versions use the Hebrew term *mamzer,* which has a more precise meaning in the Torah, a meaning that focuses on the behavior of married people.

Although the language used varies between versions of the Bible, a direct condemnation of bastards can be found in the King James Version from the 1950s (Cleveland: The World Publishing Company, n.d.):

A bastard shall not enter into the congregation of the Lord; even to his tenth generation shall he not enter into the congregation of the Lord. (Deuteronomy 23:2)

The Old Testament is full of condemnations that zealots love to quote, even as they manage to ignore the ones that apply to themselves. The Bible gives no hope for bastards. I always wondered whether the nuns' treatment of me was a reflection of the Bible's proclamation.

Christmas at the
Charrier house
where Mom worked
as a Nanny.
Circa 1950.

Cousin Jack Schmitz
holding me on a
snow bank by the
Schmitz house
where Mom and
I lived for a while
at New Market,
Minnesota.
Winter 1951-52.

My First Communion dress. April, 1956.

Inside the covers of my *Three Bears Visit Goldilocks* book
(March 1, 1951) and my *Little Black Sambo* book (December 25, 1949)
showing where my last name was obliterated.

Mom at
Yavapai Point,
Grand Canyon
National Park,
Arizona.
January 1,
1943.

L-R - Charles Schoenecker, Cyril
Schoenecker, Peg Simones, Rita
Schoenecker at Cave of the Winds,
Niagara Falls, New York. 1944.

Mom's Christian Mother Society badge.

My handmade dress and veil on my wedding day, Saturday, October 31, 1970.

Rex puppy and me at our farm, Donnelly, Minnesota. November 11, 1973.

Rex dog and me by a pile of rocks Gordy and I picked from about twenty-five acres of the eighty-five tillable acres on our farm at Donnelly, Minnesota. We piled rocks from the other fields elsewhere. There were so many rocks on the fields that we had to pick them before Gordy could plow that fall. November 10, 1974.

Gordy and I in our grain
field at our farm, Donnelly,
Minnesota. August 6, 1976.

Gordy and I with Rex dog at
our farm, Donnelly, Minnesota.
August 7, 1977.

Me fanning wheat at our
farm, Donnelly, Minnesota.
April 15, 1978.

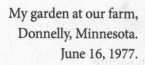

My garden at our farm,
Donnelly, Minnesota.
June 16, 1977.

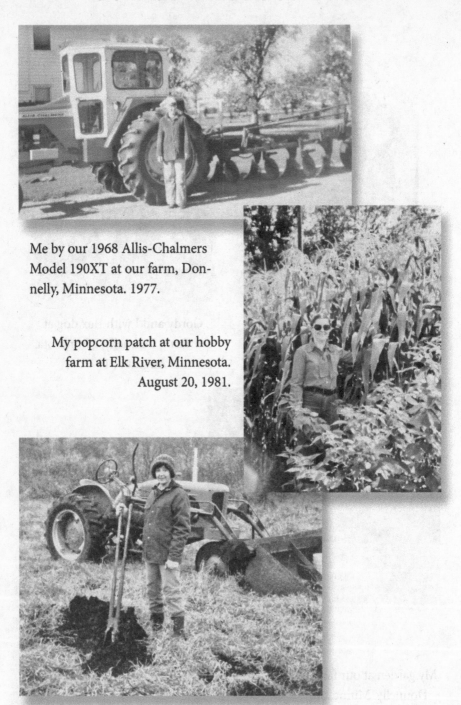

Me by our 1968 Allis-Chalmers Model 190XT at our farm, Donnelly, Minnesota. 1977.

My popcorn patch at our hobby farm at Elk River, Minnesota. August 20, 1981.

Digging a post hole as we fenced around the slough pasture at our hobby farm at Elk River, Minnesota. October 1983.

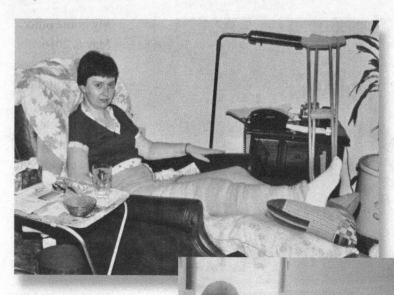

Recovering from
cancer surgery in our
apartment, Elk River,
Minnesota.
July 28, 1986.

My cubicle at work.
July 1989.

My cubicle at
work. 2008.

My home office. May 6, 2016.

In this and the previous two photos, note the many changes in office equipment that "old people" have readily accepted and quickly learned to use.

At the 2019 Minnesota State Fair, Gordy and I pointing to a photo of Johnny Cash on the exterior wall of the Grandstand. The day marked the 50th Anniversary of our first date when we saw Johnny Cash at the Minnesota State Fair Grandstand Show in 1969. Gordy is dressed in bib overalls because earlier in the day he performed his book, *If I Were a Farmer: Nancy's Adventure,* at the Twin Cities Public Television stage at the Minnesota State Fair.

BASTARD MOMENTS: A WOMAN'S TREK THROUGH A MAN'S WORLD

Part 2

INTRODUCTION

In part 1, I labeled as "bastard moments" those times when a nun, priest, or other church member reminded me—sometimes repeatedly—of my bastard status, making me feel ashamed and powerless. Ironically, this treatment also trained me how to deal with the bastard moments that life continued to offer.

In part 2, I expand the meaning of a *bastard moment* to include discriminatory treatment of women by supervisors and coworkers in the workplace, by medical doctors and clinics, and even by farmers in their attitudes toward work exchange. Experiences include sexual harassment, ageism, religious persecution, and the right to clean air. It's a glimpse into the bastard moments inflicted on me as well as other employees in the working world, which often denied women dignity, power, credit, wages, and respect, without any recourse. Some of these bastard moments robbed me of health, while others robbed my coworkers and me of thousands of dollars of our retirement funds.

However, a few bastard moments comprised humorous or tragic awakening to the realities of life. Many of you may have experienced similar moments. Either way, I hope you can laugh as you enjoy reading these stories of my bastard moments and those who perpetrated them. As in part 1, most names are aliases.

CHAPTER 9

A NEW BEGINNING

The New Job

Before our wedding, Gordy prepared a one-bedroom apartment for us on the west edge of the largest lake in Minneapolis, Bde Maka Ska, which was called "Lake Calhoun" at the time. (How did a lake in Minnesota get named after US Secretary of War John C. Calhoun, who was from South Carolina, a defender of slavery, and a perpetrator of white supremacy?)

After the wedding, we had no time for a honeymoon or even a full day off. Gordy was a sophomore at the University of Minnesota, and he worked about twenty-five hours a week at Honeywell as a draftsman. The Sunday evening following our Saturday wedding, he dutifully began practicing a speech he would deliver at his Monday-morning class. At half past five on Monday morning, he left for school, leaving earlier than usual to get a good parking place and a few hours of study at the library before class began. During that day, I contemplated my job-search strategy.

Although I was confident my experience, typing skills, and great reference from Nutting Truck & Caster Company would help me get a good job, I was nervous too. I was eager to play an important, supportive role and earn money toward moving into a home three years later, when Gordy would get his first teaching job. As luck would have it, the first place I applied was less than a mile from our apartment, and they were hiring staff to fill vacancies in a new department. The interview went well and they hired me. Two weeks after our wedding, I started work in a new department at the headquarters of Fingerhut Corporation, a family-owned company located on West Lake Street, not far from our apartment on West 32nd Street, in Minneapolis.

Working in an office in Minneapolis was a bit different from working in an office in Faribault. For example, women were not limited to wearing dresses or skirts and could wear dress slacks—much more progressive. This was the "big city," and as I expected, there was much more diversity among the employees working in the office. The difference that impressed me the most, though, was the large number of women in nonclerical positions—in sales, advertising, and marketing. Also, women filled many of the supervisory positions in all departments of the office, which was never the case when I worked in Faribault. Seeing women in nearly all available jobs was inspirational to me, and I soon found out that women were treated with respect too. Not until years later would I discover that these progressive characteristics were more a reflection of the exceptional management at Fingerhut than they were indicative of workplaces in the big city as a whole.

During my time with Fingerhut, in the early 1970s, the Fingerhut family still owned and managed the company. The employees were all loyal to the company and seemed to know everyone in upper management, including the owners. After working there a short time, I discovered that Manny Fingerhut, the owner, would walk around the office during his lunch break. If you were at your desk, he would say hello or ask how things were going, and he not only listened to what his employees had to say but also took action to rectify problems.

For example, I worked in a new department created a few months before I was hired, and because the office was crowded at that time, our department was set up in a temporary area in the warehouse end of the building. The heating did not adequately warm our work area, and it would get extremely cold inside when the big overhead warehouse doors were opened to load or unload large trucks. Although our boss had asked the maintenance crew to do something to provide better heat for our area, they told him there was nothing they could do. Our boss told us just to wear our winter coats at our desks when we got cold.

One day, one of the owners happened to walk through our area when we were wearing our winter coats. He realized how cold it was and asked us why we didn't have heat. The point here is that he didn't ask our boss. He asked us, the employees, who were working in the cold. We told him that our boss had been told by maintenance that there was nothing that could be done. The owner said something like "We'll see about that," then left. Within an hour, the maintenance department delivered brand-new space heaters for each of our desks and made sure there were adequate electrical outlets to run the heaters. Within a day or two, heavy plastic strips were hung from the ceiling to surround our work area and prevent the cold air from coming in from the open warehouse area. No longer were we freezing at our desks. This treatment made me feel like a valuable employee.

The following summer, our department was relocated within the building, which gave me an opportunity to meet more people in other departments. Most of us brought our lunch, but we had one special opportunity for lunch that most offices did not have. Directly across Fingerhut's narrow parking lot was Porky's Drive-In. Many times, one of my coworkers would say they were going to Porky's and ask if anyone wanted anything—a malt, a shake, fries, and the like. The person going to Porky's then phoned in the order for pickup and brought the whole huge order back to the office. Once in a while, I would join someone walking over to Porky's for lunch. It was a great drive-in. Inside, customers sat in their booths and used the installed phone setup to place their orders—no waiting in line.

During those days at Fingerhut, promotions were frequent and based entirely on ability and job performance, without regard for race, gender, or religion. If any employee openly displayed any discrimination, there were swift consequences. For example, one woman seemed to dislike Jews, and although she didn't say anything outright, the way she intentionally phrased comments made her feelings known to many who spoke with her. A coworker told me that the woman had put a swastika on the wall of her cubicle, claiming it was a piece of artwork. Shortly after hearing about this "artwork," we discovered the employee no longer worked there. Apparently, during one of Manny Fingerhut's lunchtime walks, he went past her cubicle. Seeing the "artwork," he stopped, wrote down her name as displayed on her cubicle, and quickly walked back to his office. When the employee came back from lunch, the head of personnel was waiting for her. She was handed a dismissal sheet and a check for her last wages, told to take her personal items, and escorted out the door. There was *zero* tolerance for discrimination at Fingerhut, and I learned the company would support those who stood up for themselves when confronted with intolerance and discrimination.

Fingerhut mostly filled positions by promoting from within, which gave employees a sense of worth and a reason to be loyal, but the company occasionally hired from outside. One such hire was my new department head. He was fresh out of college, thought he knew everything, met only with the supervisors, and never sat down to learn the department procedures from the staff who actually did the work. We had a hunch this new boss thought clericals deserved no respect, but because of our positive history with Fingerhut's management, we all thought it best to give the new guy a chance.

His first priority seemed to be to change everything. Any fool knows that procedures need to be constantly improved for any company to stay competitive, but before a change is made, the present situation needs to be totally understood. Well, this new college guy just jumped in with both feet. For example, I worked as a typist in the department that designed all the mailings. These mailings tested which inserts were the most effective. A test sample for each item would include versions using different photos or offering different free gifts and so on, and a mailing might contain three to eight different varieties of inserts. There were several designers, but the clericals were not assigned to certain designers. A designer would mark up their mailings in a folder and place it into the general in-basket for the typists. Once the mailings were typed up, the folder was placed into the out-basket. The designer would then check the out-basket for their finished folders. It sounds like a simple and effective process, right? Well, this was a busy time, and we were typing these orders as fast as we could.

One day, we were told the process had changed: if the folder in the in-basket was green, we were to type those first because they were priorities. Per our instructions, we typed up the orders in the green folder first and placed them in the out-basket. At the end of the day, the hired-from-outside-the-company manager came out of his office and spotted some green folders in the out-basket with other folders, and he started yelling at all of us typists, insisting we'd ignored his orders. Apparently, he wanted the green folders to be hand delivered back to the designers as soon as they were typed up. He accused us of ruining his new procedure and undermining his authority. Unfortunately, he wouldn't stop yelling long enough for us to explain that we weren't told about that part of the new procedure. Our immediate supervisor came out of his office and tried to calm the guy down. Even our supervisor was not fully aware of the entire new procedure. After yelling and turning red, the new manager finally stomped off to his office, with our supervisor following him. The next day, our supervisor completely explained the new procedure to us.

The new manager—who, again, had been hired from outside the company—felt himself too important to talk to a lowly typist, an attitude that, to me, resembled treating all of us like bastards. This man's ideas were often good, but his follow-through with the workers was terrible, as shown with his next idea, which was to change the forms we used to type up the mailings. The forms were legal-size, portrait format, and the width allowed space to list only three changes per page, as one-third of each page was devoted to the header, which contained the full mailing information. If there were more than three changes on a mailing, another full page had to be typed up, including the full header information, which meant a lot of typing. (There was no cut-and-paste option.)

One morning, the new manager called us into his office for a meeting— not a planning meeting but one to explain new changes. He handed new, carbonless, three-page forms to us, explaining we were to use the new forms going forward. They were legal-size, *landscape*-format forms that had room to type at least eight different changes for the mailing, which would, in theory, reduce our workload. He told us to go back to our desks and resume working, but we typists all hesitated. We knew the forms were a good idea, but there was a problem our manager had not considered.

Reluctant to say anything that would get us yelled at, we looked at each other briefly. Finally, I quietly spoke up. Trying not to sound mean, I started to explain the issue. But before I could finish my sentence, the manager became angry at me and yelled, "These are the new forms whether you like them or not!"

My immediate supervisor, who communicated well with his workers, asked, "Nancy, why can't you use the new forms?"

"These legal-size forms are landscape," I replied, "but all our typewriters are for letter-size papers only. The carriage on our typewriters can only take an eleven-inch paper landscape. To type on these, we'd need typewriters with a fourteen-inch carriage."

The new manager ran out of his office, toward our typing area. We all followed. He tried to stuff one of his new forms into a typewriter, but of course, it didn't fit. Trying to hold back his anger, he turned to us with a red face and yelled, "Just use the old forms today!" Then he ran back to his office. The next morning, when we arrived at our desks, we found that each typist had a brand-new typewriter with a legal-size carriage.

I would like to think that manager learned the value of input from the employees who actually do the work, but I doubt it. He was transferred to another department about two weeks after this incident. The way he treated us brought back my old feeling of being worthless and powerless. Although my coworkers shared my feelings, only I could put the bastard-treatment title to it. I realized that there are people who feel superior to others *all the time*, regardless of whether they have a specific reason.

I worked at Fingerhut until Gordy graduated from the University of Minnesota, at the end of spring quarter in 1973. Working at Fingerhut was a fantastic experience for me because I learned much about tolerance, intolerance, and how the company treated people with fairness. I gained confidence, which encouraged me to speak up for myself. I discovered that the working world contains many good people who do not judge others for their religion, race, or birth status. The Fingerhut family was Jewish, and throughout the year, they encouraged office celebrations for all religious holidays, no matter which religion or denomination.

However, what I didn't learn from working at Fingerhut—but was destined to discover years later—is how singularly unique the company was in terms of fair treatment of employees and maintaining a positive atmosphere among men and women throughout the company. If that had been the case in all businesses, part 2 of this memoir would be short, indeed.

My Job at Home

As you might imagine, the wife of a student works more than just eight hours a day. In addition to the obligatory housework, which included cooking, cleaning, and doing laundry, I embraced the job of typing Gordy's papers for school because, although he could type, he was not nearly as fast or as accurate as I was. And because this was the early 1970s—about a decade before word processing was available on computers—any editing on a page usually meant retyping the entire page, making speed and accuracy a must.

Because Gordy was majoring in English, much of his coursework demanded he read literature of all kinds, including poetry, drama, fiction, and nonfiction. His professors required their students to write essays on these works, which made up a major part of their final grade. Many times, Gordy would write for a couple of hours in the middle of the night, then wake me up to type it while he slept for an hour or so, then rise to write more or to rewrite what he had written, making it necessary for me to retype the piece. Although typing was almost a joy for me, I admit I did not necessarily feel joyful typing at three in the morning.

This teamwork approach to college had benefits for both of us. Obviously, it saved Gordy a lot of typing time, which allowed him to work and study more hours as well as spend some leisure time with me. The advantage for me was my becoming involved in the details of his education to a degree I hadn't imagined. I read many of the same stories, plays, poems, and novels that he did, and we discussed them. As I typed his essays, I absorbed many of his ideas as well as those of the famous authors. Also, because he was minoring in theater, he was required to work on play production in the theater department at the University of Minnesota as well as attend and review plays.

We would attend each play together and discuss it before he wrote the review. We attended plays in many of the theaters in Minneapolis and St. Paul, including productions at Scott Hall, on the University of Minnesota–Minneapolis campus; the Minnesota Centennial Showboat, a riverboat theater; Theater in the Round; Mixed Blood Theater; and the Guthrie Theater. (We became contributing members of the Guthrie and would attend every one of their productions for the next thirty years.) These early opportunities to work together bonded us in a way we had not even considered by providing shared interests, hobbies, and pursuits. It helped us grow toward being one.

In spring quarter of 1973, Gordy did his student teaching at North Junior High School, in Hopkins, in the same school district where Uncle Cyril, one of Mom's younger brothers, taught at Eisenhower High School. Although they were in different buildings and did not see each other during the day, the connection led to a few visits with Peggy and Cyril that probably would not have happened otherwise. I already felt that Cyril and Peggy were close friends of mine, but they soon became closer to Gordy too as the teacher bond grew. I didn't think of it as an intergenerational friendship at the time, but as decades clicked by, Gordy and I began to realize that Uncle Cyril provided a bounty of knowledge and a bridge to the past. For example, much of what we learned about Mom's mysterious past came indirectly from Uncle Cyril's stories.

CHAPTER 10

LIVING IN PRAIRIE-
FARM COUNTRY

Gordy's first teaching job was at Chokio-Alberta High School, where he taught ninth- and tenth-grade English and one class of senior English, directed plays, and was the assistant wrestling coach for a couple of years. There were no rental spaces available in the nearby towns, but we found a farmhouse near Donnelly to rent for thirty dollars a month from some nice farmers who owned land nearby.

Our move from the busy streets of Minneapolis to the prairies of western Minnesota comprised a contrast both stark and magnificent. When we awoke in our old three-bedroom, two-story farmhouse following our first night there, I felt transported to a kind of fairyland. After dressing quickly, we ventured outside to see low-lying fog rolling off the distant sloughs as the sun began heating the air. It was August, and a light northwest breeze carried the strangely pleasant odor of peat to my nostrils, creating an experience like sticking my head into a shallow well and inhaling deeply. Earthy smells wafted toward us from a two-acre windbreak of tall green ash trees. The hog barn, which was only about one hundred feet from our house, was home to our landlord's hogs and reminded us that this was a working farm, not a nature refuge. But even the pungent odor of hogs seemed almost sweet in the freshness of the morning. Steve, our landlord, kept about fifteen head of thousand-pound steers in the fenced area behind the hog barn. They roamed the small cow yard but could take shelter from the sun and get fresh water in a forty-foot-square pole shed.

Along with paying the low rent of thirty dollars per month, Gordy and I had agreed to do Steve's morning and evening chores each day, a task that would fall solely to me after school started in the fall. Gordy and I had discussed the matter, and I had embraced the idea. Even though I was a town kid and an office worker, the thought of the farm being my domain appealed to me. The hog feeders and waterers were automated, so chores for the hogs mainly consisted of checking the automatic waterer, watching the animals eat, and walking among them to detect any strange behavior that might indicate a disease or injury. The cattle had automated waterers too. Cattle chores included carrying a couple of bales of hay to the feeder at noon and giving the cattle several pails of corn in the morning and evening. Gordy and I did these chores together until school started. Doing them alone sounded pretty simple, but both Steve and Gordy warned me not to hurry through the chores. "Take your time and watch the animals eat," one of them said. "Look for animals that stay away from others or that go off feed. Spotting ill animals early can save a life, and saving an animal means saving money."

Feeding and petting the kittens was my favorite part of doing chores, and by fall, we'd bought a white German shepherd puppy, who became my constant companion. We named him Rex, and he loved the kittens and all the farm animals. After a year or so, he became so protective of the kittens and me that if I yelled at a steer that had gotten too close, he would go for its throat. Although Rex's protective spirit saved me in some later instances, I learned that I had to chain his collar to his doghouse when I fed the steers.

Women Get a Lunch

That fall, I had my first encounter with women being treated differently from men. Steve and his wife, Dot, owned the 320-acre farm we were on plus the 320-acre farm where they lived, about a quarter mile east down the gravel road. They were great neighbors and good landlords, with just the right amount of concern mixed with a mind-their-own-business attitude. I would see them often when one or both came over to check on their livestock. I spent my days doing chores, learning to bake bread, and becoming a homemaker to a degree I had never imagined. I loved it!

One fall day when Gordy was at school, Steve asked if I would help pick some corn by hand; he'd had to leave the corn standing in a part of one field because the ground was too wet to support his heavy combine. Steve said he would be happy to reward me for the help, and, of course, I agreed to help my neighbor—a tenet of basic kindness my mother had instilled in me. The discussion with Steve was vague, but my takeaway was that there would be some remuneration, some special reward. Although I was ready to help them for free, I fully admit to hoping for some cash. After four years of college, Gordy's teaching degree earned him an embarrassingly low starting salary, and I imagined how delighted he would be when I showed him the cash his little wife had earned through farm labor.

As it turned out, helping my neighbor pick corn meant spending three long days carrying a plastic five-gallon pail as I tramped through cornfields thick with mud that stuck to my boots, making them unbearably heavy. While the ears of corn remained on the stalk, I'd peel off the outer covering as I pulled down and twisted, tearing them from the plant and collecting them in a pail. Once the pail was full, I'd carry it through the mud, back to the wagon, which was parked on the dry part of the field. For the noon break, I had to go home to make my own meal. Although the job was a physical and mental challenge, I gave no thought to quitting. These were my neighbors and I could help them—so I did.

A few days after we finished, Dot called to invite me out to lunch, on her. She picked me up in their pickup, and off to town we went, to a small local café in nearby Morris, Minnesota. Through conversation, I discovered that this lunch was my "reward" for three days of hard labor. She vaguely explained the way things supposedly worked: that men trade work, man for man, and that women get a lunch. I had not expected much of a payment, and a kind thank-you would have been an ample reward for my helping out a neighbor, but what I found unsettling was the degree to which they seemed to think the lunch was a big deal, as if it balanced the scales perfectly. Clearly, I had yet to learn how little a woman's labor was valued, even when doing work usually allocated to a man.

The House Cat and the Puppy

Rex became my helping hand for chores that fall, and when he came romping into the barn with me on the first day, the cats were wary but curious. Rex marched straight up to the cats, his tail wagging, and they became instant buddies. From that first day on, whenever I opened the barn door in the morning, the cats would come running up to play with Rex, jumping all over him.

One morning in November, the cats did not come running when I opened the door. I noticed they were all huddled around the feeding dish located way back on the aisle. Ready to play with the cats, Rex came bounding into the barn as usual, but there was a large black-and-white cat sitting on the top board of the hog gate. I realized it was one of Steve and Dot's "house cats," which also roamed free outside. Before I could stop the cat, it viciously attacked Rex, jumping on his head, scratching and biting. I was able to grab Rex away and get him back to his doghouse, where I could clean him up and fasten his collar to a chain. When I went back to feed the cats, the big cat wouldn't let any of my feline charges come to eat. I tried to chase it out of our barn, but all I could do was get it away from the food dish so the other cats could eat. Later, I found out from Steve that Blackie, as he called her, used to roam this barn when Steve and Dot had lived in the house we'd moved into. After they built their new house on the other farm, they took Blackie with them, Steve explained, but Blackie liked to come down a few times a month to reclaim her territory. Steve thought the skirmish with Rex was funny. I didn't. When he took Blackie back with him that day, my chore routine with Rex resumed.

Blackie next appeared in the spring of 1974. Although Rex had grown rapidly and was now a large dog, he continued to have the same happy, loving puppy attitude around "his" cats. One morning, as I opened the barn door, no cats came running to greet us, and my memory went back to the last time Blackie had visited. In those few fleeting seconds, as I saw our cats cowering by the food dish, I also saw Blackie sitting on the gate of the hog pen. Rex bounded playfully to greet our cats, only to once again be attacked by Blackie, who jumped onto Rex's head. The moment became a blurry, furry mess of dog and cat, accompanied by growls and shrieks. By the time I could set down the cat food and rush to separate the animals, Rex was standing over the cat—it was dead. No longer a helpless puppy, Rex had only a few scratches on his face. It seemed he had remembered the cat that attacked him months earlier. Rex ran over to our cats, who all welcomed him, climbing all over, even licking his wounds.

I panicked as my mind raced through all the possible horrible consequences of Rex's deed of self-defense. Would Steve and Dot throw us off the farm and sue us over the death of their favorite house cat? Would they change their minds and refuse to sell us part of their farm? Would they demand we put Rex to sleep? I could not let that happen! Although an extreme reaction from them was unlikely, I knew I could not take a chance. I didn't want our chance at farming to be over before it even started, and I absolutely couldn't lose Rex, who'd become my devoted companion (at least when Gordy wasn't around).

I viewed the scene before me, calmed down a bit, and considered what I should do. As I fed the cats, I saw the shovel leaning against the wall. I grabbed the shovel, scooped up the dead cat, hurriedly carried it out of the barn, and tromped far into the windbreak of tall ash trees behind the cattle barn. It was early spring, and the snow was still deep between the trees, but I dug down until I hit the partially frozen ground, then dug a shallow hole. I placed the dead cat into the hole, covered it with dirt, and heaped snow high over the gravesite. It would be weeks before all the snow melted, and by then the ground would have settled—the remains would never be seen. When I got back to the barn, I cleaned up all traces of the fight and vowed never to tell anyone what had happened, not even Gordy.

A few days later, when Steve stopped in to check on his cattle, he asked if I had seen Blackie recently. I quietly said I had not. Blackie would usually be gone only a few days, he said, but she'd been gone longer than that. He posed that maybe the cat had come up against something she couldn't beat in a fight. I told him I would keep my eyes open and let them know if I saw Blackie.

For over thirty years, I never told anyone about this incident—again, not even Gordy. Sometime around 2010, years after both Steve and Dot had passed away, Gordy and I were reminiscing about our years on the farm near Donnelly when I finally confessed to Gordy what had actually happened to Blackie the cat. Although he was surprised, he understood why I had told no one for all those years. I emphasized that my growing up as a bastard, keeping things to myself, had trained me well.

The Pastor

To Steve and Dot, we were young people who needed guidance, and they readily took us under their wing. We appreciated their advice, especially when it came to farming and gardening. Their years of experience had given them knowledge, which they passed on to us willingly. However, they clearly wanted to be our religious mentors as well. Steve and Dot belonged to a small Lutheran church in Morris, Minnesota. Gordy and I had been considering joining a church ever since we were married. Back when he was still in college, we even attended a couple of large churches in the cities to see what might appeal to us, but we found them to be too big and too impersonal, and their sermons were always about money.

The small size of Steve and Dot's church appealed to us, and when they brought up introducing us to their pastor, I was open to it because of my positive experience with Pastor Almquist, who had married Gordy and me. Steve and Dot told us stories of the committed people in their congregation.

One young couple, whom they lauded as two of the best examples of Christians they knew, lived two miles east of us, on an old farmstead with a house that lacked running water and indoor toilet facilities. They were expecting their first child, and yet they indefinitely postponed their plans to upgrade their house so they could donate $1,000 to the church to finance one large stained glass window, which would be installed above the main church entrance. Steve and Dot praised these neighbors and credited the pastor's charismatic leadership for inspiring his congregants to serve and donate. Gordy and I said nothing at the time, but we later agreed that the church sounded a bit like a cult to us. Nevertheless, we agreed to let Steve call the pastor to schedule a meeting with him at our place.

During the meeting, the pastor explained that his church was part of the Wisconsin Evangelical Lutheran Synod. The pastor seemed nice but was quite aggressive. We explained that Gordy had been raised Lutheran, attending Highview Christiania Lutheran Church, which was not a member of the Wisconsin Synod, and that I was raised as a Roman Catholic. The pastor then detailed what we would have to do to join his church: Gordy would have to attend extensive religion classes to understand Lutheran society under the Wisconsin Synod. And since I had been raised Roman

Catholic and attended a Catholic school for eleven years, I did not have to attend any religion classes—I could join immediately.

Alarms started to go off in my mind, and I felt a pain in my stomach. Would this Lutheran church mirror the worst parts of the Roman Catholic church I'd just left? My mind flashed with images of church members labeling me a bastard. I didn't know what to say, but Gordy handled it diplomatically, explaining that the two of us would have to discuss the issue before deciding.

After the pastor left, I told Gordy I was not interested in joining a church where my Catholic training was considered a prerequisite. Gordy admitted he was not keen to take classes that would indoctrinate him into a Lutheran sect that discounted his previous training as a Lutheran. We agreed that it seemed more like joining a cult than a church, and we decided against it. But the pastor was persistent.

About a week later, the pastor showed up at our place during the day. Luckily, Gordy was home, and together we talked to the pastor in the yard. We indicated that we were not going to join, and he seemed to take the message with grace. But a few weeks later, he showed up again. The school year had started, and Gordy was at school. I happened to be out by the barn when the pastor drove in. He was aggressively friendly again, mentioning that he had been hunting duck on a parishioner's land. Indicating I should follow him, he excitedly walked to his car, opened the trunk, and displayed his prize. Lying limp on the floor of the trunk were several dead mallard ducks, heaped in a pile, their brightly colored feathers spotted with blood. He proudly said he had just shot them.

I am not hostile toward shooting and eating wild game, but I felt that the pastor displayed way too much pride for accomplishing the fairly easy task of killing ducks with a shotgun. Feeling a little miffed that he was taking my time to brag about himself as an excuse to peddle his religion, I solemnly looked at the dead birds and chirped, "Oh, to think—just an hour ago, these beautiful birds God created were flying free." The smile on his face instantly disappeared. He slammed the trunk, said he had to get home, got into his car, and sped away. We never saw him again.

Planning and Planting

By spring, we'd purchased the farmstead in our care along with 160 acres, and we planned to eventually raise calves, hogs, barley, wheat, oats, and alfalfa. I became the proud farmer that did chores during the week, when Gordy was at school. That spring and summer, I learned to drive the tractor and do field work, including tilling, planting, and baling.

From the beginning, Gordy and I embraced farming together. We planned everything as a team, agreeing on what to purchase, what to plant, and what livestock to raise. Our future looked bright and exciting. Committed to his teaching career, Gordy explained that we could grow only small grains and alfalfa, no row crops, because he would be back in school before corn or soybeans could be harvested.

The fields on our farm had been rented out for years to different farmers, and they hadn't taken the time to remove the rocks that appeared each spring. After a renter harvested his crop in the fall of 1974, Gordy had to plow the fields before winter, but we needed to clear out some of the rocks first. Rocks of various sizes lay on the fields like they owned it, and if we didn't remove them, they would ruin our machinery and limit the growth of our crops. Gordy worked at school from half past seven to half past four, and daylight hours were tapering off, so we needed to use every scrap of daylight we could.

Our work was cut out for us, but we were young, strong, and ready to do what needed to be done. Some might have thought us stupid, but that fall we picked rocks every waking moment. During the school week, we would get up before four and head out to the fields in the dark. We would pick a full wagonload, park it at the end of the field, and walk back home to eat a quick breakfast, then Gordy would clean up and still get to school on time. After Gordy left for school, I would walk out to the wagon and unload the rocks alone. Then I would drive through the fields, pick a load of rocks by myself, and unload those. While I was the only one unloading rocks, I was never alone; Rex was always by my side.

My usual chores notwithstanding, unloading and picking another load of rocks took most of the day, but when Gordy got home from school, we would head out to pick even more. We created huge rock piles at the end of the north field, where we unloaded the wagon, and we even took pictures of one pile to commemorate the magnitude of our grueling task. After we cleared the field, Gordy plowed the eighty-five acres, then adjusted the teeth on one of the two-row cultivators, closing the gap between the rows, so he could use it to level off the field—a process that dug up even more rocks, those to be picked the next spring.

In late February, long before the fields were ready to plant, Gordy and I borrowed Steve's small fanning mill and fanned oats, wheat, and barley for seed. Steve was great—he not only loaned us the fanning mill but also loaned us grain for seed, which we would repay after we harvested our crop. He also loaned us gilts (young female swine) and a boar (uncastrated male swine) so we could start our own farrowing operation and return the gilts to him as full-grown sows after we weaned the piglets.

When the fields were ready and it was time to plant our grain, we were excited to begin seeding. We had previously purchased a Ford 901 tractor, which came with some farm machinery that included an older-style, steel-wheeled grain drill. Gordy had taught me how to drive the tractor and operate the grain drill so I could seed grain during the day, while he was at school. Each morning, before Gordy left for school, we would get the tractor gassed up and pull the wagon, loaded with bags of grain seed, out to the field. Then we would hitch the grain drill to the tractor and fill it with seed. We'd split the eighty-five tillable acres into three parts, planting about fifteen acres of wheat and alfalfa, twenty-eight acres of oats, and forty-two acres of barley. We interspersed the wheat among the alfalfa to function as a nurse crop, as alfalfa is a perennial, producing a crop for multiple years.

After my morning chores, I would drive out to the field, with Rex following close behind. I would spend all day seeding, taking only a short break for lunch. Rex would follow me up and down each row, taking only a few short rests himself. Seeding was a slow process; I watched carefully, making sure the seed came out evenly and that I overlapped the last row just so.

Driving slowly down the field, talking to Rex or singing to myself, I found the work to be enjoyable and gratifying. I felt I was playing an important role in our farm operation, and as Gordy expressed his pleasure at how much I accomplished each day, I felt proud of my newly acquired skills. Although Gordy would rush home from school each day to help out—taking over the seeding so I could go make supper and do chores—the daylight was fading quickly during early spring, and he couldn't seed in the dark. I ended up doing most of the seeding, but I didn't mind at all. In fact, I loved the quiet of the field, interrupted only by the hum of the tractor, and I smiled to see my dog, Rex, running alongside.

The grain drill had a grass-seeder attachment, which we'd used to plant the alfalfa, but Gordy wanted to plant special grass seed in the lowland areas, where alfalfa may not have grown as well. During one evening when the wind was still, Gordy and I went out with our manual cyclone seeder to plant Timothy and brome grass in the low spots. Gordy needed me to act as a marker, walking a line about fifteen feet parallel to him and assuring him the seed was reaching that distance. Then I would follow my footprints as we walked the other direction to seed another strip. The cyclone seeder we used was the same one Gordy's father had used when Gordy was a little boy, when he would serve as his dad's marker.

Learning so many things about farming made this an exciting and happy time for me. I was truly an important part of our joint farming operation.

Rabbit Trails

I felt needed and respected by my husband and my neighbors, but little did I know, my field work was the topic of discussion among some of the men in the neighborhood. Our neighbor Andy rented the fields next to our farm. He was a friendly, kind man, and we had previously met his wife and their youngest son. On many spring days, Andy and I would be seeding at the same time, and we would wave as we drove close to the mutual field line, sometimes stopping to have a brief chat about weather, planting, seeds, and so on.

Several weeks later, when the seeds we had planted appeared above the dark soil in neat rows of bright green shoots, Andy stopped by as I was working in the yard, near the barn. After we said the usual hello, discussed the weather, and assured each other we were all fine, he mentioned how nice the grain looked in our fields. I agreed. Andy grinned and commented how the rows in my fields were all straight, with no "rabbit trails" between. In response to my quizzical look, he explained that a *rabbit trail* was a long, wide space with no grain coming up because the driver had not gotten close enough to the previous mark, leaving a space where no seed had been dropped. At this stage in the growing season, unplanted strips of land show up clearly and can give the farmer a reputation for being sloppy. Andy also told me that my rows did not overlap too much either, so I was saving seed and money.

Pleased at his unsolicited compliments on my seeding, I expressed gratitude, but a short silence ensued as I silently wondered why he seemingly felt compelled to frame my quality work as unusual.

Finally, he broke out into a laugh and asked, "Haven't you noticed all the pickup trucks slowing down to look at your fields?"

"No, I haven't," I replied.

"The people in those pickups are your neighbors, checking your seeding ability," he continued. "They're trying to spot rabbit trails."

Baffled, I said nothing.

"Look," he teased, "in this area, many people think seeding is a man's job and that women should never seed. They think only a man can do it right." He laughed loudly. "But I guess you showed them!"

I came to realize that Andy was even prouder of my accomplishment than I was, and when I told him I had never seeded or even driven a tractor before this spring, he was pretty amazed.

We talked a bit more, and I remember him saying, "Seeding may take some skill at the wheel, but it mostly takes patience, going slow even though you are in a hurry to get done. Women probably have more patience than men anyway. At least that's what my wife tells me, and she's always right."

I could tell he was teasing again, but this was one of the many instances that led me to appreciate Andy's wisdom and the form in which he delivered it. I'd already been feeling pretty cocky about my seeding work after Gordy's many praises, but knowing that my farmer neighbor took time to stop and tell me I was doing well gave my tarnished bastard ego a much-appreciated boost. It also proved that Gordy had not simply been stroking my ego when he said I was a valuable partner on the farm.

End of the Line

I helped Gordy with some teaching paperwork and with his theater productions, and we grew closer to each other during those years, especially while working together on the farm. Working with Gordy on the farm instilled in me a confidence and pride in my abilities that I never got from anyone else. In addition to caring for animals and doing field work, I kept a huge garden, so I learned to plant, tend, and harvest vegetables. I also learned to can and freeze garden produce and make my own ketchup and tomato sauce from fresh tomatoes. We never purchased bread, buns, or sweet rolls from the store because I mastered the art of making bread from scratch. I was really enjoying my life at home, and Gordy and I began to consider starting a family.

Out of the blue, my periods stopped for a couple of months, and I made an appointment with the local doctor, expecting to find out I was pregnant. Unfortunately, I was not. The doctor said there was something wrong, but he didn't know what.

"If you don't get a period next month," he said, "make an appointment and come back."

What? I thought. *Wait a month?*

Gordy had driven me to the appointment and was waiting in the car. When I came out crying, he knew something was really wrong. I told him the doctor had said to come back in a month if I didn't get another period.

Gordy had the same reaction I did. "What? Wait a month?"

After we got home, we continued discussing the situation, eventually agreeing I should make an appointment with a specialist as soon as possible. I called a specialist in Willmar, Minnesota, over an hour's drive from the farm, and I was relieved that the office was able to schedule an appointment within a week.

We were anxious on the drive to Willmar, but we were eager to learn what the doctor had to say. The specialist examined me, did a bunch of tests, and gave me his diagnosis: "You have stopped ovulating." He asked if any other females in my family had received this diagnosis. I thought about it and replied that my mother may have experienced it too.

After some discussion, the specialist gave me two alternatives: receive an extensive hormone treatment to restart my ovulation or do nothing and hope my body started ovulating again on its own. He laid out the pros and cons of the hormone treatment; the only pro was that it *might* help me get pregnant, whereas the cons were extensive. It would take six months or more of hormone treatments to arrive at the right dosage. During that time, the list of possible adverse reactions was long, plus, at that time, they did not know what long-term effects the treatments might have on my body. The only adverse effect of doing nothing was that I couldn't get pregnant unless I started ovulating again on my own, which was unlikely. I was scheduled for a follow-up appointment in two weeks.

Feeling downhearted, I left the office. During the hour's drive home, Gordy and I discussed the situation thoroughly. His first reaction was to comfort me and to reassure me that he loved me and wanted a long life together. We agreed that having children was not the main goal in our marriage.

When the doctor gave me that diagnosis, all my bastard feelings of insecurity flooded my mind—being a bastard, not being good enough, not being a valuable person. Yes, I wanted to have a baby with Gordy, but at the same time, I was afraid to take those hormones. I was relieved that Gordy's first concern was *my* health, not my getting pregnant.

"That we may be the end of our bloodlines is not as important as your health," he said. "You and I are good as we are."

The support and love of my husband were all that I really needed at that moment. We both feared that hormone treatments could jeopardize the great life we had together.

At the next appointment, I told the specialist that we'd decided not to do the hormone treatment. He smiled and said he thought that was a good decision. Although we might not have any children, I still had a bright future with a loving husband. Life was good.

When I next saw my mother, I brought up my diagnosis, thinking it might open up some dialogue with her. She said nothing. I pushed, asking whether she'd, maybe, had something similar, since she had been married for several years in her early twenties but didn't get pregnant until long after her divorce, when she was thirty-three years old. She tried to sidestep the issue but finally admitted she "never really had periods much." Her words alarmed me at the time, but when I tried to pursue the issue, she changed the subject. I took her response to mean she had the same condition, but her seeming lack of empathy for my situation spoke volumes. She seemed more disappointed that I wasn't providing a grandchild for her than concerned about my health. I felt like I'd let her down again, but I resolved not to let her disappointment interfere with my enjoyment of life.

Bastard Moments on the Farm

Gordy and I happily dove into our farmwork together. We were young and strong, and together we thought we could conquer anything. Our first harvest was in 1975, and we'd planted wheat, oats, and barley. We didn't have much money for fertilizer, so we'd used granular fertilizer only on the wheat and planted fields of oats and barley without any fertilizer. Gordy asked Steve about it, and he agreed we could skip a year of fertilizer and still get a good yield.

We lucked out with a good summer of rain and sunshine, resulting in excellent crops for our meager investment. The barley was plump, and it sold as malting barley for $4.20 a bushel, whereas feed barley regularly sold for less than $2.00 a bushel. All the crops were relatively free of weeds, so we were not docked much on each load. This good harvest boosted our resolve, and maybe it gave us some false confidence, especially when farming's main unknown factor in production is always the weather.

Nature is neutral. She cares not about your crops, your stock, or your buildings. And no one learns this faster than a farmer. Although the year had started well, our second summer of farming taught us humility. We hired high school kids to help pick rocks. Gordy advertised "Join Mr. Fredrickson's rock band!" We hired girls and boys, paid them well, and fed them constantly, so we had no trouble finding rock pickers (even in subsequent years). We spread granular fertilizer on all fields and finished planting our oats, barley, and wheat by the first couple of days of April. Proud of our accomplishments, we waited for rain.

As it turned out, we waited all summer for rain, but from planting time to harvesttime, we did not get one drop of rain on our fields. Fortunately, Gordy had plowed everything in the fall, which was a common practice to preserve soil moisture accumulated from winter snows and early spring rains.

Turning over the soil with a plow in the spring loosens the soil and causes it to dry out quickly during summer months. Another factor that dries the soil is deep-tilling it with a field cultivator or digger in the spring, a process that levels the field and loosens the soil, making a smooth seedbed. Most farmers had powerful tractors that pulled large diggers that easily handled deep-tilling, but our equipment was old and only able to dig into the soil a few inches.

The downside of our shallow-tilling in the spring was that our fields stayed rough, but again, the upside was that the soil retained most of the moisture it had stored over the winter. Consequently, the seeds had some moisture to aid germination, even without spring rains.

During the spring and summer, the clouds teased us by gathering in the wide prairie sky before skirting around our area without dropping any moisture. Hot sun and dry winds prevailed, sucking moisture from the plants and the soil. In late July, we began harvesting the oats, barley, and wheat, none of it ever having tasted rain. Although wheat is drought-resistant, ours yielded a meager thirty bushels per acre, but it was the cleanest wheat ever, resulting in no dockage for foreign matter. Our oats were poor but clean, with a yield of forty to fifty bushels per acre.

It was the barley, though, that gave us the biggest disappointment. Our barley had done so well the previous year, having yielded about seventy bushels per acre without adding any fertilizer. This year's barley yield was a ridiculous eight bushels per acre. Apparently, most of the seeds never germinated, producing few plants per square foot, and because the barley lacked the moisture required to fatten, the resulting thin seeds were high in protein but low in substance, making our barley unsuitable for malting. When Gordy tried to sell it, they offered only the feed-barley price of less than two dollars a bushel. He brought it back home, and we ground it up to feed to the hogs, which we sold as feeder pigs. The hogs did so well on the high-protein feed that they grew to selling weight a full week earlier than we expected. The buyer even asked Gordy, "What did you feed those hogs?"

In addition to the summer without rain, our time on the Donnelly farm included several other memorable events. Mother Nature is objective—she doesn't care whether she rains on your field or misses it entirely. She also doesn't care whether a tornado drops down on your land or her earth quakes under your house; in our five years on the Donnelly farm, we experienced both—plus a three-day blizzard that no one would forget anytime soon.

The earthquake was unusual for Minnesota, and it rocked us along with the farm buildings. Although little damage was immediately apparent, the coming weeks saw reports of damaged well pipes and mismatched sewer pipes, requiring some expensive repairs.

The tornado dropped down for a few moments, sucking up some dirt in our plowed field, but the small funnel retracted to its home in the clouds before the sheriff came to officially proclaim touchdown. We later found out that if the sheriff doesn't verify the tornado touchdown, the tornado never officially happened. The sight of it was pretty convincing to us, though. Gordy's folks were visiting at the time, and when the four of us saw the small cyclone moving toward us, across our field, we flew to the shelter of our house and scrambled down the cellar stairs.

The blizzard, on the other hand, was one for the records. Part of what would later be called "Minnesota's Storm of the Century," the blizzard raged for three straight days, during which visibility was absolutely zero; we couldn't even see the pole shed or the barn out the windows of our house. We had to run a guideline rope from the house to the light pole in the yard and then to the barn so we wouldn't get lost when we went to care for our cattle and hogs. Luckily, we never lost power, so our lights and the automatic waterers connected to our well kept working as expected. The wind blew the snow so hard that it pushed right through the puttied edges of the windowpanes in the house, causing a one-foot-high snowdrift in our living room. I wish I had taken a picture of it, but I was so horrified that I wanted to clean it up immediately.

When we investigated the damage after the blizzard, we discovered our cattle were fine, but they were not in their pen anymore. Once again, the wind was the culprit, blowing so coldly and relentlessly that snow drifted over the cow yard's fences and froze in place, hard as ice. The drifts supported the hooves on our twelve-hundred-pound Holstein steers, enabling them to walk on top of the drifts and beyond the fence line. We built a two-wire fence atop the drifts, but it required constant adjustment as the drifts melted and decreased in height.

We also found out that hog prices can be just as unpredictable as the weather. Having borrowed money to feed our first crop of hogs, we wrote monthly checks for feed bills and guessed at the animals' weight every day, aching for when they would be ready for market. Hog prices were high, and we needed the money to continue in the hog business and pay some bills. At the time, hogs were shipped to the stockyards in South St. Paul, and because that's a four-hour drive from Donnelly, the hauler picked up the hogs early in the morning to have them at the stockyard in South St. Paul sometime before noon and be sold in the early afternoon.

We listened to the market report on the radio in anticipation, hoping for a good price. Then, at noon, we heard the announcement: for the first time in the history of the South St. Paul Stockyards Exchange, they stopped buying hogs at noon. The high number of hogs in the morning had flooded the market, and demand plummeted. Buyers had to reconsider what to pay for hogs for the rest of the day. After about an hour, the hog market opened again, but the price had dropped drastically. We had to sell our hogs, even though the price no longer covered our costs and fell far below our hopes and dreams.

Farming promises nothing other than hard work and risk. Steve told us the only way one will never lose money on raising hogs is if they never raise hogs in the first place—true farmer wisdom. He added that if we were going to raise hogs, we had to keep at it through the bad times as well as the good, which convinced Gordy and me to continue raising them. We received no sympathy from our neighbors, and they never forgot the episode. In addition to gaining some farm wisdom from the hog experience, we also learned some farm humor, as the neighbors always kidded us about our closing the market on hogs. If Gordy met a farmer at the feedstore or in town somewhere, he would joke, "When are you planning on shipping your hogs, so we can ship ours a few days before you?" The remark always got a good laugh, but we understood that farmers have to laugh at their pitfalls to make life bearable.

Then there was the early snowstorm following three days of heavy rain in November. I couldn't even walk into the cow yard without losing my boots in the mud, making it impossible for me to carry a full bale from the hay shed to the hay bunk. I had to take less than half a bale at a time, which made conveying twenty bales of hay and several pails of corn a three-hour chore.

There was also the help from a stranger when we'd left our cattle in the pasture a little later in the fall than we should have. It was a cold day with pouring rain, and the cattle were not coming into the cow yard by the pole shed. That morning, before Gordy left for school, I told him that when the cattle came up to the yard, I would close the gate to the pasture for the season. By afternoon, no cattle had entered the yard, so I put on my long raincoat and boots and trekked out into the pouring rain, searching for our herd. I saw them at the far end of the pasture, over a quarter mile away, but as I walked closer, I saw that they weren't actually in the pasture; they were in the road ditch on the other side of the pasture fence, and some of them were on the road.

The fence was down at the corner, so I walked to the road to try to round up the twenty cattle and chase them back through the opening—a futile effort for one person alone. I had been trying for some time when a car pulling a small duck-hunting boat stopped because my cattle were blocking the entire road. The man slowly got out of his car and calmly asked whether I needed some help. I answered yes in earnest, thanking him. Lucky for me, this guy knew how to herd cattle. The two of us quickly rounded them up and chased them back through the fence. As soon as they got back inside the pasture, they took off at full speed, running toward the pole shed and home. I thanked the man profusely and headed home, following the cattle, but I was too exhausted to run. By the time I got to the cow yard, the cattle were all safely inside the fence. I closed the gate to the pasture and went into the house to dry off. I never got that man's name, but I will never forget his kindness.

Gordy's health remained good, but he did have back issues. When he was younger, severe back pain led Gordy to be diagnosed with scoliosis, a lateral curvature of the spine—a condition that cannot be reversed. One autumn at our farm, he injured his back and couldn't even lift a five-pound bag of flour. All chores fell to me, and the weather that year was terrible— lots of mud, lots of snow, and freezing rain. It was a long, hard battle before his back was better and he could again do outside work.

Machinery and Work Exchange

When we first started farming, we knew we couldn't afford all the farm equipment for harvesting, so we entered into a verbal work-exchange agreement with Steve. We bought a brand-new baler and hay wagon and agreed to bale all his straw and hay. In return, Steve would harvest both our farms' grain with his combine and provide the equipment for Gordy to swathe all of it. Fuel would be paid for by the landowner in all cases. Any extra hours we worked would be recorded, and compensation for hours worked would be calculated at the end of the growing season. The agreement seemed fair, but Gordy and I had lessons to learn.

I eagerly learned how to drive the baler, pulling the wagon behind as

Gordy loaded the bales. That first year, I drove the tractor and baler for both of our farms. Steve had a small field of alfalfa, which we baled for him three times that summer. I also drove the tractor and baler to harvest all of Steve's straw while he was busy doing other things, like driving the combine. At the end of harvest, we met to settle up. Gordy had kept close track of both of our working hours. His hours were measured against Steve's, one for one. But my hours essentially replaced those of an extra man, whether hired for pay or barter. When Steve started counting the hours, he did not include my hours. Gordy pointed this out and asked Steve to add my hours to the total.

"No," Steve answered, "those hours don't count." When Gordy asked why, Steve looked at him and said, "Around here, the hours women work are never counted. Only the hours *men* work are counted."

The bastard put-downs I had endured while growing up came rushing back, and my mind raced with those old feelings. I wanted to scream. I could tell Gordy was upset too. But Steve held the contract for deed on the farm, so we both kept silent.

When we got home, we talked it over, and some previous experiences started to make more sense, particularly Andy's enjoyment over my seeding ability and the "reward" lunch with Dot in exchange for three days of hard work, picking corn by hand. I remembered the words of Dorothy Parker: "Women and elephants never forget."

The next summer, when it was time to bale at Steve's farm, I always seemed to be extremely busy with "women's work" on our farm. I continued driving the tractor and baler on our farm, but I never again drove the tractor and baler on Steve's farm. Maybe growing up a bastard had hardened me to this treatment, but by that point in my life, I wasn't going to let my work be dismissed and not counted.

Generally, the work-exchange arrangement worked well for a couple of years, until it suddenly didn't. After harvest in 1977, Steve began to hint he was concerned he was wearing out his machinery harvesting our crops. This was a kick in the gut to Gordy because he was doing everything Steve asked and more. The irony was that it was Steve who had originally wanted to have Gordy help him in exchange for harvesting our crops, even saying he looked forward to having a young hand around so they could, together, achieve more than either farmer could alone. And with the way the work and machinery exchange panned out, Gordy was on Steve's farm much of the summer, helping to harvest his near 150 acres. And now Steve was worried about wearing out his equipment by harvesting our measly 65 acres!

Gordy and I discussed the issue over the next couple of days and decided we needed to hire someone else with a combine to harvest our crops or exchange work with a different neighbor, assuming we could find a neighbor who was interested. Either way, Gordy felt as unappreciated as I did when we discovered there would be no pay for my work. We approached the winter of 1977 knowing we would have to do something different for the 1978 harvest.

Bastard Moments for Gordy

Gordy's experience working in the Chokio-Alberta Public School District was great in every way, until suddenly it wasn't. He enjoyed the kids and his teaching assignment, and he found directing the plays to be fun as well as exhausting.

He especially enjoyed parent-teacher conferences, where parents would sit down with him and discuss their children's progress, among other topics. Gordy received many compliments from parents, claiming that their child had not liked English class in previous years—but liked Gordy's class. One such compliment was especially gratifying, as it came from a school board member—I'll call him "Art"—who had two boys, one in grade nine and one in grade ten. Art said his sons liked Gordy's classes and seemed to be learning a lot in English for the first time during their schooling. He added that he hoped Gordy would remain with the district and not move on, like so many teachers do. Gordy assured him he planned to stay. Actually, Gordy got those kinds of comments from parents often—and they motivated him to do even better.

During his third and fifth years of teaching, the faculty selected Gordy to be on the team of union members who negotiated the teachers' two-year contract with the district. During those sessions, the school board remained adamant about keeping salaries low, which by itself was not unexpected, but board members also boasted that they did not have to raise salaries to retain teachers because teachers could, supposedly, be replaced so easily. Although teachers, students, and parents all knew the value of continuity in education, school board members scoffed at the idea that replacing teachers every couple of years to save money detracted from the students' learning experience. Gordy became particularly discouraged when Art, the same school board member who had complimented him at the parent-teacher conferences, agreed with the other board members on the issue.

Gordy and I discussed the event after he got home that night, and I remember that he was unusually depressed about the prospect of making a career teaching the children of people who did not value his dedication and excellence enough to reward it. At the time, we tagged it as a bastard moment because, on top of being treated as if he were unwanted and unappreciated, he was essentially scorned for wanting to thrive in the profession that defined him. We ended up laughing about it—as we would for future bastard moments—but after he and I discussed our future at length, we agreed he should look for a position that would provide more opportunities and greater appreciation for teachers.

The episode with the school board happened within weeks of Steve's concern about wearing out his machinery on our land. When you go through life being praised for work well done and then are suddenly gut-punched with a comment indicating you are easily replaced, your self-worth is likely to take a hit, if not plummet. I had never seen Gordy without his usual joking swagger and energy, but during that winter, his demeanor was less jovial—yet another reason we had to make a change.

Gordy's getting a new job meant possibly selling the farm. Our contract with Steve stated we would need his permission to do so, but we decided to deal with that only after Gordy got a different job. We really did not want to move. Reluctantly, however, Gordy opened his placement file at the University of Minnesota and soon started responding to job listings he received in the mail. He got a couple of interviews, which went well, but when we never heard back, we buckled down and decided to forge ahead with plans for the farm.

That spring, we purchased a newer, larger, more modern grain drill, towing it home behind the pickup. But when we started to get it ready for seeding, we discovered it was in terrible shape, the owner having rigged it to only look good. We spent days lying on the cold, hard ground, replacing parts of the machine. In fact, I spent my thirtieth birthday—April 30, 1978, my golden birthday—out in the cold wind with Gordy, struggling to fix that grain drill. That was a bastard moment of our own creation.

We eventually got the drill running, but there was one important flaw remaining: when the operator tried to drop the disks to start seeding, only one side would drop. Normally when I came to the end of a pass, I would raise the disks to pause seed distribution, turn the tractor around, and line it up for the next pass before again dropping the disks, resuming the flow of seed—all in one smooth motion. But with this "new" grain drill, after I raised the disks to turn around—at the end of every pass, on all our fields—I found that one side of the disks would not drop. I had to stop the tractor, take it out of gear, jump down and walk behind the machine, and kick the row of disks until it dropped down. As you can imagine, I wasn't exactly singing a happy song every time I kicked those disks. It was like one long bastard moment.

In late May, Gordy got a callback for a job interview, and the principal offered him a job. That fall, he would begin teaching at St. Michael–Albertville High School in St. Michael, Minnesota. Things moved quickly after that. We put the word out that our farm was for sale, and our neighbors Don and Bonnie Gieselman immediately made an offer. So without any realty agents, we sold the farm on contract for deed to Don and Bonnie.

Steve was not pleased with the news, lamenting that he had sold the farm to us specifically because he envisioned our staying there and trading work to lighten both our loads. Gordy refrained from speaking his mind as he apologized for our leaving. It was too late to explain that we would gladly have stayed if Steve's initial enthusiasm about the work-exchange agreements had not taken a 180-degree turn when he suddenly expressed concern about wearing out his machinery on our small acreage. Our time on the farm had taught us about the different perspectives in any exchange of labor.

Another moment of truth came when Art, the school board member with the two sons who liked Gordy as their English teacher, came to see Gordy during the last day of school. He said he was disappointed Gordy was leaving and that he thought Gordy had liked teaching there. He expressed again that his sons really liked Gordy and that the whole family hated to see him leave.

"You told me you were going to stay. What will I tell my boys?"

"Tell them the truth," Gordy shot back. "Tell them how you told me you wanted me to stay during that conference meeting, and then tell them how you basically said quite the opposite during the contract-negotiation meeting, when you and the others boasted that there was no real benefit to raising teacher salaries to boost retention. 'They can easily be replaced,' you said."

"We were all just posturing for negotiations when we said that."

"And *that* is what I suggest you tell your boys. You can blame it on me if you want to, but you know it was your dishonest rhetoric that drove me away. I need to work where I can build my career, in a place that values teachers."

"We don't praise teachers when we are negotiating salaries," Art added.

"You should try it sometime," Gordy asserted. "You might find them more willing to stay, even without more pay. Instead, you expressed the opposite and expected me to continue to feel supported. I'll bet you don't do that with your family. Try telling your wife that you can easily get just anyone to cook for you, and see how that goes. You and the entire board have expressed how little you value your teachers. I believed the board members when they scoffed at the idea that replacing teachers every couple of years to save money detracted from the students' learning experience. Don't say it if you don't mean it."

When Gordy got home that day, he seemed to feel good about expressing his feelings to the board member, but I could tell he was sad too. He told me it would have cost the district nothing to dish out a little praise to teachers and that said praise would have been felt by students, recognizing their teachers' sense of self-worth.

We were sad to leave the wonderful students at Chokio-Alberta. Gordy had most of the students in the high school for both ninth- and tenth-grade English, and he and I both got to know many of them as we worked together to start a drama club and direct plays. We also hated leaving the farm and our neighbors, even Steve. We'd just barely started getting on our feet farming, and we'd been looking forward to the next growing season, but that said, we were thrilled to be off on a new adventure together.

Decades later, we now refer to our five years on the farm in western Minnesota as "the good old days." We were young and foolish and worked all the time—and loved every second of it. It was an idyllic era in our lives, really. We knew it then, but it has become more apparent every year. I think it's more than just nostalgia.

CHAPTER 11

THE MOVE

When viewed as a whole, any experience changing residences is like speed-climbing a huge mountain, instead of trekking up to the peak one step at a time. Moving from a farm is even more daunting. Luckily, we'd sold the farm quickly, after just a casual conversation with our neighbor, who was glad to pay the asking price for a farm that was only a quarter mile from his own.

We could live in the house until fall, but we needed to harvest the crops we'd planted, sell them to the grain elevator, auction off our machinery, and sell our cattle and hogs, plus I had to find a new job. In addition to these mostly farm-related issues, we had to do all the other things any family needs to do when they move, including finding a place to live, getting a loan, moving household items, and changing addresses on legal documents.

Bastard Moment at a Bank

We were looking for a place with less acreage because we knew that my working full-time and Gordy's busy school schedule would preclude doing much hobby farming. Also, Gordy's new school was located within driving distance of the University of Minnesota–Twin Cities and St. Cloud State University, giving him the opportunity to attend college courses during the summers to earn an advanced degree, which would inch him upward on the pay scale at work.

We hired a local realtor from St. Michael, Minnesota, to help line up several houses and hobby farms to see. He was not a young, smooth, fast-talking sales type. Instead, he was older, talked cautiously, and had a folksy demeanor that Gordy and I found trustworthy. We liked him. After we decided to buy a hobby farm near Elk River, our next step was to secure a mortgage. Our realtor took us to a branch of a large bank in the Twin Cities area, which I'll call "Big Bank." Since we had already received the down payment for selling the farm, we were able to pay off half the price of the place in Elk River. Our realtor told us that getting a loan for the remainder, much lower in comparison, would be no problem.

We continued with the moving process. The plan required that I get a job, and since we hadn't moved yet, I would have to stay in a motel during the week and drive back to the farm on weekends. The parents of the man selling the hobby farm to us caught wind that I needed a place to stay, and they insisted I live with them until we could move in to their son's home. They had an extra bedroom and would not take any money for it. I agreed. This was much more pleasant than having to stay at a lonely motel all week.

I found a full-time job (more on this in the next story) several weeks before our official move-in date. Seven weeks had passed since we applied for the loan, but the woman at Big Bank had not yet approved it. We insisted on another meeting with her to discover the holdup. Our realtor was with us when we met her at the bank. She was vague in answering why the loan had not been approved and whether there was an issue with our credit. We explained that I was working, so our income was going to be larger than just Gordy's teaching salary.

She gave a short type of laugh. "We don't count the wife's salary. We only count the husband's salary."

Really? Her statement completely discounted me as a legitimate wage earner, making me feel powerless—a woman in a man's world. This was a serious bastard moment. I wanted to scream at her, but I kept myself calm.

"I am already working and getting a paycheck, and my husband has signed a contract to teach this fall. But your bank does not recognize my paychecks even though my name is on the mortgage?"

She looked at us with an arrogant face and snottily explained, "That's right. We only count the wages of the husband for the mortgage."

She had no idea she was talking about a woman who had seeded grain, picked rocks, and cared for cattle during a three-day blizzard. As I imagined myself jumping over that desk and grabbing her by the throat, I remained calm, sat back, crossed my arms, and stared her down. Gordy controlled his temper, saying something like "We're out of here." As all three of us got up to leave, Gordy added, "I wouldn't expect us to ever set foot in any branch of this bank again."

Once outside, we discussed the issue. The realtor explained he was sure the reason for stalling the loan approval had nothing to do with our income. Instead, he thought it had to do with rising interest rates. The interest rate had gone up since we first applied for the loan, which meant the rate offered on the application date was the rate we would get if they approved the loan without our making a new application. The bank was greedy. If they stalled approval, they could make us apply again, using the new, higher interest rate. Gordy and I were furious, even as we asserted we would've agreed to a higher interest rate just to move things along. Always the optimist, our realtor said he was going to check with a local banker in St. Michael the next morning, when they would meet for coffee. Maybe he would give a local teacher a loan.

The next day, our realtor called and said the banker in St. Michael wanted to meet with us. Gordy drove down from Donnelly, and after I got off work, the four of us met in St. Michael. The local banker was great, and he was, indeed, interested in helping out a new local teacher. When I mentioned I was already working and pulling in a wage, he said his bank doesn't figure loans by wage percentage, adding that when loaning money to married people, he always took into account the trustworthiness of both people. This made both Gordy and me smile.

The banker said he would review the new property to assess its value and that our paying half down certainly worked in our favor—he didn't foresee any problems. Before we left, the banker added, "If the local bank can't loan one of our teachers money to buy a home, I don't know what the heck we are good for." The next day, the bank sent someone to review the property, and within an hour, the banker called to say we'd gotten the loan. Small-town businesspeople can be marvelous. There were no bastard moments in that transaction.

New Job Number One

When I first started applying for jobs in Elk River, Gordy and I drove around town, looking for businesses. I applied at the headquarters of a large power company in town, but they had no immediate openings. A large cement company had both their headquarters and one of their distribution facilities in town, and although I interviewed at their headquarters, the job would be at the distribution facility. After the HR manager interviewed me, he offered me the job with a set wage of $3.50 an hour—which, at the time, was considered good pay for an office worker living outside Minneapolis. I accepted the position, and I would start the following Monday.

My first day of work was an eye-opener. When I arrived at the cement-distribution facility, I entered the office. I only saw one other person, a woman, and she was quite surprised to hear I was starting work there. When the supervisor finally arrived—which, I would learn, he never did early or even on time—he took me into his office. My mind raced as he explained he wanted to get rid of the woman working there, the one I'd talked to, but didn't want to fire her until I was trained in. He wanted me to deceive a coworker—a terrible dilemma. As I was reviewing and signing the paperwork, I noticed that the wage offered was $3.00 an hour.

"This must be a mistake. The HR manager quoted me $3.50 an hour."

"Have you got that in writing?" he asked, sneering.

"No, but that's what he quoted."

With a final smirk, he said, "Well, $3.00 is what you're getting."

I felt powerless and demeaned. It's not a good omen to be subjected to a bastard moment at work before even clocking in on your first day, but I signed the papers and went out to start training.

The woman training me—whom I would eventually replace—was kind but seemed understandably confused as to why she had to train me on everything she did. Those days were a strain on me. I felt that the supervisor was treating her like a bastard, and I hated being part of the deception.

Relief came when, on Tuesday evening, I got a call from the HR person at the large power company—which I'll refer to as "LPC"—asking if I wanted to come in for an interview. I told her I was working at the cement company already. She asked what my hours were, and I told her I got off at four o'clock. She offered me an interview slot at a quarter past four the next day, Wednesday, and I said I would be there.

The interview at LPC went great. The HR woman said the job paid $3.65 an hour. I told her it would be appropriate for me to give my employer notice, possibly as long as two weeks. Plus, I wanted to discuss the decision with my husband. I finished the interview by saying I would call her the next day with my decision.

I called Gordy and we talked it over. I explained that after my first day at the cement company, I did not have a good feeling about the boss, especially his seeming lack of ethics. I told him I intended to talk to my boss at the cement company the next morning and see where the meeting went from there, and Gordy agreed with my approach.

As soon as my boss arrived the next morning, I asked to speak to him in his office. I told him I had a job offer from LPC that paid $3.65 an hour. He just grunted—no offer of more money or any other attempt to convince me to stay. So I just asked.

"Do you want me to leave now, or finish out the week?"

Without looking up at me, he just said, "Finish the week."

I agreed, walked out to my desk to call LPC, and told the HR person I would be there first thing on Monday morning. The woman training me heard this and asked what was going on. I told her I was taking a new job at LPC starting Monday. Then she and I made plans to go out for lunch. I felt an obligation to let this woman know about her boss's deceit.

At lunch, I told her I'd been hired specifically to replace her, that the boss intended to fire her as soon as she had me trained in. She was quite shocked and promised not to say anything about the situation to the boss during the rest of my remaining week there. I met her in downtown Elk River about a month later, and I was glad to hear she had found a better job, having abruptly quit the cement company, with no replacement trained in for her job. Clearly, the boss had no regard for the value of clerical staff and felt he had the privilege to treat them—and perhaps all women—as expendable, powerless pawns with little value, other than doing his bidding.

A Visit from Clergy

When Don and Bonnie Gieselman bought our farm near Donnelly, not far from their own, they were gracious enough to help us make the move. Don volunteered to harvest our grain and even let Gordy use his grain truck to haul it to the elevator immediately. Don also paid Gordy to help him harvest his grain while I worked in Elk River. When Don insisted on using his truck to haul some of our items to our new place, including our Ford 901 tractor, Gordy offered to pay him for the gas, but Don said he wouldn't take a dime. As I said, he and Bonnie were gracious people.

When they arrived at our place after the grueling four-hour drive in a grain truck, our possessions in tow, we treated them with all the hospitality we could muster. After unloading the items, we all settled around our dining room table for some refreshments, including cold beer.

We talked and joked about the five years we'd spent farming in Donnelly and about Don and Bonnie's future plans for the place. Then we heard a knock on the door. Opening the door, Gordy discovered a man who introduced himself as the pastor of a small Protestant church attended by our neighbors, the kind couple with whom I had stayed while we waited for our loan to be approved. We'd gotten along wonderfully during my stay, and I had enjoyed eating supper and spending time with them in the evenings. Our discussions had revealed to me that they were devoutly religious, but I did not know they'd told their minister about Gordy and me. Although I never indicated I wanted to join their church, I suppose they and the pastor figured it was their Christian obligation to recruit us. By all appearances, they had every reason to believe we were a nice young couple. We believed so too, actually.

Being a cordial host, Gordy invited the pastor in, and we each introduced ourselves as he took a seat at the table. Gordy offered him a choice of refreshments, and as we were about to continue our friendly visit with Don and Bonnie, the minister decided—quite suddenly—to take control of the conversation.

The minister's voice pitched slightly higher as he asserted, "I do not condone drinking alcohol, and I cannot refrain from condemning your drinking it here today."

During the silence before Gordy spoke, I became extremely uncomfortable. The alarms started to go off in my head again, and pain in my stomach began to grow as this man of God asserted his self-righteous superiority in my home. This was, indeed, a bastard moment.

Gordy took charge of the situation without raising his voice, telling the minister that Don and Bonnie were our guests and that they had generously made the four-hour drive to our new home, their truck loaded with our farm items, and we were offering them some hospitality for their kindness. Gordy made it quite clear that if the minister couldn't "condone" drinking alcohol, he would have to leave and *not* "condone" it somewhere else. The minister left, and we never saw or heard from him again. Although Gordy and I were concerned that the episode had alienated our kind neighbors, they never mentioned it, and we stayed good friends with them for the duration of the time we lived near Elk River.

CHAPTER 12

THE NEW JOB

The power company was a good place to work in many ways. There were opportunities for advancement in a number of departments because the company was large and still growing, making it a far better option than the cement company. Although not all supervisors treated employees with the respect they deserved, most of them did, and the clerical staff had a union that negotiated two-year contracts with the company, making the wage scale known to all and ensuring promotions were not awarded by way of favoritism.

Coffee Duty at LPC

After about one week of working at LPC, one of the secretaries informed me that my name would be added to the rotating coffee-duty roster in the break room. Apparently, all the women were each assigned a week during which they would make coffee and put out pastries first thing in the morning, then, before leaving for the day, wash out the coffeepot and clean up the tables in the break room.

I told the secretary I didn't drink coffee and that Gordy and I didn't even make it at home, then politely suggested my name not be added to the coffee-duty roster. But she informed me that it was part of my job.

"Why are only women on the list?" I asked. "Don't the men drink coffee? Why don't they have this duty?"

"Men don't have to make coffee," she barked, looking at me like I was from another planet. "Your name is on the list now, so make sure you do your week."

This was one of many moments that led me to question why some women are so supportive of discrimination against their own sex. The secretary seemed thrilled to put me in my place in the man's world she had apparently accepted, as if her having to explain it to me ensured her place above me in the pecking order.

The coffee-duty assignment didn't sit well with me. I didn't use the break room. I didn't drink coffee. I didn't even know how to make coffee, especially with one of those gigantic coffee percolators. Regardless, I accepted that I had to cover my week and asked my coworker Jane some questions on how to make the coffee. Unfortunately, her answers seemed rather vague—and I really like details when it comes to cooking.

My week eventually came up. On Monday morning, when I began to fill the huge coffee percolator with water, I noticed how dirty the inside appeared, and I made a mental note to clean it thoroughly after work. I tried to put in the proper amount of coffee by reading the measurements on the coffee can, but I threw in a few extra scoops just in case. It looked good. I plugged the machine in, set out the rolls, and left. In the late afternoon, I began cleanup. I dumped out the remaining coffee and tried to clean the pot, a task I decided needed a more intensive approach.

Tuesday morning, I came in armed with S.O.S Soap Pads and good dish detergent. I scrubbed the inside of the metal coffeepot as best I could that morning, but I didn't have much time before I had to start making coffee. That afternoon, though, I scheduled more time to clean up. When I dumped out the remaining coffee, I noticed there was a bit more than what was left on Monday. Dismissing the observation, I began cleaning the pot, this time with my supplies from home.

I continued this through the entire week. By the time I left on Friday afternoon, the inside of that coffeepot shined so brightly that I could almost see my face in it. But I kept thinking about the leftover coffee, as each afternoon throughout the week, more and more was left in the pot. I concluded that people must drink more coffee on Monday than the rest of the week.

Tuesday morning of the following week, a notice from headquarters was posted, stating that the janitor would be making the coffee and cleaning up the break room in our building from then on; the women would no longer have coffee duty. This proclamation ignited a lot of discussion throughout the building. I heard extensive tales of how terrible the coffee had been the previous week, and I was not sure how many people knew I was the one who had made the coffee. I said nothing, but I came to believe that most of them knew I'd made it. Apparently, the coffee had been so bad that all the men complained to their managers, who, in turn, complained to headquarters—everyone wanted something done about it.

Of course, no one asked my advice, but if they had, I would have told them to ensure that whoever made the coffee also drank coffee regularly, so they'd know how to make a passable brew. There's a truism from Shakespeare's *Romeo and Juliet* that reads " 'Tis an ill cook that can't lick his own fingers." The same applies to making and drinking coffee. As it turned out, my first week of coffee duty was also my last.

Sexual Harassment

In my three years of working at Fingerhut, in Minneapolis, I didn't encounter any sexual harassment, and most managers were understanding and had a prominent concern for their workers. But my experiences after my five-year hiatus from the working world were extremely different.

Shortly after I started work at LPC, in 1978, one of the first things my female coworkers warned me about was Len. Len was a department manager, which gave him authority over the clerical staff, even if they didn't work in his department. His position gave him credibility with upper management and HR by default, so he practically had the power to get people fired or even destroy their career.

Len liked women—for both touching and intimidating—and he used many devious methods to enact his will. Len wasn't conventionally attractive, but his real ugliness showed in the way he leered at women. He stood at about 5'4", but he strutted around like he was 6'10". My coworkers also explained that his wife was an extremely jealous woman, thinking all the women in the office were after her husband, and she made that known to Len's boss and to HR. Although it's hard for me to imagine her actually convincing Len's boss and HR that the women of LPC were after her husband, he probably was able to perpetuate the lies because his position of authority made him believable to other men. When my female coworkers warned me about Len, they also warned me that their formal complaints were not taken seriously.

A few weeks after I started work at LPC, I began my assigned week of coffee duty, which meant I would be alone in the break room in the late afternoons, when I had to clean up the break room. During one such late afternoon, Len came into the room. I was cleaning the big coffeepot by the counter at the end of the room. Before I could move, Len quickly walked up and pinned me into the counter and against the wall. With his entire body pressed firmly against the front of mine, he placed his hand on my ass and squeezed. I was shocked and scared, but I also got really angry. He said something, but I was so enraged that I didn't even comprehend it.

I tried to control my anger. I knew he could get me fired, especially since I had only worked there a few weeks. Gordy and I really needed this job to pay our mortgage, and I knew there weren't any jobs in the area as good as this one, but I also knew Gordy would back me up on any incident at work. All this raced through my mind while I held on to the coffeepot. Knowing this was a frightfully dangerous situation, I considered hitting him on the head with the coffeepot. Calling for help wouldn't have worked because no one else was around to hear me. I knew I had to get out of there fast and that I had to do it by myself.

Tensing up and bracing for a fight, I looked down into Len's leering eyes, declaring forcefully, through clenched teeth, "The only man who has the right to put his hand on my ass is the man who put this wedding ring on my finger. Now get your fucking hand off my ass and get away from me immediately, or my husband will be coming into this office to beat the living shit out of you!"

It didn't take long for that statement to sink into Len's depraved mind. He must have believed me, because he jerked his hand away. He jumped backward, releasing me from being pinned. I looked at him and repeated that I could call my husband and have him there in a few minutes. That seemed to do the trick. Without a word, Len turned and rushed out of the break room. I was still shaking when I got back to my office, but I grabbed my stuff and drove home.

As soon as I got home, I told Gordy about the whole horrible incident.

He wanted to go into work the next morning to confront Len, but I told him I didn't think that would be necessary and that I would call him if there was any more trouble.

Len kept his distance from me for some time, but about a month later, we inadvertently crossed paths in the hall. I had seen some of the dirty tricks he would try to pass off as innocent. One trick he played on women was the admire-the-necklace ploy, which gave him an excuse to reach out and clasp the necklace appreciatively, also taking the opportunity to push his arm against one of the woman's breasts. As Len approached me in the hall, his arm came up, and he said something about my "lovely" necklace. I instantly grabbed my necklace, angrily stared into his eyes, and loudly declared, "Yes, it is a nice necklace. It was a gift from my *husband*." The message got through to him quickly. He jerked back his hand and kept walking. After that, Len stayed clear of me, but stories of his sexual harassment toward others were common.

Comeuppance for Len

I became good friends with Len's secretary, Chris. We had purchased our house from her cousin, and her parents lived just down the road from us. Chris shared how she'd learned to defend herself from Len's advances and tricks. Her husband agreed with her methods but, like Gordy, was willing to come in to straighten out Len if things escalated.

Chris referred to the move that kept Len afraid of her as "the drawer." Back when she was fairly new on the job, Len would approach and stand behind her when she was seated at her desk. He would lean in tight, try to caress her neck, and even breathe into her ear. Due to the man's short stature, the top side-drawer on Chris's desk was just even with Len's crotch area.

So one day, as Len tried to breathe into her ear, she pretended not to see him and jerked open her top drawer as hard as she could. It hit the mark! Len was in extreme pain but really couldn't admit it to anyone. He held his crotch and slunk back to his office. From that day on, Len never tried anything on Chris again, but he continued his game of harassment with others, unchecked by management.

Harassment and Bullying

I enjoyed doing clerical work in a big office like at Large Power Company; it proved to be a good job for me. I enjoyed working with my coworker Jane, and I got along well with all the *respectful* male staff. Liking the work helped me quickly learn about the type of work done by my department, which included doing work for the outside line crews. Unfortunately, there was one person in the department who would make things difficult: Suzie, the department secretary.

All the clericals knew Suzie to be a slacker who bragged about the little work she actually did while pushing the rest of it onto others. Suzie was not only extremely good at bragging about her accomplishments, but she was also an expert at flirting with her boss, blinding him to her actual sham activities. She would regularly arrive late or leave early without punching out, and then she would fill in forty hours on her time sheet and charm the boss into signing it, even though he usually knew she was cheating.

Jane and I mostly just shrugged off Suzie's behavior and did our jobs, but what we couldn't handle was all her backstabbing. Whenever she couldn't find something on her messy desk, she would blame Jane and me, claiming one of us had taken the item without her knowledge. Of course, all these items would "magically" appear in her office later, but we never received an apology. Many times, Suzie would accuse us of answering the wrong phones or not answering the phones at all, quickly reporting *our* dereliction of duty to the boss. This constant harassment was part of her scheme to discredit us so she could maintain her preferred status with the boss.

Sometimes, her harassment brought back memories of the bastard treatment I endured during my youth. Sometimes I would try to fight back by taking the issue straight to the boss, but even when I proved myself innocent, all the boss would ever say was "Oh," and he never extended an apology for the wrongful accusation, not even a casual "Sorry about that." I questioned whether trying to make things right was worth the effort. Little did I know that the worst was yet to come.

Smoking Issue

In 1980, the company remodeled the office areas, including my department, which resulted in rearranging staff offices. I was moved from the open area

I had shared with Jane to a large room, which I would share with six men with whom I'd often worked previously. Most of these men smoked; in fact, many times, there would be five men smoking in the room at once. Their assignments often had them working with the outside crews most of the day, so they were only in the office, usually smoking, early in the morning and later in the afternoon—but their smoke didn't leave with them.

I worked closely with Ned, who worked in the office all day and smoked constantly. He would chain-smoke, lighting the next cigarette with the previous. He often lit a cigarette, rested it in his ashtray, then left for a meeting or went to the warehouse, leaving the cigarette burning. I was the *only* person who did not get to leave the area all day. Every day, I would develop a terrible headache and a bad sore throat, and when I got home, my clothes and hair stank of smoke.

I tried to talk with the men about cutting back on their smoking, but they just laughed about it. I talked to the department manager, and all he did was ask the janitor to make sure the air vent in the room was fully open. After I complained again, the department manager brought in a fan to blow the air around. That's all it did—blow the air and smoke around the room. Yet again, I asked the manager to come up with some remedy, but he said the fan was enough. Honestly, I felt like a bastard among privileged elites.

Large Power Company was a union shop for the clerical staff. We were in OPEIU (Office and Professional Employees International Union) Local 12. Through the union, I got a copy of "LPC Administrative Policy #24," dated May 29, 1979, which spelled out which areas were the designated smoking areas, written to comply with the Minnesota Clean Indoor Air Act. It stated, "Smoking will not be permitted in offices occupied by two or more employees unless all of the nonsmoking employees consent." Obviously, I didn't consent.

On December 4, 1980, I walked into the department manager's office and handed him a written memo, formally requesting that the room I work in be a nonsmoking area. He was not happy about the memo and said I should be satisfied with "all" that he had done to cut down on the smoke. I told him it wasn't enough. I had inhaled the smoke for months and would no longer put up with it. He said he wanted the issue kept within our division and that he would "talk to the guys." I informed him that wasn't enough, that if he didn't comply with my request, I was prepared to take this matter to the top—and further, if necessary. He got the message. The next day, everyone in the department knew about my request, and that's when things started to get *really* ugly.

The atmosphere in the room was extremely tense, and there was a lot of whispering among the smokers. The only positive feedback I received was from one of the line crew supervisors—another nonsmoker—who said he thought it was a good idea to have a smoke-free office. On December 8, I put a sign on the door that read "This is a No-Smoking Area. Your cooperation is appreciated. Thank You." A couple of days later, I came into work to find another sign posted under mine, this one reading "It's hard to soar with eagles when you work with turkeys."

The next day, I found out that Jack, the other line crew supervisor, had put it up. One of Jack's crew members had come to see me to express support, which Jack didn't like, leading him to have a talk with his whole crew. But apparently, Jack didn't have the courage to confront me directly about the no-smoking sign. I removed Jack's sign, but a few days later, the division manager, whose office was down the hall, stopped in the doorway, looked at me, ripped the no-smoking sign off the door, crumpled it up, and threw it into the room.

By December 15, Jack was still extremely angry with me, and he finally had the guts to say something. He accused me of disrupting the entire division with my no-smoking request, claiming I was chasing people out of the room, and asserted that the no-smoking rule made him spend too much time away from his desk. He further claimed I was discriminating against his right to smoke. I stood my ground and told him I had only asked people to put out their cigarettes when they came into the room and that I thought it was a sorry thing that he couldn't work at his desk without a cigarette. He told me he would not allow the matter to drop.

Throughout the rest of December and into January, when I would arrive at my desk in the morning, Jack and Ned would be smoking. Another smoker in the room commented to me many times that he'd be glad when I got moved out. On January 19, 1981, the department manager informed me I would be moving into a small office with Jane. I stated that I still required my work area to be no-smoking. He agreed—which was easy, since Jane didn't smoke—but he said I would not be allowed to have a no-smoking sign on the door.

"What am I supposed to do," I asked, "announce to everyone when they come in that the room is no-smoking?"

"You do that anyway!" he snapped back. "And besides, the word has gotten around."

After Jane and I moved into the small office, she told me that the move had been Jack's idea. With help from the department secretary, Suzie, Jack had written a scathing letter to the department manager about my terrible discrimination against him. In fact, he referred to me as "a baby" throughout the letter. Jane had seen Suzie working with Jack on the wording of the letter, and she was able to sneak a look at the letter when she was working near Suzie's desk. The day after we were moved, I could hear Ned singing loudly in my old work area: "I can smoke a cigarette! I can smoke a cigarette!" The department manager was in there at the time, and he and everyone else in the room seemed to think Ned's singing was funny.

I'd thought the move would mean my work area would be free of smoke—not so lucky. For months after the move, the same men would walk into my work area with a lit cigarette. Of course, I would politely remind them it was a no-smoking area and ask them to put out their cigarette. Most of the time, they would either ignore my request because they were "just getting a form" or take several quick puffs on the cigarette and quickly blow the smoke in my direction.

As this harassment continued, others in the building began to notice the rude behavior. In May of 1981, a secretary from another department was walking past when she witnessed the harassment. Later, she stopped by my desk to ask how often it happened. I tried to be diplomatic about the incident, but thankfully, Jane gave her the full lowdown about the constant harassment.

When I came into work the next morning, there was a huge "No-Smoking Area" sign on the door to that secretary's department. When I stopped in to ask her about it, her boss called us both into his office. Apparently, the division manager was sincerely concerned about the harassment and wanted me to know that he supported what I was doing. He thought that visibly declaring his department a no-smoking work area would acknowledge the importance of the issue, especially since everyone who came into the building had to walk past his department's door. Also, he was the same level as my department's division manager, the one who'd removed my sign, so he was sure no one in the building would dare remove his sign.

After all the months of harassment and stress, I was so relieved at his support that I almost started to cry. He also informed me that many departments within the headquarters building were no-smoking. In fact, the accounting department had always been no-smoking, and no one ever dared to bring in a lit cigarette. I thanked the division manager profusely for his support, and from that day on, he would often stop at my office to talk with me. His visible support helped improve my situation in the building.

Unfortunately, Ned continued his harassment whenever he could. I talked to the department manager about it several times, but nothing changed. After talking with the union steward, I wrote up a harassment grievance and gave it to the department manager. He was not happy with it and tried to give it back to me, but I refused and said the harassment had to stop, or the union would handle the grievance. The department manager talked to Ned, then returned to me, saying that Ned claimed he'd never brought a lit cigarette into my office. I said that was a lie, and Jane backed me up, explaining how often it happened. The department manager must have talked to Ned again, because his harassment eased after that.

What amazes me to this day, though, is how readily people were willing to treat me poorly. I knew of others who did not like inhaling the smoke all day, but they seemingly lacked the courage and goodwill to take my side and make their views known to management. Male managers were empowered by workers—both male and female—who stayed out of the fray just because it didn't affect them at the time. I admit I lost a little faith in many of my coworkers during that period, but I am sure that many of the women feared risking their jobs over the issue.

Union Steward Issues

During the months of harassment about the no-smoking issue, I talked to the union stewards at length about my rights and gained a better understanding of the union contract and the union in general. One of the stewards was leaving, so with encouragement from Gordy, I decided to run for the office—and I won. I was now one of the people that union members came to with questions and issues, and I had immediate access to the HR department.

Eventually, the attitude toward me among the men in my department began to reflect a bit more respect, especially after I helped negotiate a new contract in 1983. Before those negotiations were completed, however, the prevailing negative attitude toward women reared its ugly head in my dealings with Ernie, the male union representative assigned to us from the Minneapolis union office.

I heard that there had been clashes with Ernie during the 1981 contract negotiations, when he had ignored our local members' input. I didn't want to see anything like that during the 1983 negotiations, so I vowed to be ready.

Before the new contract negotiations even began, we union stewards held meetings to get input on what local members wanted us to work on for our new contract. The stewards combined the input into categories, then had members vote on them to determine which concerns were the most important. We typed up the member-approved requests and handed the document to Ernie.

The contract negotiations were held in the large conference room in the headquarters building, where we all sat at the huge conference table. On the management side of the table were LPC's general manager, HR manager, HR assistant manager, chairman of the board, and two board members. On the union side of the table were Ernie and two union stewards who were lowly clericals. Walking into a meeting in which we were outnumbered six to three was intimidating for us, but even worse was the fact that Ernie, who was supposed to be on our side, seemed to be more on the side of management.

Ernie would joke with the management side, refer to us as "girls," and not listen to what we had to say during negotiations. We would try to discuss points with Ernie, but he seemed to concur with everything that management suggested. At one point, we union stewards were trying to discuss a matter with Ernie, and we wanted to leave to discuss the matter in private. Ernie refused to leave and suddenly agreed to one of management's suggestions that we stewards disagreed with. He then continued on to the next item. As Ernie happily carried on talking with management, the other steward and I stood up and said we wanted to talk to him outside. Then we walked out. This action stopped all discussion, and Ernie finally followed us out to the hall.

After a heated discussion with Ernie, he agreed to reopen the last point, the one he'd inexplicably agreed with management about. We went back into the conference room, where the matter was discussed again, and management finally revised it to meet the union's requirements. After several days of negotiations, our members voted to accept the new contract. But trouble soon followed.

In late June, a bookkeeping clerk retired from the department, and the company stated that the clerk's position was being eliminated from the department. Yet a clerk in that department was given the retiree's duties as well as a raise, making her wages equivalent to those of a bookkeeping clerk. This action prevented the posting of what would otherwise be an open position that others could apply for. Reassigning a position without posting a job opening was in violation of the union contract. We stewards contacted Ernie about the violation, and he started to investigate.

On June 23, Ernie came down to address our members at a union meeting. At the meeting, he asserted that the reassignment was valid because the job was "an upgrade" and the reassigned clerk was the "incumbent" in the job. We tried to explain to him that it was not "an upgrade," and we told him that the term *incumbent* was not in our contract. But Ernie would not listen to any opinions from our members. When he ended the meeting, we all left with the understanding that there would be more investigation and we would have another meeting. But Ernie told HR that the members agreed with him and management.

When we found out what Ernie had done, we were livid. He had once again ignored our opinions. We called a member meeting, and everyone agreed that our next step was to file a formal grievance against the move by management. After we typed up the grievance, every union member signed it, and we sent it to HR. We also sent a copy to our union office in Minneapolis, complete with a cover letter detailing how Ernie's actions had damaged Local 12's relationship with the management at LPC.

The union office took notice, and Ernie was forced to reopen the investigation. The union office eventually agreed with our members, and the job was finally posted per the union contract. We took that as a real win for us, the underdogs, especially since we were able to overcome our pro-management union representative, who seemed more interested in his relationship with the company managers than in his relationship with his actual constituents.

Ernie and the Girls

Ernie's pro-management attitude continued to strain his relationship with our union. Getting ready for the 1985 negotiations, we stewards had an idea that we brought up to our members at the first pre-negotiations meeting: Since management brings in two volunteer board members, why don't we bring in two volunteer union members? These volunteers wouldn't have to do any of the paperwork—the stewards would do that. But they could see how negotiations work and would be there to help answer any questions that might involve their area of expertise. The members thought it was a great idea, and we voted in two volunteers. After all, five against six would be better odds for the union at the negotiation table.

As usual, Ernie did not come down beforehand to find out what the union members would be requesting; instead, he arrived just shortly before we had to go into the conference room. He was furious at us for having the two volunteers, claiming it was not acceptable. But we pointed out there was no wording in the contract against it—so we won that issue. As we walked in, we could actually see the mouths drop open on the general manager, HR manager, and assistant HR manager. We politely explained who the volunteers were and that it was within our contract rights to have them attend. No one objected.

Large Power Company's board members were from areas in outstate Minnesota, and because negotiations would take several days, they stayed in a hotel nearby. On the second day, we discovered that Ernie had gone out for drinks and supper with the general manager, HR manager, and all three board members.

As we all gathered in the conference room before the meeting started, I was standing by one of the board volunteers. He asked why none of us had joined them for drinks and supper. I smiled politely and said that I'd had to get home after work to feed my cattle. Plus, when I got home, the electric-fence controller for the pasture had shorted out, and I had to find the short and fix it before the rainstorm hit.

He got this totally shocked look on his face, then asked, "You have cattle? You farm?"

I explained that my husband and I both had jobs but also had some acreage and raised some steers. I added that before we moved to the area for

Gordy's new teaching job, we owned a quarter section of land, and I raised cattle and farrowed hogs.

With that, the gate to the fence separating us opened, and he and I had a wonderful discussion about farming and cattle. I discovered that this board member also had a job outside his farm, but he and his wife were raising a small herd of cattle. From that moment, this board member started to see our union members as people to whom he could relate. We were no longer those strange women who live and work in "the cities." He even started to speak up and defend us during discussions. By the next day, the other board volunteer started to see our side of things too.

Negotiations are always difficult. We still had trouble with Ernie, who continued to be on management's side in all matters. We threatened to walk out of negotiations if he didn't listen to us. That threat usually got him to settle down a bit. When the discussion finally rolled around to wages, things got heated between the union and the company.

The general manager looked me straight in the eyes and screamed, "We can get any idiots off the street to do your jobs!"

"Go ahead," I said, smiling politely. Then I quietly described all the positions that would be eliminated, including in payroll. "After all," I added, "everyone likes to get their paycheck on time." During the next several days, we agreed to a contract we would take to our members for a vote.

Ernie's bullying tactics against our members continued, even as he read the new contract aloud to the lot of them before they would vote. As he read, members would raise their hands with questions, but he told them there was no time for questions, and he would continue reading. Later, when the questions were asked again, he became angry and indignant and refused to answer. We stewards stepped in and answered as best we could. When any member suggested we not vote to approve the contract, Ernie used the old management threat, "It's going to cost you!" Against Ernie's objection, we let the members think about the contract overnight and had our voting meeting the next night. The contract was approved.

Our whole union was still upset over Ernie's behavior and pro-management attitude—well, except for Ernie. The other union steward and I put together a long statement against Ernie, listing our grievances and showing how he supported management, not our local union, and how he disregarded the requests of our union members. We explained that he never ran any meetings according to Robert's Rules of Order—a widely utilized guide to parliamentary procedure—and how his referencing us as "girls" was extremely demeaning. The typed-up grievance was signed by all members, and we sent it to the union office in Minneapolis, a move that stirred up a hornet's nest.

The Minneapolis office took notice of our local, and Alan, a new union representative, came down for a meeting. This guy was good. First, he apologized to our local for the union not supporting us fully. Ernie would no longer be representing our local. Instead, Alan would be our new union representative. He said that if we thought he was not supporting us fully, we should let both him and the union office know immediately—that the union was there to serve its members, not the other way around.

This was quite a change. No longer did we "girls" get the bastard treatment. We were treated as valued union members. Alan was knowledgeable and accommodating, and he returned our calls swiftly, always with answers to our questions and ready to share information from the main union office. This was what we'd been missing out on.

Changing Departments

It was October 1984, and the yearly budgets for 1985 were being written. Managers announced layoffs, additions, and so on to department employees during this process. Nothing was said to us about any big budget changes, so we continued working per usual.

One day, I had to go over to the accounting department to handle some money items, since the secretary was out on vacation for the day. As I was getting money from the petty cash clerk, she asked how my job search was going. Confused, I asked her why I would be looking for another job. She said that the department secretary, Suzie, had come over last week and told everyone that my job was cut from the department budget for the next year. Shocked at the news, I told her I didn't know anything about it, then went back to my office.

When I told my coworker Jane what the petty cash clerk had said, she was totally shocked. She hadn't heard a word about any cuts to the department. The boss was out for the rest of the day, so I had to wait until the next day to find out what was going on. I was worried. If my job was cut anytime in the upcoming year, there might not be a good open position to which I could transfer.

That night, Gordy and I discussed the issue, and I explained my two options. Option one was to use my seniority to bump the least senior person in my category. According to the union contract, if my job was cut, my seniority in the "bookkeeping clerk" category would allow me to take the job of the least senior person in that category. But I didn't want to force that person out, as I would appear cruel to my fellow union members, even though the procedure was written into the contract to protect long-term members like myself. Option two was to apply for a recently posted bookkeeping clerk position for which I was qualified, and I probably had the seniority to get it.

I also knew that "Suzie the Slacker" had probably used her "talents" to influence the boss's decision on which position to cut. She knew full well the union procedures regarding position cuts, and getting my position cut was one way she could get back at me for speaking up for myself to the boss about her lying about me. I realized that I was in a tough spot, but I hoped the cuts might just be a rumor.

The next morning, I marched into the boss's office. I recounted what Suzie had said and asked him if it was true that my job was being cut. He hurriedly got up from his desk and closed the doors to his office.

He said it was partially true. After I asked what that meant, he clarified, saying that my position was only in the budget for the first six months of the year. I looked him in the eyes and asked, "Just when did you plan on telling me about it?" He mumbled something about sometime near June. I was quite angry, but I controlled my temper and suggested that maybe his secretary shouldn't have told the entire accounting department about it before he bothered to inform me about my position being cut. Again, he mumbled something about the fact that she shouldn't have said anything to anyone, which I agreed with. But I asserted that his decision to wait until June to tell me was unprofessional—not to mention just plain mean—and would rob me of the opportunity to file early for an open position.

I informed him that I was going to apply for the open bookkeeping clerk position in the accounting department, for which I was qualified. Without waiting for a reply, I walked out, went to the bulletin board, and signed the posting. The fact that I was the most senior clerk in the category ensured I would get the position, and I would not have to bump another clerk out of her job in June. I knew the job transfer would take place in a couple of weeks.

Jane was shocked when I got back to my desk and told her what had transpired. Actually, everyone in the building was quite surprised when they saw my name on the posting, even after I explained the situation.

During my interview for the accounting position, my future supervisor expressed concern about my being the union steward and working in accounting, with access to the company payroll. However, there was nothing in the contract against it. With my qualifications and seniority, I got the position and moved to the accounting department on October 11, 1984. I was happy to get away from Suzie, and I was eager to start work in the accounting department—where smoking was not allowed.

CHAPTER 13

PLANS TO MOVE

Health Issues and Travel

The years in Elk River were good years for us. Gordy was teaching English and directing plays at St. Michael–Albertville High School. I helped him as much as I could with the plays, and I typed papers for his class handouts and tests. After we fenced our land, we were able to raise a few head of cattle and hogs. We had developed friendships with several of the teachers and their spouses, and we were able to continue attending plays in the Twin Cities, including all the plays at the Guthrie.

Our health was basically good, but a few issues arose over the seven years we lived in Elk River: More than once, Gordy's spine rendered him immobile for a few days, but he was always able to exercise himself out of it. After a spell of about six years where I didn't ovulate, my body suddenly started again, which seemed to require me to need a dilation and curettage procedure. Although I found the simple, outpatient procedure to be a bit scary, there were no bad results. Soon after, I had a brief scare when the doctor found a lump in my breast, but it was benign.

Without having to deal with farming in the summer, we started traveling, sometimes with friends and sometimes just the two of us. Our destinations included Ontario, Canada, for the Shakespeare-centric Stratford Festival; both sides of the border at Niagara Falls; and Tennessee, to visit friends. Given our proximity to St. Cloud and Minneapolis, Gordy started taking evening and summer classes, and after earning quite a few credits, he entered a master's degree program at the University of Minnesota. Life was good.

Buying the Farm

Although living in Elk River put us much closer to the Twin Cities and our parents than when we lived on our farm in Donnelly, the drive to visit our parents still took over an hour and a half. Assisting one or the other set of parents was often a once-a-week event. On one visit to Gordy's folks in late 1984, his mom and dad announced they wanted us to buy the remaining 70 acres of their 120-acre farm.

I have to admit that the offer hit us by surprise, but the enthusiasm shown by both of Gordy's parents got us excited about the prospect. We would have to build a house so his parents could continue living in their farmhouse, and this would take a bit of thinking and planning on our part. We didn't agree immediately, but buying the farm was all we could talk about on the drive home and late into the night. We both agreed that we wanted to do it, and his parents were happy to hear our affirmative answer. Gordy and I looked forward to living closer to our parents so we could visit and help them more often.

As we started to plan, we realized the process would take a couple of years. First, we would sell our place in Elk River and move into an apartment while we built a new house on the farm. After we moved, we would keep our jobs and together drive the fifty-five miles to Gordy's school plus another ten miles to my job at LPC. After we were settled, I would look for an office job close to our new house, and Gordy would look for a teaching job nearby too. We needed to be careful, though, because jobs in either of our fields were not plentiful. But we decided it was worth the risk. We put our house on the market and soon found an apartment in Elk River. Our farm equipment was moved to the new farm, and our furniture came with us, to the apartment, where we planned to live for a year while Gordy finished his master's degree at the University of Minnesota and while the new house was built on the farm.

Our First Computer

In late 1985, while we were living in our Elk River apartment, LPC announced an incentive plan for employees to purchase personal computers. The offer was for up to a $2,000 loan with interest-free payback through payroll deductions. For several years, I had been working at computer terminals for LPC's internal systems for inventory, purchasing, accounting, and payroll, but I knew nothing about the emerging personal computers and systems. Here was a chance for us to get into this new technology. I was the second employee to sign up.

After much discussion with the teachers at St. Michael–Albertville High School who taught and used these new computers, we found that Apple provided the easiest systems to learn, especially for word processing. In January 1986, we purchased an Apple IIc plus all the software offered with it. We also decided to buy the best dot matrix printer available, because in the college classes Gordy had been taking, professors would not accept papers printed on dot matrix printers unless the dot pattern was on the denser side, better mimicking a typewriter.

With no farm chores, I had plenty of time to learn how to use the computer. For practice, I typed up every single class outline, schedule, handout, and test that Gordy wrote for all his English classes.

The Big C

The next two years were hectic, but selling our place in Elk River and moving to the apartment went smoothly. In the spring of 1986, we started to build our new house on the farm.

Gordy had been attending summer sessions at the University of Minnesota to get his master's degree in English education, thinking it would aid him in getting another teaching job once we moved. And I had been saving up my vacation hours at work so that, during the summer, I would be able to do all the inside painting and staining at the new house, saving us money. And my parents would be happy to have me stay with them in New Market while I worked on the new house. Everything was in place, as we had planned, but it seemed life had something else in store.

Before I started my vacation, I had my annual physical, and the doctor removed a mole from my right calf and sent it in for testing. The following week, when I was back at work, the test result came back stating I had "superficial, spreading, *malignant* melanoma cancer, Clark's level 2," which sounded scary, but we didn't know exactly what it meant. After urgent phone calls with my doctor, my cancer specialist, and the American Cancer Society, Gordy and I digested the meaning: melanoma is a cancer that kills quickly. Luckily, mine was only level 2, which meant it had not yet reached my bloodstream, but it also meant I needed surgery as soon as possible.

I received that first test result from my doctor on Wednesday morning. Later that day, the cancer specialist called to recommend a plastic surgeon, and the surgeon was able to fit me in for a consultation the next day, Thursday, in the afternoon. Apparently, they weren't kidding about the "as soon as possible" part.

Thursday morning, the surgeon's office called me at work to verify that my husband would come with me to the appointment. They said it was vital he attend with me, but how could I contact him? Gordy had classes in the morning and then would go straight to the new house to check on the construction. There was no such thing as a cell phone, and there was no phone at the building site.

Hoping Gordy would stop in to see his mother, Helen, before he checked on the construction, I called her to let her know that Gordy had to be back in Elk River by half past one to pick me up for the doctor appointment. She said they would watch for Gordy, and if he didn't stop, his dad, Gordon, would drive up to tell him. Lucky for me, Gordy did stop in, and Helen gave him the message. He rushed back to pick me up, and we were off to the plastic surgeon.

The appointment scared the hell out of us. Prior to this whole ordeal, we'd had no idea melanoma was so deadly. The doctor detailed how much of my leg he would have to cut out and explained the skin graft that he would put over it. He scheduled the surgery for early Saturday morning, the earliest possible opening. I would be in the hospital about two or three days, and I would be on crutches for at least six weeks after the surgery. The surgeon informed me that there is no treatment other than surgery for melanoma. If the surgery did not remove all the infected tissue, I would have less than a 40 percent chance of living for five more years. We were stunned and seemed to drift out of his office in a trance. Suddenly, the new house and the move meant nothing. Our entire future together was in jeopardy, and I didn't want to die.

There was no time to console ourselves. I had to get back to work to let my supervisors know what was happening. I had a pre-op exam scheduled for Friday morning, while Gordy would be in class again, plus the house was still being built. We had to inform our families. Gordy's mom was understandably concerned but very supportive, asking that we call her as soon as the surgery was over. When I called to tell my mom, her reaction was not what I expected; she seemed more interested in talking about her neighbor's problem than the fact that her only daughter was having cancer surgery the next day. After I hung up, I felt disappointed and sad about her reaction, but I knew that denial was how she handled most negative events in her life.

Everything moved quickly. Early Saturday morning, July 19, 1986, I was wheeled into the operating room, where the surgeon removed a section of my right calf measuring about six inches long by five inches wide and about half an inch deep. He had to not only remove the skin and tissue directly below but also cut off the top part of the muscle. He covered the open wound with a large graft of skin taken off my right buttock and secured it to my leg with about forty-five stitches.

Three days later, after receiving physical therapy covering how to correctly use crutches, I was sent home with a soft cast of cotton batting and elastic bandage, stretching from my right foot to my right hip. I had strict instructions not to bend my knee because, if bent, the skin graft would be pulled and not heal properly. We were greatly relieved a week later when the test results came in. The cancer had been found only in the mole itself. No further cancer cells were found in any of the skin, tissue, or muscle—great news!

CHAPTER 14

AFTER SURGERY

I needed to heal so I could get back to my job. I had the vacation days saved, but I'd only painted for a week prior to my surgery. And now I couldn't do anything but stay home, sit in the recliner with my leg propped up, take my pain pills, and rest. Gordy still had to finish his classes at the University of Minnesota in the mornings, but now he also had to spend every afternoon and evening painting and staining the new house, which left me alone in the apartment all day. There was the danger of me falling as I tried to use the bathroom alone. And with no cell phones yet available, contacting others was tricky, especially if there was an emergency.

Lucky for us, I worked with Melissa, the wife of Gene, the maintenance man at our apartment complex. Since he was still in college, he was home during the day all summer. He had a key to all the apartments and would come over if I called him, but Gordy and I had to come up with a plan in case I couldn't get to the phone. We devised a system for checking on me: When Gordy left for college each morning, he would get me up, help me bathe, dress me, make me breakfast, and settle me in the recliner, with the phone next to my chair. Each day at noon, I would call my mother-in-law, Helen, but just before I called her, I would get up, go to the bathroom, and bring my lunch over to my chair. If I didn't call her at noon, she would know something had happened to me, so she would call Gene, and he would come over to help. Luckily, nothing bad ever happened. Although I never needed to call Gene for an emergency, he or Melissa would come over once in a while just to check on me. They would knock and announce loudly who it was, and I would yell back, telling them to come in. Knowing these two friends were there to help really made me feel more secure during my recovery.

I received many get-well cards from relatives and coworkers, which helped cheer me up. But the only people who actually came to see me—at least from outside our apartment complex—were Deb and Dan, a couple from work. I had worked with Deb, plus we had served as union stewards together, and Dan worked in the IT department. Shortly after my surgery, they arrived at our apartment with an arrangement of flowers in a chicken-soup bowl. Their visit really cheered me up. I still have that bowl, and whenever I use it, I think of their friendship and support.

In addition to working on the house every afternoon and evening, Gordy still had to complete his master's degree final, part of which involved creating and printing out a full layout for an English class, including daily class outlines, handouts, tests, and quizzes. I usually did all the typing for Gordy, but in my condition, I was not able to sit at a typewriter. But I remembered the many documents I'd created while learning how to use our computer, which I'd saved on a floppy disk (look it up if you don't know what that is). All I had to do was bring up the file, add the appropriate heading for his college course, and print it out. We adjusted the computer table to accommodate my elevated leg, and I was able to print out Gordy's materials in short sessions. Gordy was able to hand in his final and finish the course. Thank goodness we had that computer.

The oncologist had said the only option was immediate surgery, and there were no chemotherapy or radiation treatments for my melanoma cancer; they either got it all or they didn't. All I could do to prevent another melanoma outbreak was to avoid the sun, wear appropriate clothing, use lots of sunscreen, wear sunglasses (to avoid melanoma of the eye), and get yearly checkups with a dermatologist. I had to see the surgeon regularly for the next eighteen months, after which I would be eligible for reconstructive surgery on my leg.

After the eighteen months passed, the surgeon explained, in detail, all the pros and cons of the reconstructive surgery, which would involve placing a silicone implant in my leg and covering it with yet another skin graft. At that point, I really couldn't face having another surgery. Gordy and I agreed that the scar wasn't something grotesque; instead, we saw it as a wonderful reminder of how lucky we were to still be together after my close brush with death, so we turned down the reconstructive surgery. Many years later, we discovered that the type of silicone implant they would have used in my leg was the same type used in breast reconstruction, which often broke, causing pain, cancers, and death in many patients.

During my recovery, we also had to move from the apartment to the new house. There wasn't much I could do to help, but we set up a packing system for me. Before Gordy left in the morning, he would set several empty packing boxes on tables or cabinets in rooms, and I would stand and pack the boxes with items that were easy to grab without bending down or getting on a step stool. But in the end, Gordy did most of the packing. On moving day, Gordy's nephew Bob Tornio came over to help. He and Gordy did all the lifting and moving of boxes and furniture, whereas all I could do was stand and hold a door open as needed. This was an extremely frustrating experience for me, someone who had enjoyed being a strong worker and farmer.

Harassment at Work

My recovery was going well. I had progressed from using the cast of cotton batting and elastic bandage to a prescription Jobst stocking that came up to my hip. This stocking was much tighter than a normal one, meant to hold the skin graft in place and facilitate proper healing. It was also designed to keep my knee from bending, which would pull at the skin graft. I was only allowed to remove the stocking when I went to bed at night, after replacing it with a tight elastic bandage. For me to return to work, the doctor said, I had to be able to walk without crutches. I worked hard to handle walking, and I was finally cleared to return to work on Monday, August 25, 1986, six weeks after my surgery.

On Thursday of the previous week, my supervisor from LPC, Sam, had called me at our apartment in Elk River. Sam had always been a detached, cold supervisor who proudly displayed his muscled physique by wearing tight, short-sleeved shirts. He seemed to take pride in being unfriendly and abrupt, but I always managed to get along with him, and I looked forward to going back to work.

My feelings toward Sam and going back to work took a sharp turn when he called me and initiated a demanding and rude conversation. He made no inquiry about how I was doing or comments about my cancer, not even a polite hello. Sam just informed me that when I returned to work, I would *not* get my regular job back. Instead, I would have to learn a new job in the same division, under his supervision. Because both positions were the same level and classification, this would be allowed under the union contract. I was to take over for the person going on maternity leave in November, and Sam would hire a temporary person to handle my payroll position.

Sam made it extremely clear that this was *not* a request. His exact words were "You have no choice. The decision is made. You will do Lori's job." Sam almost shouted all this at me, never seeming to take a breath or give me a chance to respond—no chance for any discussion. Basically, all I could do was say I understood and that I would be in the office on Monday. With that said, Sam hung up. I had no objection to the new assignment, but I wondered why Sam had basically treated me like a bastard. Sure, he had been cold and detached with me before my surgery, but this kind of aggressive dismissal of my humanity was new.

The phone conversation left me shaken. My recovery had involved not only physical healing but also getting a grip on my emotions about the cancer and the possibility of my own death. I had been told that if the surgery didn't remove all the cancer, I would have less than a 40 percent chance of living five more years. I didn't need Sam's sympathy, but I had hoped he would treat me like a human being. Instead, he bullied me into agreeing to what could easily have been presented as a new opportunity. I tried to calm myself, but I knew that now, in addition to being worried about handling the pain of walking and sitting without bending my right leg at work, I would have to deal with the stress of learning a new job with a boss who was clearly hostile toward me. Gordy and I discussed the nature of the call, which helped some, but there was nothing either of us could do or say to prepare me for the harassment that would come once I returned to work.

When I arrived at work on Monday, most people were happy to see me back, but again, there was not one word of greeting or empathy from Sam. All he did was curtly inform me that Marge would be taking my place; he wouldn't even give me a date as to when she would start. Until then, I had to do payroll and all my other regular duties.

During the many greetings from my coworkers, I found out that none of them knew anything about my taking over for Lori during her maternity leave or about Marge taking over my payroll position. When I asked Sam about this, he said he would hold a division meeting to announce it sometime later in the week. Feeling that was unfair to me and everyone else in the division, I pressured him to have the meeting sooner, and he agreed to have it the next day, Tuesday.

At the meeting, Sam delivered the news to everyone in the same blunt, abrupt manner he had to me over the phone. He said he had made the decision, and that was that, seeming to give everyone who worked for him the bastard treatment. Again, he would not give a specific date when Marge would start my job.

On Wednesday of the next week, September 3, Sam came to my cubicle and informed me that Marge would start in my former position the next day and that she would be taking over my work area and computer terminal. He said that I would have to move all my things out immediately, including my personal items. When I asked where I would be moving, Sam barked, "Find someplace else to sit until Lori leaves, in November."

I was shocked. Why was he treating me this way? Granted, Marge would be doing my payroll duties, but I needed a space of my own to sit, organize all my files and journals, and work at a computer terminal; plus, I was also assigned to sit with Lori and learn her duties. Sam also informed me that he did not want me to sit in Marge's work area while doing any of my new duties because I would, supposedly, disturb her. And he did not want me to train in Marge because he was going to do that. Again, he said I needed to find somewhere else to sit.

That was too much for me. I pushed back, demanding that he find a work area for me. Finally, he said I could use the desk of his supervisor, Max, since he was out on medical leave for the next several months. But Sam insisted I not move any of Max's stuff. After I explained about needing space for all the files I had to take with me, he said he would clean out one drawer in Max's desk for my files.

The next day, before my shift started, I moved all my files and journals into Max's office, bringing no personal items with me. Even after I filled up the one allotted desk drawer, the top of the desk was still completely covered with files and printed journals. As I started to work, the people in this area of the accounting department would stop to welcome me to my "new home" and ask how I was feeling after my surgery. Each greeting helped lift my depression.

When the other accounting supervisor, Gil, joined several of his workers to welcome me to his area, he looked at the mess on the desk and told me to pack up Max's things and take over some storage space. When I explained Sam's strict instruction not to move any of Max's things, Gil looked a bit surprised. He said Max was out on medical leave, recovering from a heart transplant, and that the earliest he could be back at work was May of 1987, long after I would be out of there. Just as Gil started taking things off Max's desk, Sam entered the office, demanding to know what was going on. Gil told Sam his plan to move Max's things to give me more space to work. Sam looked angry but he couldn't argue with an accounting supervisor who was a level above him, so he just glared at me and growled, "How much room does she need?" Although Gil ignored what Sam said and continued to clear off the desk, I knew Sam's statement comprised a direct threat to me, a warning that I had better not move anything myself. Clearly, Sam felt I had already overstepped my bounds.

After getting settled in Max's office, I went to sit with Marge for a quick orientation about payroll entry. When I told her Sam intended to do the actual training himself, she looked puzzled; apparently, Sam had just told her that I was to do the training. I went to check this out with Sam, but he was not in his cubicle, so I went back and sat down to train Marge.

These next few weeks were extremely difficult for me. I was trying to train Marge and do all my other duties at the same time. Many times, this was physically challenging because the limited desk space in her cubicle left no room for the files I needed to reference, forcing me to walk back to Max's office, where my files and journals were located, then walk back to Marge's cubicle to assist her. Walking was still painful for me, and when I sat, my right leg needed to be elevated, per my doctor's instructions, making getting up and sitting down time-consuming.

Sam's harassment never seemed to ease, becoming more difficult to endure every day, and I had no idea why he felt the need to treat me that way. Whenever I requested time off for my many mandatory doctor appointments, he became irritated but grudgingly approved the time off.

But when I was in the office, often training Marge, he would keep reminding me that all my other duties still needed to be completed. Then, on top of everything else, he suddenly gave me two special projects that he needed completed "right away." When I reminded him that I also had check vouchers to complete, he just said, "Work on it!"

The next day, Sam came into Marge's cubicle, where she was entering time sheets and I was working on my check vouchers. He demanded to know why I wasn't also entering time sheets. When I told him that there wasn't another computer terminal available, he said nothing, turned, and walked away, which led me to think he'd been more interested in yelling at me than in actually having me enter time sheets.

I finished training Marge in payroll, and in November, I took over Lori's duties, as planned, but I also continued doing all my other duties. The pressure was immense at times. I kept hearing rumors that I was the floater clerk for the whole accounting department, which was not the position I had been promised *before* my surgery, and it was definitely not the position that Sam had told me I would come back to *after* my surgery.

I confronted Sam about the rumors, and he confirmed that when I returned from my surgery, I had, in fact, been assigned to the floater position, not a bookkeeping position. When I asked why he had lied to me, he just said that the decision was made, it was all according to the union contract, and that's all I needed to know, as if doing things according to union contract gave him permission to keep me in the dark. It was his way of wielding his power. Sam also told me that once Lori returned to work, I would be assigned to another area of accounting, working under Gil, but Sam would continue to be my direct supervisor.

I discovered that working with Gil was a welcome reprieve from Sam's constant harassment. And as Gil and I worked on special projects together, I learned a great deal about different aspects of accounting. Gil was easy to work with and kind, which encouraged me to tell him about Sam's behavior toward me, especially how he'd handled placing me in a new position without my knowledge. When I told him about Sam's rude phone call, Gil was shocked. He said that his understanding of my position move was that Sam had asked me about the new position and that I had agreed to it. (Gee, more lies from Sam.) I told Gil exactly what Sam had told me—that the decision had been made and I had no say in it.

Gil then told me the full story: He had wanted me in the floater position because he knew I was a good worker, I could learn new skills quickly, and everyone in accounting liked to work with me. He had personally requested that the position be offered to me. Wow, what a difference in attitude! Here was a supervisor who valued me for my skills, and yet Sam had purposely withheld that bit of praise from me. I'm not sure of Sam's purpose in lying to me, but perhaps it was his method of control. His actions reminded me of the motivate-by-intimidation method used by the nuns when I was at school. Or maybe it was like the school board members at Gordy's first teaching job, who felt that degrading their employees would gain them an edge. Likewise, Sam was a supervisor who didn't want to make me feel like a valuable person or employee.

By this time, I had heard so many different tales about which job position I actually held that I needed verification from the accounting manager, so I asked for a meeting with him. At the meeting, I explained my understanding of the whole story, adding how the confusion and harassment was affecting my ability to do any job well. The accounting manager seemed surprised. He explained that I, indeed, held the floater position and that, according to Sam, I had agreed to the change. I explained to the manager that although I had no objection to the position, I took issue with the way Sam had handled the whole process—keeping me in the dark and never offering me a choice. The meeting ended with me knowing I was now the floating accounting clerk. I thanked the manager for his honesty.

The accounting manager must have had a meeting with Sam after our meeting, because Sam stormed up to my desk and demanded a meeting with me in the conference room. He was furious. He accused me of stabbing him in the back, undermining him, and going over his head after he had already explained everything to me. I maintained that he had lied to me and kept me in the dark.

During his tirade, he kept contradicting himself. Apparently, his own lies were confusing him. He then went into a long attack about how bad the office union was and how poorly we union stewards ran it. I simply said I would not, could not, discuss any union business with him.

Sam went on to accuse me of not liking him, saying he couldn't understand why.

"After all," he asserted, "my wife and kids like me." That statement shocked me. What in the world did that have to do with work?

I responded by saying, "Maybe you treat them nicer than you treat me." That ended the meeting. I returned to work as the floating accounting clerk for Gil, which I enjoyed because his group was great, plus it taught me more about accounting. I began to enjoy working again.

I think Sam's rant after my meeting with the accounting manager revealed the basic weakness that made him mistreat me. He hated that unions empowered individuals and decreased what he thought was his right as a boss to make decisions based on favoritism and whim. Unlike a confident, effective supervisor who knows how to motivate people without intimidation, Sam was lost without his ability to bully and demean others.

During my time as the floating accounting clerk, I became good friends with all the accountants. And I learned so much from each of them about the company's entire accounting process. By late summer in 1987, Marge had left the department, and I was permanently assigned as the payroll clerk, with Sam as my immediate supervisor. Sam's supervisor, Max, had returned from his medical leave in the spring and was back as an assistant manager, with Sam reporting directly to him. Insecure about his supervisory and accounting abilities, Max was easily manipulated by an aggressive male subordinate like Sam. Max's lack of competency was exemplified when, one time, he entered a figure as a credit instead of a debit. It took two accounting clerks over an hour to convince him that his entry was wrong and another hour to convince him he needed to debit the amount not once but twice to correct the error.

When I moved back to payroll, I asked Sam and Max who they would be assigning as my backup and when I could start training them in. They said they would inform me when I needed to know. I knew that, sooner or later, I would be requesting vacation, and over the next seven months, I kept reminding Sam and Max about the need for a backup payroll clerk. They always told me that they would tell me when I needed to know. I didn't understand why they kept putting it off.

For seven months, I didn't take any vacation or sick leave near a payroll deadline, but it was now 1988, and I wanted to take some vacation. In January, I asked to take three days off in February. After I handed in my written request, Sam stormed into my cubicle and told me I didn't have a backup for payroll, so he was going to deny my vacation request. I told him I had accumulated several weeks of vacation time and had every right to use it. I reminded him that I'd asked about a backup many times, with no action taken on their part. I also played the union card, specifying that I had the vacation time coming per the union contract and that if he didn't approve my vacation time, I would take it up with the accounting manager and/or HR.

Sam yelled at me, saying he was the supervisor and he could refuse any vacation request he wanted—more of his dictatorial behavior. My bastard training kicked in, and I calmly replied, "Go ahead and refuse it, then." Sam grabbed the vacation request and marched down the hall, to Max's office, and slammed the door. Everyone in the near vicinity could hear loud voices coming from Max's office. Suddenly his door burst open as both Sam and Max rushed down the hall, toward the accounting manager's office, shooting me deadly glares as they passed my cubicle.

After only a few minutes, Sam and Max quietly left the accounting manager's office and slinked back to Max's office, with all onlookers witnessing their strange behavior. A short time later, while I was busy working at my computer terminal, a piece of paper came flying at my head. I turned around to see Sam standing in my cubicle. He glared at me and growled, "Train Jean as your backup." Then he abruptly turned around and stomped away. The paper he'd thrown at my head was my approved vacation request—unbelievable! Although I felt insulted by Sam's unprofessional delivery, the action was consistent with his past unprofessional behavior. I knew this was how I was going to be treated from then on, but I also knew I could handle any bastard moment he threw at me.

The next day, the accounting manager's secretary stopped at my cubicle and asked where I was going on my three-week-long vacation. I was stunned! After I said I wasn't taking a three-week vacation, she looked puzzled and said that Sam and Max were in her boss's office the day before, expressing outrage because I was asking for three weeks of vacation. Surprised, I explained, "I put in for three *days* of vacation, and they weren't even consecutive." She laughed loudly and exclaimed how ridiculous it was for Sam and Max to have such a fit over someone requesting three days of vacation. I wondered whether they had even read my request and whether they even knew what they had approved.

I continued serving as a union steward and tried hard to conduct meetings during breaks, lunch, or after work, if possible, but any union business handled with HR had to be done during working hours. Yet every minute I spent on union business was criticized by both Sam and Max, who berated my position and accused me of handling union business on company time. This accusation was made during department meetings and in discussions with other supervisors. Any time there was a mistake made, Sam tried to blame me for it, and I would have to defend myself, even for the mistakes he had made. Every time anyone stopped to talk with me, Sam or Max would quickly walk to my cubicle to eavesdrop, hoping to catch me talking about personal stuff. Whenever I requested vacation or sick leave, they thoroughly questioned the need and the amount before giving approval. The constant harassment was brutal, and it took a huge toll on my health.

I was fortunate that during my dealings with the accounting manager, the position had been held by two different men, who were both solid, experienced professionals. These men could recognize the lies and misdeeds of their subordinates and were confident when making bold decisions. The first had occupied the office during the no-smoking controversy, and the second during the period that Sam was harassing me. Without their positive management skills, events could have turned out much differently.

One Coworker's Critique of My Scar

Regarding my cancer issues, as you might expect, my coworkers were generally kind and sympathetic, but not everyone at work was understanding about what it is like to face death from the Big C. One bookkeeping clerk, in particular, subjected me to a number of bastard moments through her comments.

After my doctor told me I no longer had to wear the Jobst stocking, my surgery scar became visible. It was a large, indented area on the calf of my right leg, nearly a half inch deep, six inches long, and five inches wide. The skin graft covering the wound was pinker than the rest of the skin on my leg, and the stitches had left marks around the wound. I wore slacks most of the time, but the graft was sensitive to touch, and slacks sometimes chafed, so I would occasionally wear a long skirt that covered most of the scar.

Many people were honestly curious and asked me if they could look closely at the scar. No one made any disparaging comments, except for a young, single bookkeeping clerk in accounting who lived with her domineering boyfriend. She didn't like my scar, and she made sure I knew how she felt. The first time I wore a skirt, she told me how horrible it was for her to be forced to see my scar. She claimed it was so disgusting to look at that it made her want to puke. She vehemently expressed that I should be more considerate of the people who had to work near me, saying I should wear only slacks or really long skirts to hide the horrible scar.

The first time she threw this accusation at me, I was so shocked and hurt that I just wanted to crawl away and hide. It took all my effort to not break down and cry. For someone recovering from cancer surgery, statements like this are extremely devastating and cruel. Contrast her behavior with those kindhearted folks who get their heads shaved in support of cancer survivors who have lost their hair. No, I didn't want anyone to cut a chunk out of their leg to show support, but I could never understand the point of her cruelty. If my scar bothered her, she needn't look at it.

Some time passed before I had the courage to wear a skirt to work again, but by that time, her cruelty didn't have the same effect. From then on, I would only stare back at her or just reply that she's lucky it was me that got the cancer and not her.

The Funny Side

I learned not to view all my cancer moments as depressing; instead, I looked for the humor. For example, after wearing the Jobst stocking and not bending my knee for six months, I'd experienced severe muscle loss in my right leg, especially around the knee. The doctors did not prescribe any type of physical therapy, just telling me to "work on building up strength." Yeah, I didn't know anything about physical therapy at the time, and apparently neither did the doctors.

I bought a stationary bike with adjustable resistance, thinking it could help. I started using the bike to build up my knee strength, but due to how long my leg had been stabilized, progress was slower than I would have preferred. During this time, I continued work as normal, and sometimes my weak leg would get me into some strange circumstances. One day at work, I needed a particular form, so I went into the supply room to get some copies. The form I needed was, of course, on the bottom shelf, only a couple of inches off the floor. I knelt to grab some copies, and then it hit me—I couldn't get back up. I had no strength in my right leg, and I couldn't balance well enough using only my left leg. I couldn't grab on to the shelf because it was merely lightweight metal and would fall on top of me if pulled. There was no one else in the supply room, and the nearest cubicle was far enough away that I would have had to scream for help, which I would've found too embarrassing.

"Okay, okay, don't panic," I said to myself, wondering whether I should just relax and wait for someone to come in for supplies. *Heck, that could take all day or longer*, I thought. *What else could I do?* Looking around, I saw a sturdy table near the door, at the other end of the supply room. *I could use that to pull myself up*, I thought, *but it's all the way over there. How could I reach it?* Yeah, you guessed it. I crawled on my hands and knees—which was actually rather painful on my right knee—all the way across the room, dragging those stupid forms with me. Once I got to the table, I was able to grab the top edge and pull myself up using my left leg and both of my arms. It wasn't pretty, but it worked. I got up, brushed myself off (that floor needed cleaning), and looked around, embarrassed, hoping nobody had seen what had just happened.

Then it hit me—this entire episode was funny. In fact, it was downright hilarious. I started to giggle, then I broke out laughing. Just then, a coworker walked in and looked at me—all alone in the room, standing by the table, laughing—and asked what was going on. I told her the whole story, and she started to laugh too. Before the end of the working day, everyone in accounting knew about the incident. From that day on, we would bring up the story when we needed a good laugh.

Len's Retirement Party

In 1987, nine years after my sexual harassment encounter with Len, I was still a union steward. Things were changing in the world for women, and I had learned a great deal about our legal rights from the union representative out of the Twin Cities. Len's secretary, Chris, no longer worked at LPC, and I had moved to the accounting department in the headquarters building. Len was scheduled to retire the next Friday, and the staff in the headquarters cafeteria busied themselves baking cakes for an all-employee party to send him off, sending delicious aromas wafting around the building.

On Tuesday of Len's retirement week, one of the staff from the mail department, which was in the headquarters building, came to me, her union steward, with a problem. It seemed that the new mail girl, Lily, was being harassed by Len whenever she went to that building to deliver mail. Lily was young and afraid of losing her job, making her unwilling to talk to me on her own, but her coworker told me the frightening story of how Lily had been terribly harassed by Len. I called the other union steward to inform her of the problem, and we decided to meet with Lily that day.

We convinced Lily to confide in us. Apparently, Len had immediately taken an amorous interest in Lily when she started at LPC. Every day, when she did her morning and afternoon mail runs to the other building, Len would greet her at the door. He would follow her around the building, trying to get physically close to her and making her extremely uncomfortable. She asked him to leave her alone, but he ignored her requests. Lily said that, one day, Len even waited in his car, which he'd parked right next to hers, and then followed her home. She saw him do this several more times, and he even drove past her house over the weekends. Lily said she'd reported all of this to her immediate supervisor, but all her supervisor said was the standard "Just stay away from him when you are in that building." Now Lily was extremely worried about what would happen when Len retired. Would he be waiting for her at her home when she returned from work or from shopping?

The other union steward and I agreed this was serious. We asked Lily to come with us to HR to report it. She was understandably hesitant, as her supervisor hadn't taken any action, and she worried about losing her job if she went to HR. Telling Lily we'd get back to her, the other union steward and I called the union representative at the OPEIU and asked for advice. The representative said the issue had to be reported to HR, and since the union member had spoken to us, her union stewards, we could report it to HR and file a grievance on her behalf. He added that the situation comprised a serious legal violation by Len, and if it was not properly handled, the company could face legal trouble. After we shared this information with Lily, she agreed to come with us.

That Wednesday, the other union steward, Lily, and I met with the assistant HR manager to lodge a formal grievance against Len. As we told the assistant HR manager the story, her eyes kept getting larger, and she became nervous and on edge. After we explained that Lily's supervisor knew about the harassment and had done nothing, the assistant HR manager jumped up and said she would be right back. After several quiet minutes of waiting, she returned with her boss, the HR manager. Both seemed nervous.

We related the entire story again for the HR manager, who asked Lily several clarifying questions. The HR manager asked us to stay there while he and his assistant manager went back to his office for a few minutes. Soon, the assistant HR manager returned with the security team leader, a former county sheriff who had been assigned to provide full security for the company and all its power stations throughout Minnesota. The security lead informed Lily that he or one of his assistants would be following her home each night to make sure Len did not come near her. He also said he had reported Len's harassment to the Elk River police and the county sheriff, including the make and model of Len's car as well as the license plate number. The police said they would be making regular drives past Lily's house to make sure everything was good. She was to call the police immediately if she sensed any problems.

After more discussion, the security lead left, and the HR manager came back to talk with us. He apologized to Lily that she had to endure such terrible treatment and that her supervisor had not supported her when she reported it. He assured all of us this would be handled immediately and that he would personally work hard to make sure nothing like this ever happened at LPC again. More apologies came from the assistant HR manager, with assurances that if Lily needed anything else, she should come to HR immediately. The HR manager said he would follow up with the union representative after our meeting, and we said we would do the same. After more discussion, the meeting broke up and we went back to our desks.

That HR leaders were tripping over themselves to apologize to Lily demonstrated to me that they knew the company could be found in violation of Lily's rights, especially since she had reported it to her supervisor and nothing was done. At this point, I had no idea what would happen to Len, but it looked like he could be in serious trouble. I held hope there would finally be some justice for women in the working world.

When I returned to accounting, the place was buzzing with excitement, and I was immediately surrounded by my coworkers as they asked about the meeting. I said the meeting was confidential, so I couldn't discuss it, but I asked them what the heck was going on to cause such commotion. They were happy to tell me everything they'd heard and seen. First, there would be no retirement party on Friday for Len. The cafeteria staff had been told to stop baking cakes, to put what they had in the freezer, and to cease all other party preparations for Friday. Second, the HR manager, accompanied by security personnel, had gone to Len's office and told him he was fired— not retired, but fired! He was to leave the company grounds immediately. Len was informed of the harassment charges against him, that the charges had been reported to the police, that he was never to go near Lily again, and that security would also be following Lily home and making sure Len did not go near her. If Len went near Lily, he would be arrested, and the company would file charges against him. Len was then escorted to his car and followed off the company grounds. Other employees had witnessed all this activity, and everyone in all the buildings was talking about it.

I also found out that Lily's supervisor had been called into HR with her boss, the accounting manager. With much crying, apologizing, and groveling, the mail department supervisor was able to save her job, and after that, she was one of the most steadfast supporters of workers' rights. No one ever harassed anyone in her department again.

Seeing Len finally meet his demise as a habitual sexual predator was a spectacular moment for all the women at LPC, even though it was way overdue. I was one of many who were overjoyed to see him leave in disgrace. I still feel frustrated when I think about all the women he harassed for so many years, many of whom were single or had no support from a husband at home. I wish I could have done something sooner. We need to remember that workplaces that support those fraternal-like, good-old-boy environments will continue to exist as long as misogyny is legitimized by business and political leaders and allowed to become something to which young men should aspire.

Transition and Insurance

Gordy and I had transitioned to our new home in the fall of 1986, and from then on, we drove to work together. Gordy got out at St. Michael, and I drove on to Elk River. During the summers, when Gordy wasn't teaching at St. Michael, I drove to work alone. The trip took one hour in the morning, but the trip home in the afternoon would take up to two or more hours because of traffic. Changing jobs was not an immediate option for me because of my cancer surgery; my diagnosis meant I was not eligible for new insurance. We learned this hard fact when we tried to get mortgage insurance on our new home. The agent told us that because I'd had cancer, no insurance company would insure me. Most insurance companies required that a person be cancer-free for a minimum of eight to twelve years before a policy would be approved. Luckily, our agent found a clause in our current mortgage insurance that stated it could be rolled into a life insurance policy without any conditions. It wasn't the best, but it was something. We took it.

Getting medical insurance was another problem. I had medical insurance through LPC, and Gordy had medical insurance through St. Michael–Albertville School District. Getting on Gordy's insurance without an exclusion for cancer treatment could only be done at certain times during the contract years. The next such period wouldn't happen until late in 1987. Consequently, I had to continue working at LPC and continue buying their medical insurance, but Gordy added me to his medical insurance as soon as I was eligible. We also had to verify that my cancer was covered on this insurance before we dared to have me change jobs. By May of 1988, we were able to verify that Gordy's medical insurance was covering me for everything, opening up the possibility of changing jobs. On May 19, 1988, I turned in my official resignation letter, stating my last day of work at LPC would be Friday, June 3, 1988.

In recognition of my status as union steward, I was given an exit interview with the HR manager. During that interview, I detailed the treatment I had been subjected to from Sam and Max. The HR manager was, of course, a company man and was more than a bit defensive as he tried to support Sam and Max. I added that I had the notes and evidence to support my grievance. That seemed to put some fear into the HR manager. I warned him Sam was a terrible supervisor and that he would continue to be a detriment to the work environment in accounting. For me, though, that was LPC's problem, because I was leaving and off to a new adventure. In July of 1988, I was offered a job at a nearby telephone company.

A Call from My Replacement

During my final year at LPC, there was a huge push from management to pressure the clerical staff to dissolve their union. I had campaigned strongly against this, but after I left the company, management succeeded in convincing the clerical staff they no longer needed the union, and the members voted it out.

Often, those who benefit from the sacrifice of others take things for granted, perhaps thinking, *I'm sure the managers will treat me just fine. I don't need a union because I am talented and can negotiate on my own.* I suggest they remember that people died so that others could have a forty-hour week and be treated fairly. The high wages in many labor-intensive jobs were negotiated because people joined together, not because each employee visited the boss to explain how valuable they were. If you give someone absolute, unchecked power over you, they will abuse it. History shows that to be true in every case.

A few years after I left LPC, I received a call from the woman who had been hired to take my place as the payroll clerk in accounting. She explained her current situation—that her treatment from Sam, my former and her current supervisor, had been so nasty and unpleasant that the stress caused her to become ill; that she'd had to go out on disability; and that she no longer worked for LPC. Without a union contract supporting her and her disability, LPC was easily able to terminate her employment. Now, although she was getting back on her feet, she was still unemployed, and she had contacted a lawyer to file a lawsuit against LPC, naming Sam.

She knew from talking with other employees that I had experienced similar issues with Sam. She said her lawyer wanted to discuss my issues to add credibility to Sam's history of treating employees unethically. Apparently, Sam had become even more unreasonable after the union was voted out (surprise, surprise!), and the clerks no longer had a union contract to protect them. I agreed to speak with her lawyer. I had kept all my extensive notes concerning my treatment from Sam, but it took me a few days to go through them. Her lawyer called about a week later, asking many detailed questions. I explained my experience, including my warning about Sam to the HR manager during my exit interview. The lawyer seemed happy with my story and said it provided proof of previous employee mistreatment by Sam. I never heard back from the woman or her lawyer.

CHAPTER 15

LIVING ON THE HOME FARM

A New Routine

Neither Gordy nor I have ever been averse to change. Change is as much a part of life as breathing, and nothing stays the same for long. However, it seems the changes that are the most inevitable are also the most dreadful, like watching parents lose some of their independence as they age.

After we moved to the farm where Gordy had grown up, we quickly settled in and learned to love the place. We had built the house on a hill in one of the fields where Gordy had helped his parents till the land, pick rocks, plant crops, cultivate corn, shock grain, and haul hay. The only downside was that because it had been a field, there were no trees. So in 1987, which was our first spring living there, we planted over five hundred trees to make a windbreak northwest of the house.

During the first few months on the farm, I learned to live with the threat of cancer returning, and I thought of the possibility often as we continued driving the long distances to our jobs. The long drive ended when I took the job at the telephone company, which was only a ten-mile drive from our new home. Wages and work conditions were good there, and I was now able to get insurance coverage for both of us. Also, Gordy would be free to look for a new job without being concerned about a gap in insurance coverage.

In the spring, Gordy opened his file at the University of Minnesota so they would send him job applications from Minnesota schools. We soon discovered that jobs were scarce, especially if the candidate had a master's degree and many years of teaching experience, two of Gordy's qualifications that, by law, mandated a higher starting salary. Gordy had several good interviews, but he always returned from them expressing disappointment, saying the school districts were more interested in what he could do for the extracurricular program than what his exceptional classroom experience and knowledge of his subject could offer the students in the classroom.

Resigning from a job without having first secured another is not a good plan, but after two years of driving to his job in St. Michael and applying for jobs elsewhere, he decided to resign anyway, risking his teaching career. A month after he resigned, the state department offered him a lucrative job that paid nearly double what his teaching job had—a truly exceptional offer. Gordy was excited about the prospect of working for the state, and he liked the job description, which would have required him to travel to schools all over the state, with expenses paid. But when we discussed it, we agreed that a traveling job would defeat the purpose of living close to our folks. It would mean being away from me, our folks, and the place we were learning to love more and more. When he turned down the job offer over the phone, the man at the state department exclaimed, "I can't believe you're turning it down!" Such was Gordy's commitment to being around our folks.

Now, I had to get used to being the main breadwinner of the family because every job he took after that paid significantly less than I was making. Determined to make the better of it, I settled in to enjoy the gift of living in a new house on the farm where Gordy was raised.

We were in our forties, a time when it is easy to become complacent with the term *middle-aged*, as if one actually had another forty years of youth left. We took for granted any advancements in work and successes on the farm, and we framed setbacks as "a bit of bad luck we can overcome." As we often said—and still do—life was grand.

We visited our folks often, and Gordy's mom, Helen, would call me at work to leave a voice mail a couple of times a week. I'd check my voice mail and hear her sparkling voice. "Stop by and pick up some fresh cinnamon buns," she'd say, or "I baked some kolaches. Stop by and pick up a bagful." Other times it was apple pie or some kind of bars. To those who asked how I liked living so close to my mother-in-law, I would just say, "Yeah, it's really tough. Twice a week, she bakes us fresh pastry. They invite us over on Friday nights and insist we drink their beer and eat their snacks." Gordy's folks were really fun people to visit, always joking and laughing and sharing stories. Gordy and I often look back at the great times we had with them every Friday after work.

Gordy was able to mow their lawn in the summer and clear their snow in the winter. He had made a special driveway from their yard to our driveway so we could visit and drink a few beers without driving on the main road to go home. Gordy also rigged up the waterers and cattle feeder so his dad, Gordon, could do the chores easily, which kept him feeling useful and gave him some good exercise. Visits to my folks' place also grew in length and frequency, and Dad enjoyed coming out to hunt on our land. Mostly, I think, he just enjoyed walking around on it.

Those first few years working at the telephone company were great. The supervisors appreciated skilled clerical workers, and as I progressed in the company, I had new learning opportunities. For example, in the 1990s, I was instrumental in setting up the equipment for the first videoconference between schoolchildren, who were visiting our offices, and the NASA training center in Texas. Things were going well at my job.

Dad's Death and the Halloween Blizzard of 1991

Our move to Gordy's homeplace also made it much easier to assist our folks with their paperwork for insurance, medical appointments, house repairs, and other needs. Our house was only about two hundred yards from his parents' house and only five miles from New Market, where my folks lived. My parents started depending on us to review, explain, and answer all letters or calls they received from insurance companies, doctors, and other businesses. This took pressure and stress off their minds, and although it put some added stress on us, we were glad to be there for them. It had been the primary reason we moved back to the area, after all.

On October 20, 1991, my folks, Gordy, and I were invited up to the home of Cyril and Peggy Schoenecker (my uncle and aunt), in Hopkins, for an afternoon. We all enjoyed the visit, and I took several photos. Everything was fine when we drove my parents home, but sometime after ten that night, we got a call from Mom saying Dad was not feeling well. She was understandably upset and scared.

When we arrived, Dad was sitting in his chair, looking really pale. Mom explained his symptoms, which we thought sounded like a heart attack, but Dad insisted it couldn't be a heart attack because his left arm wasn't tingling. We finally convinced him to let us drive him to the ER in Farmington. There, we explained his symptoms to the ER doctor, but Dad kept insisting it wasn't a heart attack, citing the lack of tingling in his arm. After the doctor did an EKG, he informed us that Dad would be immediately admitted to the hospital.

Once Dad was settled in his ICU room, he insisted we all go home. When I called the hospital the next morning, I was informed that Dad had a massive heart attack around three in the morning, but because he was in the ICU, the staff was able to help him within seconds. He was now resting comfortably. The doctor asked a cardiologist to review Dad's condition, which required additional examinations and tests over the next several days.

When the cardiologist called me with his assessment, he said Dad was terminal. Apparently, Dad had been having small heart attacks for the last twenty years or so, each one destroying a small piece of his heart. When I asked about surgical options, the cardiologist said that Dad didn't have enough heart muscle left on which to operate. In fact, he couldn't explain how Dad was still alive with so little heart muscle. His recommendation was for Dad to stay in the ICU, where they could monitor him for the little time he had left.

After explaining Dad's condition to Mom, I asked whether she knew about any small heart attacks. She explained that shortly after I got married, Dad didn't feel well and went to the local doctor. The doctor told Dad he was suffering from indigestion and recommended he take Alka-Seltzer. Well, that story explained why Dad was always taking Alka-Seltzer, tapping on the left side of his chest, and saying he had indigestion. I had wondered why he tapped the left side of his chest, which is the heart area. Indigestion, specifically acid reflux, is felt in the middle of the chest. Obviously, that doctor's diagnosis was wrong, but Dad never retreated from the diagnosis of indigestion. The doctor certainly should have known better, especially since Dad had been seeing him for this problem for over twenty years.

It was hard for all of us to hear that his diagnosis was terminal. We adjusted our schedules as best we could to visit him every day. Mom would visit by herself during the day, I would come right after work, and Gordy and I would pick up Mom and head to the hospital for evening visits as a group. Dad was a big baseball fan, and the Minnesota Twins were in the World Series at the time. We had brought Dad a Homer Hanky from home, but one of the ICU nurses brought in another for Dad to have at his bedside while he watched the games on TV. I remember watching some of those games with Dad when I got there after work, which created comforting memories for me.

After Dad had been in the hospital about a week, I began wondering why no one else was visiting him. Finally, I called his nephew Dennis Simon, thinking maybe he didn't know Dad was in the hospital. But Dennis said he'd called and talked to Dad several times. Dad had told Dennis he would be going home soon, so Dennis thought it would be better to visit Dad once he got home. Sadly, I had to inform Dennis that Dad wouldn't be coming home. Dennis said he and his wife would be at the hospital the next day. If Dad told Dennis he was coming home, I assumed he had told others the same story. I called some of the other relatives, and it seemed they all thought Dad would be home soon. From then on, Dad got many visitors.

The weather reports forecasted that a huge winter blizzard would hit the Midwest on October 31, Halloween. Many relatives thought they might not be able to visit Dad during the blizzard, so the day before, on October 30, 1991, Dad had visitors all day plus that evening. His room was packed for much of the day. When we left that night, I said good night to Dad and promised to see him the next day. In good spirits, he said, "See you tomorrow." I thought he seemed at peace. Maybe his faith was working for him.

Gordy and I went to work the next day, as usual, but at about nine o'clock, I got a call saying Dad had just suffered a massive heart attack and passed away. We both left work, picked up Mom, and drove to the hospital. From there, we called the mortuary to make arrangements. While we were on the phone with the mortuary, the first snowflakes started to fall. That day, we made all the arrangements for the wake and funeral, went to the florist to order flowers, and called the relatives who would serve as pallbearers. We had arranged for Dad's wake to be held on Sunday, at the funeral home in Lakeville, with the funeral the following Monday, at the church in New Market. By the time we left Mom's house that Thursday night, the blizzard was raging—we barely made it back home. Since Gordy and I were on bereavement leave from work, we did not plan on going to work until after the funeral.

By Friday, the blizzard was in full swing. The airport, schools, offices, even all the shopping centers, including Burnsville Center—all closed. The formidable storm dumped about twenty-eight inches of snow in our area over a three-day period. That Saturday, we realized the snow was so deep on the pole barn's roof that we should shovel it off before the roof collapsed onto our cattle. Gordy and I shoveled for most of the morning.

When I came in shortly after noon to take a break, I got a call from the florist. Because of the blizzard, she couldn't get any flowers delivered, and all she had for Dad's funeral was enough for one casket bouquet. This hit me hard, and I broke down in tears. I just couldn't let Dad have a wake and funeral without more flowers. I started calling every florist in the area, with absolutely no luck. Every place was closed. Finally, I called Lakeville Florist, and when someone answered, I told her my situation and asked if she had flowers to make at least one large floral funeral arrangement. She timidly asked whether I wanted any particular flowers. "No, it can be any type or combination of flowers," I quickly said. At that, she said she had enough to make a large funeral arrangement and that she could deliver it to the White Funeral Home in Lakeville by Sunday afternoon. I gave her my credit card number and thanked her profusely.

By Sunday morning, the snow had stopped. The roads were partially plowed, and Gordy plowed out the yard and driveway. He shoveled snow off the roof of his folks' house, and I helped him shovel snow off our roof. That afternoon, we picked up Mom, whom we hadn't seen since Thursday, and the three of us headed to White Funeral Home for Dad's wake. The roads were terrible, but we made it.

As promised, Lakeville Floral had delivered the large floral arrangement. It was beautiful! It contained every type and color of flower that you can imagine. The florist later explained to me that she had to clean out her entire cooler of flowers to make it. I told her she did a wonderful job of putting it together and that I would always remember her kindness. She didn't know me personally, and she could have said no during this major blizzard, but she understood my situation and was determined to serve her customer. We continued to do business with her for many years, including for Gordy's parents' funerals.

On Monday, the sun was shining for Dad's funeral, but the temperature was frigid. Many people were unable to attend the wake and funeral because the roads were still covered in snow and slippery. After the funeral and burial, we took Mom back to her house in New Market. We knew that Mom's roof would need to be shoveled off, so we had brought along our chore clothes and shovels. We climbed up on the roof to discover waist-deep snow in most places. We shoveled for hours, unafraid of falling off the roof because the deep snow on the ground served as a perfect safety net. This was quite a workout, not a normal after-funeral chore.

The next day, I drove Mom to several appointments to handle some legal items regarding Dad's death. Again, the roads were deep with ice and ruts, so driving was terrible. It was lucky that we finished our appointments in the morning because another snowstorm set in. Gordy had returned from leave, but he had to take some time off without pay for the funeral. I was much more fortunate. My supervisor at the time told me that since I, too, was an only child, he understood all the legal issues that I had to handle. The company officially allowed for three bereavement days, but he told me to take as many days as needed and that he would sign my time sheet for full pay. To have a supervisor be so understanding and generous was a great comfort. At a later time, I was to experience a supervisor at the other end of the empathy scale.

CHAPTER 16

MURPHY BROWN AND THE VICE PRESIDENT

Murphy Brown was a comedy television series that originally aired from 1988 to 1998. Candice Bergen won five Emmys and two Golden Globes for her portrayal of the title character, who was single, independent, a reformed alcoholic, and a top news reporter. In the 1991–1992 season, Murphy discovers she is pregnant. After learning the father didn't wish to marry, Murphy decides to have the baby and raise the child on her own.

As these episodes were being aired, Vice President Dan Quayle, in an effort to claim family values in the presidential campaign, publicly condemned the show as well as single mothers across the country. He criticized the series by saying, "It doesn't help matters when primetime TV has Murphy Brown . . . mocking the importance of fathers by bearing a child alone and calling it 'just another lifestyle choice.'" Critics quickly responded that it was unrealistic to insist that family values could not exist without a man in the picture, and my memory went back to my years in grade school, where the nuns emphasized that a family must have a father in the house.

On Thursday, May 21, 1992, three pictures topped the front page of the *New York Times*: Vice President Dan Quayle, Candice Bergen (as Murphy Brown) cradling a baby, and White House Press Secretary Marlin Fitzwater. Below the vice president's photo was his statement from his speech two days prior, and below that was a statement he'd made the next day, in response to the criticism: "I have the greatest respect for single mothers. They are true heroes." Apparently, someone had reminded him that single mothers can vote.

Wednesday morning, however, Marlin Fitzwater stuck to a hard message, saying, "The glorification of the life of an unwed mother does not do good service to most unwed mothers who are not highly paid, glamorous anchorwomen." But only a few hours later, the White House softened the message by adding, "The Murphy Brown Show [exhibits] pro-life values which we think are good."

However, when Candice Bergen won another Emmy that year, she thanked Dan Quayle. In one episode of season 5, the character actually addresses the VP as she looks into the camera. She says, "These are difficult times for our country, and in searching for the causes of our social ills, we could choose to blame the media, or the Congress, or an administration that's been in power for twelve years . . . or we could blame me."

I confess that the national condemnation of a mom raising her child without a father really hit me hard. Although I was forty-four at the time and had put my bastard identity behind me, I felt as if my family was being nationally scorned by the vice president and the party to which he belonged. I wondered whether this was how all Republicans felt about single mothers and their children, about my mother and me. Granted, I should have had more confidence in my friends, and it may have been unfair to take the VP's comments personally. But honestly, was there any other way to take it? Should I have assumed Mr. Quayle was referring to all other single mothers and their children, but *not me*? That would be quite a stretch.

CHAPTER 17

CHANGE, LOSS, AND NEW CAREERS

After my stepfather died, in 1991, I thought Mom might feel freer to enlighten me about her past and my beginning, that she might finally be able to tell the truth and not worry about Dad's feelings or his focus on his standing with the church. I was never more wrong about anything in my entire life! Mom lived until 2009, eighteen years after Dad died, and she never volunteered to piece together the story of her past for me. Regardless of how delicately I brought up the subject, she would simply say she didn't want to talk about it. Apparently, she was prepared to take her secrets to the grave.

In the years that followed Dad's death, though, her demeanor was lighter. The pressure of pleasing her neighbors and other church members seemed to decrease a little, and our conversations were less tense. She was free from dealing with Dad's anxiety, which had begun to drag her down over the last decade or so of his life.

In the 1990s, although Gordy and I were busy with work and farming, we enjoyed visiting Mom often. She was happy at her house, yet she longed for more company. Mom had always been social, talkative, and eager to visit with people, and although she attended senior functions and church functions, living alone in the house provided her few opportunities to see other people. We encouraged her to sell the house and move to a senior living apartment, but like most elderly homeowners, she proclaimed her love for the independence her home afforded.

During the same general time frame, we continued regular visits with Gordy's folks. But by the mid-1990s, our visiting slowed down considerably. Helen had to have a pacemaker installed, and her eyesight continued to weaken, making it more difficult to cook, clean, can, and garden. Gordon found that feeding our cattle had become a bit too much for him, so we sold the cattle and just raised hay for sale. By 1996, he'd worn out the artificial hip installed eighteen years prior, so he needed a new one. After the surgery, he never seemed to fully recover from the anesthetic. He spent some time at Mala Strana, and when he returned home, he was slow to recover.

Accustomed to working hard all their lives, Gordon and Helen continued to pitch in wherever they could, and they especially enjoyed working together, which they'd done for much of their life together. It was no surprise, then, that when Gordy and I started a big garden in 1987, they eagerly volunteered to mark the rows. Marking the rows of a big garden is time-consuming, as each row can measure fifty feet long or more. Although we loved gardening, neither Gordy nor I especially liked marking rows, but Gordon and Helen loved it. I think it took them back to the days when they worked outside together and took great pride in their physical ability to get things done. They usually were still marking the garden when I got home from work. As I started planting, I could visit with them at the same time. With their help, I was able to spend more time on the parts of gardening I actually enjoyed. And they seemed happy as long as they were working in the garden together.

Although we both worked long hours, Gordy and I continued to attend every play produced by the Guthrie Theater, and we found time for a couple of vacations to attend the Stratford Festival, in Canada. We also visited Europe a few times: London in 1993, Dublin in 1997, and Lyon (France) in 2004. Other trips over the next couple of decades included nine of the Canadian provinces, all fifty of the United States, and a couple of trips Gordy won at work, one to the US Virgin Islands and another to Arizona. We visited many national and state parks as well as Wine Country, in California. Life was grand.

The Big C, Again

In October of 1998, doctors discovered a tumor in Gordy's colon, and surgery to remove it confirmed the tumor was malignant. The good news was that the cancer was totally contained in the colon, meaning no radiation or chemotherapy was needed. The effects of having over a quarter of his colon removed, however, would stay with him for the rest of his life, but he was glad to be alive.

Gordy's Mom Passes Away

A few days after Gordy returned from the hospital, his mother, Helen, entered the same hospital for her heart, which was no longer able to handle her body's fluids—a hereditary heart condition. She was in and out of the hospital and nursing home for a few weeks and enjoyed the company of the other people and the nurses. It's a tragedy Helen didn't get to enjoy the nursing home experience for long, because no one appreciated being cared for more than she did—she had never experienced the leisure of having others cook and clean for her. Every time we visited her, she told Gordy how wonderful everyone in the hospital or nursing home treated her. She told the staff too, and they loved her for it.

In mid-December, after spending a few weeks at home, Helen was taken to the emergency room with heart issues. Children and grandchildren waited in an adjoining room as a trusted doctor told Gordy she didn't have long, but they could keep her comfortable with drugs for quite a while. Gordy remembered his mother's telling him she would like to live to be eighty years old, and he informed the doctor, Dr. Mark Berg, of her wishes.

"When is her birthday?" asked Dr. Berg, keen reverence in his voice.

"She will be eighty in about three weeks, on January 10," Gordy said evenly.

"That's doable," the doctor replied gently.

Gordy had the tough conversation with his mom, and she grasped the news with her usual, direct manner of handling all things real. Soon, she was transferred to Mala Strana, where she received good care from their kind staff.

Although she was on her back in the hospital bed and bridled to oxygen tubes, Helen was in high spirits when we presented her cake on the morning of her birthday. I'd made her favorite: a two-layer yellow cake with chocolate frosting and coconut generously sprinkled on the top and sides. She broke into a wide grin when she first saw the cake, and she bit into a piece with the energy of a ten-year-old. Although she was unable to eat much of it, she put on a good show to let everyone present know how much she enjoyed the cake and their company—the best of hostesses, even until the end.

The small birthday celebration brought back wonderful holiday memories. Every Christmas Eve afternoon, we would visit Gordon and Helen—gathering around the kitchen table, opening gifts, and enjoying her wonderful homemade cookies and candies. Gordy and I loved her special homemade buns, cinnamon rolls, and—my favorite—poppyseed crescent rolls. Helen loved that their kitchen window faced ours, providing a great view of the colored Christmas lights I hung there every year, and she made a point of saying as much. That was Helen—appreciative of every detail. She passed away on February 7, 1999, at eighty years old, but I continued to hang those Christmas lights for her long after she was gone.

Gordy gave a moving eulogy at Helen's funeral, and afterward, Mom told him, "Do you suppose you could find some kind words to say about me after I die?" Gordy and I were both struck by her sincerity and directness. Gordy quickly replied that, of course, he could, and it was then that Mom told us she didn't want a church funeral, only a ceremony at the funeral home in Lakeville. She also requested that we ask her nephew Ambrose Eischens, a Franciscan Brother, to come and say some prayers. She made it clear that Gordy should give her eulogy.

I had no idea at the time, nor could I have ever imagined, that our complying with Mom's wishes would result in my being condemned by my Catholic supervisor at work, creating bastard moments for weeks before I retired. More on that later.

Challenges for Gordy's Dad

Gordon was lost without his companion of over sixty years, and why wouldn't he be? They almost never went anywhere without each other, and their teamwork on the farm was legendary.

Gordy didn't know what to do for his father. Yes, they were close as father and son, but the hole in their hearts left by Helen's death could not be filled. We had meals brought in for him, and a nurse visited to handle his medical needs twice a week. Gordy's sister Judy lived nearby and tended to their father when she could, and their sister, Joyce, who lived farther away, visited him with family members too. Gordy helped him bathe regularly and spent time visiting with him daily. But nothing was enough to ease his pain, which he expressed only by being uncharacteristically reticent.

Gordy checked on his dad before going to work in the early morning, and he stopped to visit with him after work every day. We both feared something might happen to Gordon during the long hours he was alone, but he was closed to the idea of moving to a nursing home. Our fears became reality one day when Gordy stopped by for his after-work visit and found his dad on the floor. "I've been here since this morning," he exclaimed, "and I can't get up." His artificial hip prohibited him from maneuvering to rise, and he had lain on the floor for over seven hours, exhausting himself as he kept trying to get on his feet. As Gordy picked him up to carry him to his car, Gordon asserted, "I want to go to the nursing home where Mom was."

Gordon recovered quickly in the emergency room, and Gordy, after discovering Mala Strana had a waiting list, searched for another suitable place. Within a few days, Gordon was transferred to the only home available, a huge, understaffed facility, unable to give the homey, personal care that Mala Strana offered. Gordon didn't like it there because they did not allow him to walk around on his own, but Gordy convinced him to be patient because he was next on the waiting list for Mala Strana. After a month, Mala Strana had a place for him, and he transferred there. Over the next year or so, Gordon enjoyed the freedom of walking around and visiting everyone. The nurses and other staff loved his spirit and how he always brought joy to everyone. That was Gordon. He passed away on March 6, 2001.

Changes for Mom

In 2001, Mom injured herself when she fell while getting up from her easy chair. She called me at work. I told her I would come to her immediately, but I insisted she call 911 after hanging up the phone because the first responders could get there sooner than I could. She was hospitalized with a dislocated shoulder and eventually needed surgery and physical therapy. She lost some functionality in her arm and spent some recovery time at Mala Strana. To her surprise, she found she liked living there and elected to stay—the place was perfect for her. Nurses handled her regimen of medication, and whenever she wanted company, she could walk the few yards to the commons and find a card game, a table with a jigsaw puzzle, or a group that just wanted to talk. Some of her old friends from New Market were there too, so she had people with whom she could reminisce.

For us, visiting her at Mala Strana was much preferable to visiting at her house, where she always had tasks for us to complete. Of course, we were happy to help her in whatever way we could, but a visit at her apartment meant no tasks and more time for relaxing discussion. I had been doing her laundry since Dad died, and I continued to do so as she lived at Mala Strana. She was in a happy place, and our lives were all better for it.

New Careers

During one of our first driving trips, we visited the Buffalo Bill Center of the West, in Cody, Wyoming, where we saw the original farmhouse where William Frederick "Buffalo Bill" Cody was born. The house had been moved from its original location, in Scott County, Iowa, to be near other tributes to Bill Cody in the town he'd built and named after himself.

Although Gordy and I were from a "Scott County," in Minnesota, we'd been unaware of other instances of the name. Later, while Gordy drove to our next destination, I checked our road atlas and discovered a total of eleven Scott Counties in the United States. Even more interesting to us, the states in which they were located were contiguous: Minnesota, Iowa, Missouri, Kansas, Arkansas, Mississippi, Tennessee, Kentucky, Virginia, Indiana, and Illinois. Gordy and I loved road trips, so it was only reasonable that we decided to visit every Scott County in the United States. Over the next several years, we managed to accomplish this task, meeting many interesting local residents and discovering fascinating places far from any regular tourist path.

A decade earlier, after Gordy moved from teaching to the business world, he finally found the time to try his hand at writing. He started writing a novel during his lunch hour and at night. During this time, we had my Apple IIc computer, so every night I would take Gordy's handwritten pages and type them up. After he finished his first novel, he decided to search for a publisher. We sent the manuscript off to publishers and got back rejections, many of which were based on the fact that the novel was set in rural

Minnesota and/or had a farm-related subject. That discouraged Gordy, but he kept writing and thinking of different stories.

After Gordy's mom passed away and his dad was moved to a nursing home, he decided to write a story that took place on a small farm. He considered the kind of novels written by Laura Ingalls Wilder, but he thought he wanted something shorter, for young children. He came up with his idea on the Friday after Thanksgiving in 1999. I took this day off every year, freeing me to decorate for Christmas. On that day in 1999, when Gordy came home from work, he discovered my collection of old Christmas books, which I had displayed on a table near the Christmas tree. On top was my old copy of *The Night Before Christmas.* Gordy grabbed the book, stared at it, and then paged through it.

This book was written in 1822 by Clement C. Moore, but like millions of other people, we read it every year. The fact that people were still buying Moore's book in 1999 inspired Gordy's idea: a heartwarming family story based on a special Christmas when he was a little boy on the farm. It wasn't long before he put together his first children's book in rhyme and meter. We called it *County Road Christmas Eve.* For the illustrations, we tapped a former neighbor (from Donnelly) we knew did some cartooning, and he accepted the job.

With the words and illustrations completed, we set out to find a publisher. Unfortunately, most of the publishing companies were in New York City, and none of them seemed interested in a Christmas story set on a small Minnesota dairy farm in 1950. After much discussion between the two of us, we finally just said, "Fuck New York publishers!" We knew we had a great story, and we decided to publish it ourselves. Gordy registered the copyright with the Library of Congress. We found a printshop that would print out the pages, and being an experienced office worker, I was able to put them together using a comb punch and plastic comb bindings. With our books complete, we set out to sell them.

We had previously started a company with friends called Two Guys from Scott County Inc., but after Gordy and I decided to work on selling our own books, we wanted to legitimize the business endeavor and sell books under the name. We discussed it with our friends, and they agreed to sell their half of the company to us. We knew that the book alone wouldn't draw many eyes at a vendor booth, so we created other merchandise to sell. We came up with several clever ideas for T-shirts and caps, and after some research, we bought heat-press equipment and made the merch ourselves. Stocked with shirts, caps, and our new book, we registered to sell at local events.

We quickly learned to manage our sales expectations. One vendor told us we were a decade late. "Things turned sour after 2000," he said. "In the 1990s, people swarmed to vending booths with their wallets open, ready to buy anything. But not now." We struggled to make sales at events, but we did learn which events were profitable and which were a waste of time and money.

People seemed to like our book, and a good friend of ours, Diana Sawdey, asked Gordy if he would put together a presentation of his book for her third-grade students—she was sure they would not only enjoy the program but also learn some details about farming. As incentive, she said Gordy could offer the book for sale to the students before the presentation. Another friend, Nancy Terhark, wanted Gordy to give the same presentation to her third-grade students. In December 2000, Gordy gave his first school presentations for both teachers' classes. The teachers and students loved it, and Gordy had a great time too. Plus, we sold some books! We credit Diana and Nancy with initiating the start of Gordy's new career doing presentations at schools, libraries, historical societies, club meetings, and farm shows. (Over the next several years, he would do programs at over one thousand different places, for over fifty-two thousand kids and adults.)

For the next eight years following our early success, we kept busy doing presentations and selling books, T-shirts, and caps at events. I expanded our merchandise to include tractor calendars and note cards that I made from my photographs. Gordy kept writing until we had ten titles for sale. By this time, we had purchased new computers and a color laser printer, so I not only assembled the books but printed all the pages.

In late 2007, we realized we needed a more professional format, including a barcode as well as a more durable binding. Things had been changing in the publishing business, and small publishing companies were emerging in Minnesota. I did some serious internet searching and found a local company that sounded good. We submitted a copy of *County Road Christmas Eve* and got a call back, asking us to come in for a meeting—which turned out to be the beginning of a long and prosperous relationship.

Milt Adams, the founder of Beaver's Pond Press, liked our book and Gordy's goals for it. Milt envisioned a niche audience of thousands who would enjoy farm stories. Even though Milt was a city guy, he had worked on his relatives' farm and understood the need and the market for farm stories. One piece of advice from Milt that I will always remember was printed on a huge sign above his desk: "Think outside the bookstore." (We continue to take this advice and focus on schools and craft shows, rather than trying to market our books to bookstores.)

We signed on to publish with Beaver's Pond Press. Gordy rewrote *County Road Christmas Eve* to be a bit more professional and gave it a new title: *A Farm Country Christmas Eve.* Gordy hired a nationally known watercolor artist to illustrate the new version, and professional editors and layout designers from Beaver's Pond Press put the book together and sent it to a Minnesota printer. Knowing the publishing business, Milt gave us wise and practical advice for marketing and selling that remains valid two decades later.

Unfortunately, Milt left us way too early, passing away in 2012. We continued working with Beaver's Pond Press, redoing our existing books and producing new ones. By 2020, when we published our fifteenth book with Beaver's Pond Press, the company had gone through much growth, a couple of new owners, and many staff changes. But through it all, the company retained its personal relationship with us and other authors.

During all those years that we produced books, we maintained full-time jobs and faced many obstacles. Nurturing Mom through her final days and dealing with our own medical issues led to a number of serious bastard moments, some of which challenged and changed our lives.

CHAPTER 18

THE FLU SHOT SAGA, 2000–2008

When the needle slid into my arm on November 29, 2000, I couldn't imagine the challenges it would force me to confront in the years that immediately followed, and I never expected the moment would change my life forever.

For several years, the phone company where I worked had offered employees a flu shot at a discounted price, with the company paying for most of it. I always signed up for the opportunity because it was a good deal and convenient. We simply had to walk upstairs to the boardroom to get a shot, which was professionally administered by a nurse from a nearby medical center (later referred to as "MC-1"). The shots at the phone company had become a routine with predictable results. I knew my arm would be sore for a few days before the pain subsided to stiffness, then eventually disappeared.

I stood next to a coworker as we both received our routine flu shots, and we chatted as we walked out together on our way back to our department. Within twenty minutes, I started feeling extreme pain at the site of the shot. I dismissed the pain at first, thinking it was normal, but it increased overnight. At my annual OB-GYN checkup, the next day, the nurse noted that my blood pressure was higher than my normal low range. Over the next week, the pain continued to increase, and I decided I needed to see a doctor about it.

The following is a list of episodes that I label as bastard moments, dished to me over an eight-year period by doctors and clinic staff who seemed to see me as someone of no value, an unimportant old woman not worth listening to. Fortunately, the medical profession also abounds with excellent professionals, and their influence is what saved me from total disability.

The blow-by-blow account of my flu shot saga is long and tedious, which is why I decided to first provide a summary of the bastard moments, listed as B-1 through B-8. If one or more items in the summary raise questions in your mind, you can read my more detailed accounts, following the summary.

Flu Shot Saga, Summary

B-1: "Flu shot denial" by medical professionals caused needless delay in my diagnosis and subsequent treatment, resulting in permanent damage to my health.

B-2: One doctor—intentionally or unintentionally—failed to report my contaminated flu shot to the Centers for Disease Control (CDC), which set back my recovery and my settlement for years and may have endangered the health of others who received the contaminated vaccine.

B-3: A convenience-care doctor prescribed moist heat instead of ice, exacerbating my pain for days.

B-4: When I tried to follow up on my care, the clinics misdirected me—and it did not seem accidental. It felt like they hoped my complaint would just go away.

B-5: A clinic obstructed my treatment by withholding information about where the doctor who had diagnosed me with nerve damage had transferred to, delaying my medical treatment and allowing damage to my nerves and muscles to progress, unchecked.

B-6: After the cause of my pain and disability was correctly diagnosed—contaminated flu vaccine—another doctor dug deep in his medical bag of knowledge and blamed it on my "advanced" age. I was fifty-six.

B-7: A clinic obstructed my treatment by lying to me about not having records.

B-8: As time passed, my body suffered more damage, yet several doctors did not seem to grip the urgency. Instead, they delayed appointments. They failed to see that time between visits put me in more pain and caused more permanent damage.

What follows is a more detailed account that I constructed from a log of appointments and results, which I faithfully updated after each doctor visit. Unlike in B-1 through B-8, I include the positive experiences as well as the negative ones. I refer to the offending medical centers involved as MC-1 through MC-5 and name the doctors according to the order in which I started seeing them. Of course, I use real names for the clinics and doctors who actually listened and followed through.

First Doctor Visit—December 7, 2000, Dr. One, MC-2

I told Dr. One I'd received a flu shot on November 29, that pain started in the exact location of the shot twenty minutes later, and that the pain had continued to increase. Her reaction to my suggesting the pain was caused by the flu shot was to treat me like a fool, proclaiming, "The pain cannot be from the flu shot!" After her superficial examination, she gave no indication as to what else the cause could be. Her solution was to treat the symptoms, not the cause, prescribing a regimen of Advil and Tylenol.

I didn't know it then, but this was the beginning of what I eventually came to call "flu shot denial." My flu shot saga would last nearly eight years, but it could have been handled within a few months if the doctor had taken my specific complaints seriously.

Second Doctor Visit—January 23, 2001, Dr. One, MC-2

Dr. One remained deaf and blind to any possibility that my pain was from the flu shot, despite my repeatedly asserting that the pain started at the spot of injection just twenty minutes after the needle went into my arm. She began doing tests.

The first test revealed I had high blood pressure. (Months later, it was determined that the constant pain in my arm caused high blood pressure.) She took X-rays, which showed nothing, and she ran blood tests for muscle diseases that, no surprise, revealed no muscle diseases. While she continued shooting down the possibility that my pain was caused by the shot, she did finally admit she did not understand the problem entirely. She gave me a "tennis elbow" brace, put my left arm in a sling, recommended a regimen of Advil and Tylenol, and referred me to Dr. Two, who specialized in muscle problems.

My assessment of Dr. One's diagnosis—massive flu shot denial. Visits with her were nothing but bastard moments for me, and as she muddled through them, the contaminated vaccine continued to cause more permanent damage to my muscles and nerves.

Third Doctor Visit—January 30, 2001, Dr. Two, MC-2

By this time, the pain engulfed my entire left arm, from my shoulder to my fingertips. I was having trouble sleeping and was unable to do anything with my left hand, including typing, driving, or holding anything.

I was relieved when, in less than five minutes, Dr. Two concluded that the cause was, indeed, the flu shot. Someone had finally listened—and then believed me! He said the vaccine must have been contaminated and could therefore not be absorbed by my body. Instead, the contaminated vaccine remained in pockets of puss in the muscle of my upper left arm, causing inflammation. The inflamed muscle was causing a chain reaction of pain throughout my arm and shoulder. He said that without treatment, this chain reaction would spread throughout my entire body. Terrified by this prognosis, I listened carefully as he continued. He said that because it had been over two months since the shot and the pain had spread to my arm, hand, and shoulder, they needed to test for nerve damage before any treatment could start. Acknowledging the urgency, he scheduled an EMG for February 1, 2001, with Dr. Three.

Dr. Two said he would register the incident with the CDC and that, before he could do so, I needed to contact MC-1 to get the shot details— the manufacturer and lot number. He prescribed the same Advil-Tylenol regimen plus using ice on the arm. Later that day, I called MC-1 and got the required information, which I called in to Dr. Two.

I had been struggling with little to no sleep at night, and the day after seeing Dr. Two, the pain in my arm increased so much that I completely broke down crying at my desk at work. I called Dr. Two, who sent a prescription for Vicodin to my pharmacy. These pills decreased the pain enough for me to get some sleep.

I would not discover until three years later that Dr. Two failed to register the contaminated-vaccine incident with the CDC. He'd been on the right track, but he didn't follow through on this important step—another bastard moment for me.

Although Dr. Two's diagnosis momentarily ended the "flu shot denial" period, the attitude was quickly replaced with the beginning of "flu shot runaround" or "professional passing of the buck." Meanwhile, the contaminated vaccine continued to do more permanent damage to my arm. This medical muddling would drag on for another seven years.

Fourth Doctor Visit—February 1, 2001

Dr. Three administered the EMG. During the follow-up with Dr. Two a few days later, he prescribed ultrasound on the muscles around the site of the original injection, followed by electronic stimulation. Between February 14 and April 2, I received six effective treatments at MC-3. This was the maximum number of treatments covered by my medical insurance. By the end of the treatments, I no longer had to take Vicodin for pain, but my left arm remained extremely weak.

During my last treatment, the therapist mentioned having treated another patient for the exact same symptoms, also from a flu shot, but patient confidentiality prevented them from releasing the name to me. At the time, I considered that patient confidentiality was a convenient way for clinics to withhold incriminating facts.

My employer did not have sick leave, only paid time off (PTO), so between January and April of 2001, I used a major portion of my PTO for appointments, tests, treatments, and time at home, as sometimes the pain was so severe that I couldn't work at all. Because of my workload requirements, I had to make up much of the time I'd taken off, which was a real challenge because I could only type with my right hand, as I had to ice my left arm.

After the treatments, I never regained full strength in my left arm or full grip strength in my left hand. My blood pressure decreased some, but it remained in the high-normal level, never returning to its pre-shot level. My muscles continued to hurt constantly, but whenever the pain became intense, Advil and Tylenol would help. I also used the tennis elbow brace and ice packs on a regular basis. I continued this routine for over two years, until June 2003, when the extreme pain returned, requiring me to seek medical help again.

Flu Shot Problems Return

When I awoke on June 29, 2003—two years and seven months after the initial flu shot—my left arm was starting to hurt, and by the next day, I was in extreme pain again. The next day, I called for an appointment with Dr. Two, but I was unable to get one. His nurse told me to seek a convenience-care clinic right away.

I went to MC-2, where the convenience-care doctor told me I was suffering from tendonitis. He gave me a brace and told me to put moist heat on the arm. I questioned the moist heat because Dr. Two had said to use ice. But the convenience-care doctor insisted I use moist heat, and he also prescribed Vicodin.

When I picked up the prescription, I discovered it was generic Vicodin, because my insurance would only cover the generic formulation. I got home, took the generic Vicodin, and put on the moist heating pad. The pain did not decrease, and I felt weak, nauseous, and dizzy. All I could do was stumble to the bed, collapse, and let myself pass out. The convenience-care visit to MC-2 was a waste of time and a setback in my treatment. Once again, the doctor did not listen to me.

The next morning, July 1, I was again in extreme pain. I tried the moist heat. It didn't seem to help, so I decided to try a pain pill again. Within a short time, I again felt weak, nauseous, and dizzy and had to get to bed before I passed out. I decided not to take any more pain pills. I resumed using ice on my arm and taking Advil and Tylenol as previously directed, which helped a little. Praise goes to Dr. Two's nurse, who called to check how I was doing. I told her exactly what had happened, and she suggested I come in to see Dr. Two the following Monday, July 7.

Somehow, I made it through the setup and cleanup of our annual Independence Day celebration, hosting over a hundred friends and relatives at our hobby farm. I honestly don't remember much about the day itself. I know I was in pain, but tried to keep a brave face. I don't think anyone except Gordy knew how difficult it was for me. He checked on me often, but there was not much anyone could do to help.

Doctor Visit on July 7, 2003

I saw Dr. Two at MC-2. He diagnosed me with tendonitis in the lower arm, which he explained was a result of the buildup of scar tissue in the upper arm. I asked about moist heat, and he emphatically said, "Use ice!" He thought I'd been having a severe allergic reaction to the generic Vicodin, which he listed on my chart. He also recommended a few stretches for my arm but no weight-bearing exercises. The tendonitis brace, Advil-Tylenol regimen, ice packs, and exercises helped me through any pain flareups until early 2004.

My takeaway from this is that Dr. Two prescribed pain relief but did nothing to actually treat the cause. Why not recommend a neurologist? Nearly four years had already been wasted with nontreatments.

Doctor Visit on February 9, 2004

I went to see Dr. Dan Berg, a general practitioner at Parkview Medical Clinic–New Prague, for a bad sinus infection. He prescribed the antibiotic Levaquin. After taking this drug for only a few days, my sinus infection cleared up, but I had severe adverse reactions to the Levaquin. I felt weak and had trouble breathing, my heart was racing, my shoulder muscles ached, and I couldn't maintain my balance. I wasn't dizzy, but when I thought I was walking straight ahead, I would veer left, walking into walls, the bed, or furniture. I was so sick that I could not even read; I would look at a word or letter, but I could not tell what it was. When I fell asleep, I would only stay asleep about forty-five minutes before waking up in a panic.

Doctor Visit on February 16, 2004

Dr. Berg said I was having an extreme adverse reaction to the Levaquin, and he added Levaquin and all fluoroquinolone antibiotics to my list of drug allergies. He was also worried about my unusually high blood pressure. He instructed me to monitor it at home or use the public blood pressure station at the pharmacy. He advised, "If it does not return to the safe range in a few weeks, come back in to see me."

Doctor Visit on March 16, 2004

When I saw Dr. Berg again, he prescribed hydrochlorothiazide to keep my blood pressure under control, and he wanted to know more about my medical history. I didn't realize it at the time, but seeing Dr. Berg and his taking an interest in me as a complete patient would be the beginning of effective treatment for my flu shot issues.

I explained the entire flu shot episode to Dr. Berg, adding that the pain had returned to my left arm during the past year. I emphasized the constant, sharp pain in my upper arm and how the muscles in my lower arm hurt when flexed. As the pain increased, I lost all grip strength in my left hand, and again, I was unable to type with my left hand.

Dr. Berg listened carefully and insisted I see Dr. George Adam, a neurologist. Dr. Berg also said he would check on the report Dr. Two had (supposedly) sent to the CDC, then report back to me. Dr. Berg was thorough—later that night, he called to say he couldn't find any record of the report on my flu shot with the CDC, but he said he would report it now. While still on the phone, Dr. Berg brought up the form on his computer, and we answered all the questions together, enabling him to officially file the report.

I came to really appreciate the personal concern and total follow-up of Dr. Dan Berg. His actions resulted in my being contacted by Marla with the Vaccine Adverse Event Reporting System (VAERS), a program comanaged by the CDC. After I shared the details of my story, she contacted every clinic involved to get copies of my medical records. When I asked about the report Dr. Two said he would file, Marla verified that no such report had been received. She said that the CDC follows up with a phone call if a case appears to warrant it. In my case, if the report had been filed in 2001, the CDC would have called me shortly after. The CDC continued to follow up with me annually for many years, and only after it was declared a "permanent condition" did they cease.

I continue to wonder whether Dr. Two or his clinic was at fault for failing to report the contaminated vaccine. Was that oversight an accident, or intentional? If intentional, who were they protecting? What were they afraid of?

I need to express my deep appreciation for the thorough follow-up provided by Dr. Dan Berg. He and his brother, Dr. Mark Berg, who worked at the same clinic, are known for *listening to their patients*. Gordy and I were so impressed with the two of them that we continued using that clinic for many years, despite other clinics being closer.

First Visit to a Neurologist

On March 24, 2004, I had my first appointment with Dr. George Adam, a neurologist at MC-4. Before examining me, Dr. Adam wanted to go over my history and symptoms. When I explained the first medical appointments following the shot, he asked when I had first seen a neurologist. He was completely amazed when I said he was the first I'd seen. He was further surprised and a bit upset that I had not been referred to a neurologist following my appointments with Dr. Two and my EMG in 2001.

After examining me, Dr. Adam thought I may have an almost classic case of Parsonage-Turner Syndrome, which in my case was caused by the contaminated flu vaccine. He also wanted me to understand that since it had been so long, over three years, since the vaccination, I would never get full muscle restoration in my arm and shoulder—it was too late for repair, and the muscles were gone.

Before Dr. Adam started any treatment, he wanted me to have a new EMG to determine the exact damage. His office scheduled it for April 13, with Dr. Four at MC-4, and over the next few days, I began absorbing the fact that my left shoulder, arm, and fingers were now permanently damaged. Never again would I be able to type or perform any tasks with the speed I had gotten used to before receiving the contaminated vaccine.

At this point, I felt my doctors had me on the right path to healing. Dr. Adam was a godsend and more, but I had no idea that my association with MC-4 would begin a long and nasty string of bastard moments.

Call from MC-4

On April 1, 2004, nearly two weeks before my new EMG, I received a call from MC-4 informing me that Dr. Adam was no longer with the clinic. If I agreed, Dr. Four would do the EMG follow-up. This was a kick in my gut because Dr. Adam had listened to me and understood my medical situation.

Of course, I agreed to see the new doctor because I knew scheduling with a different doctor would just further delay treatment. What choice did I really have? Also, per a request from Dr. Four, the scheduler had to change the time of my April 13 EMG. They changed it, but then on April 12, I got another call from MC-4, saying Dr. Four had a "family thing," and they moved my appointment to later in the morning.

Doctor Visit on April 13, 2004

At quarter to noon on April 13, the nurse took me to a room and commented that Dr. Four didn't have the EMG machine set up yet. Sometime after noon, Dr. Four finally arrived. I waited for the lengthy time it took him to set up the machine. The entire test was uncomfortable and at times quite painful. After the test, Dr. Four announced that everything was normal, but because the rotator cuff in my left shoulder was causing tendonitis, he urged me to see Dr. Five, at the clinic next door. The receptionist was to give me the information when I left.

I asked Dr. Four, "Since Dr. Adam indicated I had Parsonage-Turner Syndrome, did he think that could be causing the pain?"

Dr. Four snorted, and with what sounded like extreme disdain, he replied, "Dr. Adam may have diagnosed that, and you may have had that three years ago, but that would have cleared up within one year."

I asked if he thought the flu shot had caused this.

"Absolutely not!" he angrily replied.

I asked what he thought would cause this.

He condescendingly replied, "You're old. Old people can have problems develop."

I looked at him and proclaimed I had *not* injured the shoulder, I had *not* fallen, I had *not* been hit, and I had *not* strained anything.

He coldly said, "Old people can get this for no reason. People get carpal tunnel for no reason. You have a spur hitting the tendon to the shoulder, and you may need surgery. Dr. Five will determine that."

After hearing those responses, I didn't feel Dr. Four was worth talking to anymore. I stopped talking and just stared at him in an effort to absorb yet another bastard moment. Why was he treating me like I knew nothing? Was he trying to wave off issues related to the flu shot in an attempt to blame all my problems on routine aging? Absurd. "You're old" was his professional diagnosis. I was a couple of weeks short of being fifty-six years old, and he seemed to merely see me as an old lady. I'm not sure if he treated all women like this, or just those he considered "old," or whether the delay to see me and the scorn about Dr. Adam's diagnosis were planned subterfuge to distract from the clinic's errors in my flu shot treatment. In that moment, I realized my treatment had taken gigantic steps backward, but in addition to "flu shot denial," they added "old age" as a catchall cause of all my maladies. As I was experiencing this bastard moment, Dr. Four mumbled on about Dr. Five, then said he wanted a follow-up with me on May 4.

On my way out of the clinic, I stopped at the desk to get Dr. Five's information, and I asked about Dr. Adam. All the receptionist would say was that Dr. Adam was no longer with the clinic. I knew I never wanted to return to Dr. Four or MC-4, so the next day, I called the clinic where Dr. Five worked. When I asked for an appointment with Dr. Five, the scheduler asked me what part of my body had the problem. I said Dr. Four referred me to Dr. Five for problems in my left shoulder and arm. She then asked why Dr. Four would do that, since Dr. Five specialized in knees. She offered that Dr. Six specialized in the shoulder area and asked whether I would prefer to see Dr. Six. I agreed, and she scheduled me to see Dr. Six on April 21.

This left me confused and angry. Why would Dr. Four want me to see a doctor who specialized in knees when he clearly knew my problem was in my shoulder? After talking it over with Gordy, I decided I had no confidence in Dr. Four and would cancel my May 4 appointment with him after I saw Dr. Six.

Doctor Visit on April 21, 2004

On April 21, I saw Dr. Six at MC-5. After an X-ray, an examination, and a long discussion about my medical history, Dr. Six determined there was nothing wrong with my bones. He seemed sure that the pain, weakness, and other issues with my muscles and tendons all stemmed from the contaminated flu vaccine in 2000. He said I needed physical therapy to regain some muscle strength, but he did not think I would get all the strength back. Wow, even a bone specialist knew the pain was from the muscles!

At this point, I canceled my appointment with Dr. Four—what "old lady" of fifty-six would want to see him again?—and I inquired about Dr. Adam once again. They gave no new information, but I was determined to find him. After many phone calls, much internet searching, and almost begging the people at MC-4, I finally found someone willing to explain that Dr. Adam had moved to the Minneapolis Clinic of Neurology—eureka! I'd once again found the one doctor who knew what to do.

I called the neurology clinic and spoke with the scheduler. She said the earliest appointment he was taking was for July 19. Although that was nearly two months away, I grabbed it. She also asked whether I would take an earlier appointment if one became available, and I responded in the affirmative. She said, "That's what all his patients from MC-4 say." Sensing a pattern, I suggested that the other patients may have had as much trouble locating Dr. Adam as I had because MC-4 wouldn't tell me what clinic he moved to. She was shocked to hear this. The people at Minneapolis Clinic of Neurology had no idea that MC-4 was refusing to inform Dr. Adam's patients where he had moved.

A question I did not ask the scheduler, but one that remained on my mind, was *Why would MC-4 want to keep Dr. Adam's new location a secret from his former patients?* Was it because Dr. Adam was the only neurologist who clearly understood how MC-4 had bumbled my treatment—and possibly the treatment of others—after the flu shot? I immediately requested all my medical records from MC-4 and MC-5 be transferred to Dr. Adam at his new clinic. The long, painful wait for my appointment with Dr. Adam would be worth it.

Doctor Visits, July–December 2004

I resumed seeing Dr. Adam on July 19 and continued seeing him as scheduled until my last appointment with him, on December 3. During those visits, I underwent many tests and months of physical therapy. Besides the EMG, I had two MRIs, a lumbar puncture, scores of blood tests, and many X-rays. One MRI showed a lesion on my spine. Dr. Adam also referred me to Dr. Randall Schapiro, a neurologist and one of the best multiple sclerosis doctors in the Midwest, and Dr. Ralph Shapiro (no relation), an immunologist.

All three doctors agreed that all my pain and weakness resulted from the contaminated vaccine and the delayed treatment. They agreed my condition was permanent. I would have to have physical therapy and train myself to live with pain, but before I could start physical therapy, the cycle of pain had to be interrupted. To accomplish this, Dr. Adam tried several different prescription medications, including prednisone and nortriptyline. The prednisone helped with my pain, but once I stopped taking it, as planned, the pain returned even worse. When I tried nortriptyline, I had a severe adverse reaction to it. It was then added to the long list of medications to which I am allergic. Luckily, in the short time I took nortriptyline, it managed to interrupt my pain cycle enough that the pain did not return as intensely. Hoping the flu shot saga was over, I started physical therapy in August 2004.

Doctor Visits and Recommendations for Vitamins and Food

By December 2, 2004, my physical therapy was complete, and I had my final appointment with Dr. Adam. Like Dr. Ralph Shapiro, Dr. Adam suggested I start taking really good vitamins—not the ones available at grocery stores, often containing fillers—to rebuild my immune system.

Dr. Adam also wanted to treat my frequent migraines, which he thought were due to an allergy. He suggested I stop eating processed sugar and only use natural sweeteners, like honey and maple syrup. He explained that processed sugar is made using a chemical that leaves residue on the finished product, which he thought was a likely cause of my migraines. He also said it would be fine for me to see a good chiropractor to help with minor pain flareups.

On December 28, I started seeing Dr. Loren Stockton, DC, and I started taking the multivitamins available through his office. The price of these special vitamins was high, but I needed to take them without fail. It would take years to build up my immune system again, and because it was so weak, I was unable to fight off many illnesses.

Between December 2004 and the end of 2006, I developed many infections in my sinuses, ears, and throat, and I got pneumonia in both lungs, which spread so thoroughly that doctors needed to give me a lung biopsy to verify it wasn't lung cancer. During the first sinus infections, my immune system was so weak that I required a shot of one antibiotic and two oral courses of another, Zithromax, to get me through. Because it took so long to get over these illnesses, doctors required me to have many X-rays and CT scans to ensure the illnesses were not getting out of control.

Research and Settlement

During 2004, I did some internet research about the flu vaccine I had received in November 2000. With the information from MC-1, I was able to look up the pharmaceutical company and discover where my vaccine had been manufactured. The manufacturer was in England, and they'd been closed down for "unclean practices." According to my research, the specific vaccine I received had been banned for sale in Europe, but someone got it approved for sale in the US, and it could, apparently, be distributed without having to inform recipients about any issues. (Gordy and I joked about some sleazy mobster calling US clinics saying, "Hey, I can get you a deal on flu vaccine.")

At the end of my last appointment with Dr. Ralph Shapiro, he had advised me to contact a law firm about my adverse reaction to the flu vaccine, and he gave me a name and number to call. It was the law firm of Conway, Homer, and Chin-Caplan, in Boston, Massachusetts. In November 2004, I called their office and was told they would take my case. The federal government had just changed the rules for applying for compensation from adverse reactions to vaccines to include the flu vaccine. A law passed by Congress and signed by President Reagan in 1986 had excluded pharmaceutical companies from being sued, but compensation for sufferers had recently been added and was retroactive for up to eight years. I fit into the time frame.

Because the changes to the law were so new, it would take the law firm a while to completely research my case, and they told me it would be quite some time before they got back to me. I was just happy they were handling my case. My case became active by June 2006, and I worked closely with the law firm through 2008, when my application for compensation was approved by the judge.

During these years, I gathered and sent everything concerning my shot—medical records, written statements from my supervisors and coworkers, plus affidavits from two coworkers who witnessed my receiving the shot. Yet not everything went smoothly. I experienced what I would definitely call bastard moments from three different sources.

The first source was MC-1. When I called them to get copies of the shot records, listing the lot number and manufacturer name, I was told that information was unavailable. I found that odd, as they had given me the information over the phone back in 2001. After several more phone calls, one supervisor stated those records had been destroyed. That seemed strange, so I researched the Minnesota law covering such practices. According to what I found, the records in question were far too recent to have been destroyed. I was ready to file a formal complaint with the Minnesota Attorney General's Office, but I first decided to call the law firm for advice. The law firm told me to try one more threat, and if that didn't work, they would initiate legal action against MC-1.

The next day, I called the same supervisor back and told her my lawyer said if MC-1 didn't find the record, my law firm would file a subpoena for all the labor records for all their nursing staff for the week I had been given the shot, in an effort to prove there were two nurses from MC-1 at my workplace the day I received the shot. The supervisor was quick to end the phone call, but within twenty minutes, I got a call from the records department saying they had "just found" the medical records concerning my shot and would fax them right over. Gosh, that was fun.

Gordy always reminds me of a line from Shakespeare's Henry VI, Part II—"The first thing we do, let's kill all the lawyers"—said by a criminal named Dick the Butcher. In context, it is not meant to disparage lawyers but, instead, indicate that criminals fear lawyers because they are the only avenue to justice for the common person.

The second source of bastard moments was my medical insurance company, Blue Cross Blue Shield (BCBS). One day in the midst of all of this, I got a call at work from them, telling me that any payment I received from my lawsuit against the pharmaceutical company would first be applied to my medical bills through BCBS. This really made me angry. I corrected the BCBS rep and explained what I'd learned—I wasn't suing any pharmaceutical company, because pharmaceutical companies were immune from lawsuits per a 1986 law, but funds are set aside by the government for special issues with vaccines. I told her that if they wanted payment for those medical bills, they could sue the pharmaceutical company themselves. Then I hung up.

Later, I called my law firm and asked if BCBS would actually try to bill me if I got a settlement. The lawyer assured me that was absolutely illegal, that any compensation money I received was tax-free and that BCBS had no right to try to claim any of it. Because of the flu shot, I would have to take blood pressure medication and expensive vitamins for the rest of my life, so I wanted any money I received to go, in part, toward covering those expenses, and the fact that my typing skills were dramatically reduced put my office job in jeopardy. The effects of the flu shot negatively impacted my career and would continue to do so.

The third source of bastard moments—this one was especially clear—was Dick, my former supervisor at the telephone company. The law firm had asked for statements from the supervisor who witnessed my struggle with pain, my absences due to doctor visits and physical therapy appointments, and how all of this affected my work performance. Dick had been my supervisor during that time, between 2004 and 2005, but when I approached him about the request, he refused, saying he couldn't get involved because it would not be in the company's best interest. I explained that I was not suing anyone, only applying for compensation from the US government, but Dick still refused, adding that he was "loyal to the company," a statement I never understood. Luckily, when one of the supervisors under Dick heard about his refusal—I had worked directly with her, and she had witnessed all my issues—she stepped up. She wrote a convincing affidavit outlining how she saw me struggle through every day and almost lose my job. My current supervisor also stepped up and supported me with an affidavit.

Many years later, when I was still working at the phone company, I had the opportunity to confront Dick about his decision. By this time, I had worked in another department for several years, and Dick had just returned to work after having surgery on his neck. I met him in the hallway and said it was good to see him back at work. When I asked about his surgery, he was happy to tell me all about it. He said he'd had severe pain in his arm and lost all grip strength in his hand, so he couldn't play golf, but it was all fixed with surgery. The pain was gone, he had full grip strength back, and he would be on the golf course soon.

I looked Dick in the eyes and said his condition sounded exactly like the shoulder pain, arm pain, and lack of grip strength I had suffered while working for him. He looked a bit piqued but agreed. I then reminded Dick how lucky he was that surgery could cure his issues, something that was not possible for me, whereas I had to learn to live with pain I would feel every single day of my life. His face lost some color—possibly from his reflecting on his complete lack of empathy and support for me during my days of suffering and seeking compensation. I hoped he remembered it, but I saw no use in reminding him. Making a full recovery and returning to the golf course probably hadn't made him more empathetic toward others not so fortunate. I just left without saying another word.

The results of being injected with contaminated flu vaccine—constant pain, food limitations, and expensive vitamin requirements—will be with me for the rest of my life. Also, my doctors told me to never again get a flu shot derived from the same substances as the contaminated vaccine I received in 2000. I cannot get the regular flu vaccine each year, but fortunately, I could take the COVID-19 vaccines because they were developed using a different method.

As I sit at my computer here, in December 2020, writing this memoir,
I have had to stop typing several times to massage my sore left arm.
I occasionally try to remember what it was like to wake up without
pain. The morning of November 29, 2000, was the last I was pain-free.

My flu shot saga presented many bastard moments perpetrated by doctors, clinics, and insurance companies, and I am pretty sure many readers can recall their own negative experiences with doctors and clinics. However, Gordy and I owe our lives to the many great medical professionals who practice listening to patients and acting in their best interest, which often means sticking their necks out to do the right thing. General practitioners have saved our lives with their quick thinking and by recommending appropriate specialists, surgeons and nurses and anesthesiologists have saved our lives by removing cancerous tissue from our bodies, eye doctors have operated successfully to help us retain our vision, and various other medical professionals have guided us through recovery from a number of other issues. In general, Gordy and I hold medical professionals in high regard, but we feel qualified to give every reader a piece of advice: if your doctor or clinic is treating you like a bastard, find a clinic and doctor who practice medicine that puts the patient first; there is a growing number of them out there.

CHAPTER 19

MERGERS AND BUYOUTS AND LIES, OH MY!

My career at the telephone company coincided with several company reconfigurations. In 1988, I started at what I'll call "Tel One," a company with loyal employees who were treated well and trusted each other. The company became Tel Two in 1992, Tel Three in 1994, Tel Four in 1999, and Tel Five in 2001, each name reflecting some kind of merger or buyout. I retired in 2010.

The reconfiguration process would have been funny if the results didn't hurt so many hardworking, innocent people. Normally, the changes resulting from any company reconfiguration follow a similar story line: First, management tells employees the sale will make the company better, that it is good for the employees, that there will be no changes to their 401(k), and that no employee layoffs will happen as a result. Soon, representatives from the company taking over show up and reiterate the same line, reinforcing the idea that everything will be better after the sale. But employees soon learn that none of that is totally true, and the layoffs come quickly after the reconfiguration paperwork is signed, often resulting in a reduction in customer service and a big bonus for one or more company leaders. In 1999, when Tel Four bought Tel Three, we employees had already experienced these changeovers, and we knew what was coming. However, what happened over the next five years was something far beyond what we'd expected.

When I first heard that Tel Four was based in Bermuda, not the US, I smelled something rotten. The message management put out to employees was that Tel Four was employee-owned, which, if true, should have encouraged all employees to eagerly buy stock in the company. A new policy said the company would match employee 401(k) contributions, but the company's portion was to be given *exclusively in company stock*. Management encouraged—even pressured—employees to put their contributions into company stock as well, sending several emails and letters and posting bulletins. These messages also stated that any 401(k) stock purchases could not be sold for a minimum of five years. I did not like that idea, so I left my contributions in the stable value fund. Fortunately, the law was on my side, and no one could make me change my contributions.

Most employees, especially managers, got caught up in the stock fever, and anyone who didn't put all their 401(k) into stock or didn't purchase extra stock was made to feel like an outsider and a disloyal employee. Being raised as a bastard, however, I found it easy to resist this peer pressure. I was used to being treated like a pariah. But all the pro-stock propaganda worried me, especially when Tel Four also changed their policy to mandate that all bonuses paid to employees must be issued in the form of company stock. Soon, all special awards given out to hourly employees—for meeting certain goals in sales or work achievements—were suddenly switched from cash or branded items to stock shares.

In 2001, Tel Four decided to sell to Tel Five. Since Tel Five was based in the US, I felt better about it than the previous sale, but we were again bombarded with the same changeover story line: better company, no changes, no layoffs. One good thing was that our 401(k) stock was to be changed to either Tel Five stock or cash. But after the dust settled, we discovered that Tel Four had not transferred control of employee 401(k) money that was in their stock. The big push to buy stock started to make sense—Tel Four executives now controlled our 401(k) savings, and they wanted to keep it!

It took a while, but Tel Five finally had their lawyers pressure Tel Four to transfer the funds. But it was too late. Tel Four had filed for bankruptcy on January 23, 2002—one of the largest bankruptcies in history. Every share of my Tel Four stock was suddenly worth zero. This took a large bite out of my retirement savings, but I still had the money I'd put into the stable value fund. Unfortunately, the employees—both current and former—who'd fallen for Tel Four's pro-stock propaganda lost everything. Yet somehow the

Tel Four executives were able to secure a free pass that ensured no one could file criminal charges against them.

Several months later, though, all former Tel Four employees were contacted by a law firm that was filing a civil class action lawsuit against the company for the misinformation and lies told to their employees about their 401(k) stock. Like so many of my coworkers, I filled out the forms and sent backup paperwork (emails, company notices, etc.) to join the lawsuit. In March 2004, the executives settled the lawsuit. Later that year, employees were paid a few cents on each dollar owed to them, which left me and many others with a large gap in our retirement plans.

Even after the settlement, employees felt that justice was not served. Executives had lied to all of us, withheld employee 401(k) money when the company was sold, and sold over $700 million in personal stock just before the bankruptcy was announced, during a period when regular employees were not allowed to sell stock. Yet the executives' only punishment was to pay back a comparatively small sum of $25 million of their own money in the settlement. The bulk of the settlement money came from other sources. I chalk this up as one of the bigger and nastier bastard moments of my working career.

Clearly, if someone had taken a hundred bucks from the corner grocery, they would be locked up, but white-collar crimes committed by rich white guys seem to get a pass. The bottom line is that the executives took from my bottom line to increase their own—standard business practice for the wealthy, I guess.

CHAPTER 20

CONFRONTING HARASSMENT, DISCRIMINATION, AND DEATH

Ageism

In 2009, I was in a position I liked at the phone company, and my immediate supervisor was great. I planned to stay in that position until I retired, at sixty-five, but one of the managers, whom I'll call "Kat," forced me to move to another department, working under a different supervisor, whom I'll call "Kit."

Kit was a self-declared "good Catholic woman" whom I had known for many years at work, but we had never worked in the same department before. When she got married in 1994, I was surprised to learn the ceremony was held at St. Nicholas Catholic Church in New Market, as there were a number of other Catholic churches in small towns closer to where she lived. She told everyone at work she had moved the ceremony to St. Nicholas because her favorite priest, Father Harry, was assigned there. She embraced his views on religion and extolled his hard stances against abortion and commingling with Protestants. Up until that time, I had not heard of anyone in the last half of the 1900s being against Catholics commingling with Protestants. In fact, local leaders in the Catholic, Protestant, and Jewish faiths had recently made efforts to reach out to each other with a good deal of success.

After I was transferred to Kit's department, I was harassed daily about my age—and not the good-natured kidding many of us expect and even enjoy. Instead, it consisted of mean, untrue statements regarding an older person's ability to perform. I'm sure the treatment of older workers varies from company to company and maybe even from department to department, but both Kit and Kat considered the older clerical workers to be dumb and slow, and they regularly subjected me to statements such as "Old people don't accept change" and "Old people can't accept new ideas," both of which are no truer of older workers than of younger workers.

For example, being sixty years old and having worked in an office for forty years, I'd accepted, adapted to, and implemented more changes than the younger employees had. If you've worked in an office for five years or less, you may just be settling in to methods and technology that you think will be the norm forever. Well, don't get too comfy—no method or technology will last forever.

When companies allow ageism, they stifle the sharing of wisdom. For example, when a new manager wants to implement a change and asks if there are any questions, chances are that some of the older workers would love to tell them why the "new" idea didn't work when the previous leader tried it a year prior, or how it *could* work this time if *x* were to happen. But the older employees know that if they say anything, they will be labeled as pessimistic and against change—so they say nothing. This is how wisdom is wasted and how the same mistakes keep getting made again and again. Repeating past mistakes has more to do with the failure of leaders to listen than with any other factor.

In one of Kit's first department meetings I attended, she stated—as if a fact—that people in their fifties and sixties don't work as fast as people in their thirties, which set a hostile tone toward me. I was sixty-one at the time and the only person on staff over sixty. As I cautiously looked around the room, I felt eyes on me. She repeated this erroneous "fact" many times in my presence and in the presence of younger people in the department. The repetition seemed to make it true, and no one stated anything to the contrary. What good would it have done?

Low Morale

At about the same time Kit's leadership was cementing bias against older workers, the company distributed an employee survey to gauge morale. The results were clear: morale was low. The company mandated that every department have a meeting to address the issue. In our department's meeting, Kit blamed her employees for having low morale, as if having low or high morale was a choice and we had stubbornly chosen for ours to be low.

In a stern, authoritarian manner, Kit glared at us all as she exclaimed, "Low morale! Well, what are *you* going to do about it?"

Like the others in the meeting, I sat and listened to her anger in disbelief, and even though I was upset at her absurd conclusions, I couldn't help but smile inwardly as I thought of a particular comic strip from the series *The Wizard of Id*, which pictured a man being publicly whipped and the king proclaiming, "The beatings will continue until morale improves." I am pretty sure that meeting was a bastard moment for all who attended.

Mom Passes Away

During this time, my mother was at Mala Strana Assisted Living. On Thanksgiving morning, November 26, 2009, my mother had a severe stroke and was taken to the hospital. We received a call and went straight there, where the doctor informed me she may never wake up. But Mom was strong, and that afternoon, she woke up for a couple of minutes, long enough for her to know that both Gordy and I were there with her. Then she slurred that she was tired. I leaned in and told her it was okay to close her eyes and rest. She looked at me, closed her eyes, and never woke up again.

The doctors said she may linger in that state for days and that she had to go into hospice care. For last rites, Gordy called the priest associated with the hospital, whose office was just across the street, but he said she wouldn't need him to visit because clergy regularly gave last rites in nursing homes every week. (So much for all those movie scenes where priests rush to the bedsides of the ill to give last rites during all hours of the night.) I was disappointed and mentioned to Gordy that in the nine years Mom was at Mala Strana, the priest from her own parish hadn't visited her even once. Certain members who were high in church hierarchy, however, visited Mom several times each year, trying to guilt her into donating money to the church on a regular basis. *Typical*, I thought.

We needed to move Mom to hospice care immediately, and lucky for me, I had already taken the Friday after Thanksgiving as a vacation day, making me available the entire weekend. Her doctor would keep her in the hospital over the weekend while we handled her affairs. Gordy and I had to clean out her apartment by the end of November lest we pay an extra month's rent; Mom no longer had personal money to cover the cost. We spent the entire holiday weekend cleaning, packing, and moving everything from her apartment to a shed on our property. On Monday, Mom was moved to Mala Strana's attached hospice center as planned.

Early Monday morning, I called work to speak with Kit, my supervisor. I told her everything that was happening and that my mother was dying.

I didn't get a single word of sympathy from her, not even a quick *Sorry 'bout that.* All she said was, "Well, is that going to take you all day? It's the end of the month, and you have a lot of work to do."

When I explained that it would take me all day, Kit then informed me I had better be at work on Tuesday morning. I realized I wouldn't be allowed to sit with my dying mother without losing my job. After work on Tuesday, I rushed over to sit with Mom for a while, but due to my own poor health, I couldn't stay long because I had to get home and rest so I could get to work the next day. Later that night, the nurse called to inform me that Mom had quietly passed away.

When I called in on Wednesday to tell Kit that Mom had passed away, Kit coldly informed me I would only get three days of funeral leave for parental death. She emphasized that she expected me to be at work the next Monday—again offering no condolences for my mother's death. Her coldness stood in great contrast to the actions of my former supervisor when my stepfather had died, in 1991; he had told me to take as long as I needed. Huge difference! At the time, I wondered why Kit seemed compelled to treat me heartlessly.

We held Mom's funeral just as she had planned: at a funeral home, not at a church. Gordy delivered a wonderful eulogy, and my cousin, a church deacon, led some prayers. It was a lovely ceremony, and many friends and relatives told us such. For some reason, both Kit and Kat showed up at the funeral. I was surprised to see them there because neither one had expressed any sympathy to me otherwise—and they didn't say anything to me at the ceremony either. I considered that, as my superiors, maybe they thought their attendance was expected.

Kat Disapproves of Mom's Funeral

When I returned to work on Monday, I received lots of condolences and sympathy greetings from my coworkers, including my previous supervisor, who expressed surprise that I was back to work already. Losing Mom was hard for me both emotionally and physically, but the worst was yet to come.

The next day, my second day back at work, I worked the early shift and was scheduled to leave at half past three. Before I ventured out into the cold, I decided to use the restroom. As I was washing my hands and getting ready to leave, Kat walked in and stood directly between me and the door.

"Why didn't you have a full Catholic funeral mass for your mother?" she demanded.

Shocked at her attitude, I said, "Because Mom said she didn't want one."

"Well," she said, "if that were my mother, I would not have followed her wishes. I would have had a full Catholic funeral mass for her."

I matched her gaze and bluntly said, "Well, I believe in following my mother's wishes."

Kat went on to lecture me on the importance of having a full Catholic funeral mass, then attributed my decision not to do so on my being a "nonpracticing Catholic." I wanted to scream at her that it was none of her fucking business what type of funeral I had for my mother, but I knew if I said anything, she could fire me on the spot for insubordination.

Kat continued her attempt at schooling me about what she viewed as my failure until another woman entered the restroom, forcing her to move. Taking advantage of the moment, I scooted around Kat, bolted out of the restroom, grabbed my coat, and ran for the parking lot. My mother had just died. I was understandably emotional, and the encounter with Kat upset me terribly. I cried all the way home. I knew I should have pulled over, but I hadn't exactly planned on crying. When I got home, I told Gordy about the incident. He asked whether there was any recourse. I said I really couldn't handle it right then but would think about it.

On Wednesday and Thursday, I was able to avoid both Kit and Kat. I kept to my cubicle all day and tried not to talk to anyone, but a memory kept going through my mind: *Who's your father? What's his name? Who's your father? What's his name?* Here I was, cowering in my cubicle, experiencing the same feelings of fear and shame I had felt as a child, crying as my tormentors chanted through the locked screen door. At sixty-one years old, I was still being tormented by Catholics who seemed to think their religion gave them the right, or even the obligation, to bully me. This time, though, was even worse because the tormentors were my supervisors.

On the drive home that day, all these thoughts ran through my mind. I exclaimed aloud, "I've had enough of this treatment!" I realized I needed to stand up for myself—and for my mother. It was time to fight back. I thought back to when I was a union steward, and I knew if this had happened to a union member, I would have been there, fighting for that person. Shouldn't I fight for myself? There are laws that protect people from this type of harassment, but although the law was on my side, I knew there would be huge consequences for me if I tried to defend myself.

As soon as I got home, I told Gordy I wasn't going to let Kit and Kat harass me. We talked over all the types of consequences I would probably get from both of them. Gordy's strong support gave me the courage to carry on. Besides, Gordy had already retired, and he had urged me to retire by my next birthday, when I would be sixty-two. We discussed how I could accurately describe to HR what had happened—who said what, and why I hadn't taken the issue to my immediate supervisor, Kit. I went over it in my mind all night, and by morning, I was ready. I resolved to meet with HR and file a formal grievance. I was ready for the backlash I would receive from Kit and Kat. I was ready to stand up for myself.

First thing Friday morning, I called down to HR to schedule a meeting as soon as possible, stressing the urgency. When I explained the incident to the HR manager, he nearly fell off his chair. He seemed to understand that this was a big deal, as he confirmed it was illegal to judge and confront any employee about their religion. When he asked why I hadn't gone to my immediate supervisor, Kit, I told him she had often made it quite clear she was a "good practicing Catholic." I added that Kit and Kat were friends and of similar mind about their Catholicism and that I didn't think Kit would have understood the gravity of what had happened.

The HR manager realized the magnitude of the situation and talked with me about next steps. When he asked whether I wanted an apology from Kit and Kat, I said no, that I never wanted either of them to talk to me about my mother again. He said the grievance would have to be reported to Kat's supervisor, the regional general manager, and it would go on her permanent record. Then he assured me there would be no repercussions from this report. I looked him straight in the eyes and said, "Oh, yes, there will be. Kat will try to get even with me for this." He assured me that wouldn't happen, but I knew the type of person Kat was, and I knew she had already misused her power, and she would do it again.

Retaliation started immediately. Kat avoided me at all costs, letting her "lieutenant," Kit, lead the treachery. Kit went out of her way to express her disdain in subtle ways. When she came to work, she would walk down the hall, past all our cubicles, and say, "Good morning," to everyone except me. If she saw me anywhere but my cubicle, even if my duties pulled me elsewhere, she would ask, "Don't you have work to do?"

One day in early January, I worked so intently to finish up my projects that I lost track of time, working over four hours straight without a break. I was finishing up at the copier in the hall when the other woman in line, whom I'd let do her few copies first, brought up my mom's death. Kit walked down the hall, looked in my direction, and yelled, loud enough for people in other areas to hear, "Unless you're on break, I suggest you stop visiting and get to work!" Then, before I could answer, she rushed to her office and closed the door. This was my reward for working four straight hours to get things done and help keep her department numbers looking good.

The increased harassment at work affected me more than I'd thought it would. I began having headaches all the time, I couldn't sleep, and I realized the stress was severely affecting my health. Gordy suggested I retire as soon as possible. I would turn sixty-two on Friday, April 30, 2010, which seemed like a great day to retire. Of course, that would mean having to buy my medical insurance until I was sixty-five, when I would be eligible for Medicare and a supplement policy. The crappy, high-deductible insurance would cost over $500 a month, but Gordy persisted, saying that maybe my health would improve without all the stress. I took his advice and filed for retirement.

The written company policy stated that an employee must give a full four months' notice of retirement to receive their pension on time. In early January, I submitted my written request for retirement, effective April 30, 2010. January was review month, when everyone submitted a self-evaluation that their supervisor then uses to "write" the review. As expected, Kit collected my self-evaluation, threw out everything positive, and rewrote it to make me look bad. Yes, this was a twisted, vicious, nasty review of my performance.

Per company policy, the first half of my review should have been written by my previous supervisor since almost half of the year was spent working under her. But I later found out that Kat hadn't allowed my previous supervisor to review me—another act of revenge. This was the first bad review I had received in the twenty-one years I worked for the company—and the first bad review I had received in all the years I had worked anywhere!

In my review, Kit claimed I was "not a team worker," citing my short daily meetings with a coworker training me on a new task, asking for clarification. I'm not sure how else I was to receive training if I couldn't ask questions. She also verbally stated, "Since you are retiring, any raise is a moot point. No raise." I refused to sign the review, which was my right according to company policy. This shocked Kit, as my not signing the review made her, too, look bad to HR.

I went straight to my desk, wrote down my notes on the meeting, and sent an email to the HR manager, asking whether, per company policy, my upcoming retirement disqualified me from getting a regular annual raise. He must have panicked and called Kat, who contacted Kit. The HR manager wrote back later that day, saying I must have "misunderstood" what my supervisor said—that she had cited not my upcoming retirement but my poor performance. Apparently, both Kit and Kat had lied to HR. No surprise there. Kit and Kat used this review to justify denying a raise, which would negatively affect my social security earnings for the rest of my life. This was obviously another act of retaliation.

Later, when I was leaving the company, my previous supervisor called me in for a farewell visit. That is when I found out she hadn't been allowed to review me. She was horrified to find out I had been given such a bad review and no raise.

Company policy stated that if a retiring employee had been with the organization for at least twenty years, their manager was to bring their entire department out to lunch. Well, that didn't happen either, but Kat devised an even greater insult for me. Retiring employees of at least twenty years were also given an on-the-clock party in the office, a benefit for which I qualified.

Kat's administrative assistant always arranged the in-office retirement parties. When the assistant talked to me, she courteously explained that they normally provided ice cream and cake, but since she knew my allergy to refined sugar would not allow me to eat either of those items, she had ordered several fruit trays instead. I was impressed by her kindness and understanding and told her so. But a few days before the party, she called to inform me that Kat had canceled the fruit trays, saying, "No special treatment. She'll get cake and ice cream like everyone else."

After word got around that there would be no free lunch for our department and that Kat had canceled the fruit trays for my party, my coworkers took things into their own hands. The people in my department, the people in the other departments I had previously worked in, and all the people on the entire floor where I worked decided to have a giant potluck lunch for me that day. Since all the other supervisors on the floor agreed to the "Potluck for Nancy," there was nothing Kit or Kat could say to cancel it, though neither one of them participated. How petty could they be?

Harassment comes in many forms, as I'm sure most people alive during the #MeToo movement already know. When your boss wields power over you unfairly for any reason, it tears into your self-worth and demeans you. It's incredible how often management and HR fail to realize how harassing workers and treating them unjustly negatively affects production. Personally, I think a lot of the bullying is done because some people feel they must put others down to appear superior. For some men, women provide an easy target. But that doesn't explain the treatment I received from Kit and Kat, both of whom were women.

One thing that sticks in my mind is how Kit totally worshipped Father Harry, who wrote about the negative impact of Catholics commingling with non-Catholics. Apparently, that can work both ways.

Exit Interview

I insisted on having an exit interview with the HR manager before I left that last day. I held his gaze and said, "I told you she would get her revenge." Then I explained everything that Kit and Kat had done to me and told him I had written post-review notes. This interview may not have changed much of anything, but it gave me great satisfaction to stand up for myself. And the kindness expressed by my coworkers made my last day extremely gratifying.

CONCLUSION

When I was a child, Catholic clergy, nuns, and some of the "faithful" church members seemed compelled to remind me I was not worthy of their approval; similarly, when I was in my sixties, my supervisor and her manager made it their business to discriminate against me. Those periods are bastard bookends of sorts. I can think of no reason for the ill treatment other than the perpetrators being inspired by their own interpretation of what their faith demanded of them.

Personally, I don't believe that the Catholic Church intends to inspire or empower clergy, nuns, or church members to abuse and disparage other human beings. I think the individuals use it as an excuse for their innate meanness to surface. And I hope that, someday, members of the church will hold such malefactors accountable and demand better behavior. If you have a choice—and we all do—why not be kind?

ACKNOWLEDGMENTS

I thank those who willingly shared their stories with me as I strived to discover the facts surrounding my mother's life, including my cousin Mary Jo "Mitz" Brunner, my late cousin Roger Stockinger, and my late uncle Cyril Schoenecker.

I especially thank Ron Zweber for his researching of names, dates, and documents. His discoveries initiated much rewriting.

I thank my publisher, Beaver's Pond Press, and the many professionals who worked on the book, including my project manager, Tina Brackins; my copyeditor, Kris Kobe; my proofreaders at ScriptAcuity Studio; and my layout designer, Dan Pitts.

I especially thank my husband, Gordy Fredrickson, who listened to my stories over the years and encouraged me to write everything down. Without his constant support and guidance, my experiences would have fallen into the category of "A story *not* told is lost forever."

ABOUT THE AUTHOR

In 2018, Nancy A. Fredrickson and her husband, Gordy, moved from their hobby farm to a townhome less than twenty miles from where they grew up. Nancy began writing *Out of Wedlock, 1948* in earnest in 2020—the same year they published their fifteenth book and celebrated their fiftieth wedding anniversary, and the year that COVID-19 caused all their performing and vending engagements to be canceled.

Nancy continues pursuing her hobbies, photography and quilting, and Gordy works on writing poetry, novels, plays, nonfiction, and children's books. You can purchase any of their sixteen books as well as view a current list of the upcoming craft shows where they sell them at gordonfredrickson. com. They'd love you to stop by and visit.

CPSIA information can be obtained
at www.ICGtesting.com
Printed in the USA
BVHW080256230922
647805BV00004B/140